I Want to Be Left Behind

NOVELS

River of Light

Becoming the Enemy

Duck and Cover

Animal Heart

NON-FICTION

Living by Water

Nature and Other Mothers

Sister Stories

Build Me an Ark: A Life with Animals

Sightings: The Gray Whale's Mysterious Journey

Singing to the Sound: Visions of Nature, Animals, and Spirit

Pacific Northwest: Land of Light and Water

ANTHOLOGIES CO-EDITED

Intimate Nature: The Bond Between Women and Animals

The Sweet Breathing of Plants: Women Writing on the Green World

Between Species: Celebrating the Dolphin-Human Bond

Face to Face: Women's Stories of Faith, Mysticism, and Awakening

I Want to Be Left Behind

Finding Rapture Here on Earth

BRENDA PETERSON

A Merloyd Lawrence Book
Da Capo Press
A Member of the Perseus Books Group

The first chapter of this book appeared in slightly different form in *Orion* magazine, January, 2008

"Shall We Gather at the River" appeared in very different form in the anthology *Face to Face: Women Writers on Faith, Mysticism, and Awakening* (Farrar, Straus & Giroux) edited by Brenda Peterson and Linda Hogan

"Render to Them Their Desserts" appeared originally as a sketch in *The Seattle Weekly* and was collected in the author's essay book *Nature and Other Mothers* (Ballantine)

Some descriptions of the gray whale lagoons in Baja, Mexico, appeared originally in the author's magazine article "Woman and Nature" in the August, 2003 issue of *O: The Oprah Magazine*

Designed by Jeff Williams
Set in 12-point Weiss by the Perseus Books Group

Library of Congress Cataloging-in-Publication Data
 Peterson, Brenda, 1950-
 I want to be left behind : finding rapture here on Earth / Brenda Peterson.
  p. cm.
 "A Merloyd Lawrence book."
 ISBN 978-0-306-81804-2
  1. Nature—Religious aspects. 2. End of the world. 3. Peterson, Brenda, 1950—Religion.
4. Peterson, Brenda, 1950—Philosophy. 5. Peterson, Brenda, 1950—Childhood and youth.
6. Novelists, American—20th century—Biography. 7. Baptists—United States—Biography.
8. Seattle (Wash.)—Biography. 9. Spiritual biography. I. Title.

BL435.P48 2010
204.092—dc22
[B]

                                                                        2009022803

First Da Capo Press edition 2010

Published as a Merloyd Lawrence Book by Da Capo Press
A Member of the Perseus Books Group
www.dacapopress.com

Da Capo Press books are available at special discounts for bulk purchases in the U.S. by corporations, institutions, and other organizations. For more information, please contact the Special Markets Department at the Perseus Books Group, 2300 Chestnut Street, Suite 200, Philadelphia, PA 19103, or call (800) 810-4145, ext. 5000, or e-mail special.markets@perseusbooks.com.

10 9 8 7 6 5 4 3 2 1

For Sarah Jane Freymann,
whose spirit and keen eye helped shape this book

There is another world, and it is this one.

—PAUL ELUARD

Contents

Prologue

The Trumpet Shall Sound

(1 Corinthians 15:51)

"WITH 9/11, THE BLESSED COUNTDOWN FOR THE RAPTURE HAS BEGUN," my neighbor George informed me almost casually.

He caught me off guard. After decades of giddily anticipating the end of the world and getting no response from me, most of my relatives have stopped asking if I'm ready to be swept up midair with them. Plus, this was the last place I expected to be proselytized. George and I sat perched on driftwood, keeping watch over a seal pup that had hauled up onto our backyard Salish Sea shore, just south of Alki Beach. Our Seattle community beach is precious to harbor seals—a place where they can give birth, nurse, rest. Late summer through September, mother seals leave their pups here while they fish. We neighbors stay the respectful one hundred yards away from the pups, as advised by the Marine Mammal Protection Act, keeping watch on the vulnerable pups in shifts of usually four hours. It's a startling stretch of time to spend together with people we usually whiz past in our busy lives.

"Hmmmmm," I answered in a whisper, hoping that my neighbor would lapse into the companionable silence we usually enjoy together while seal sitting, as we call our beach communion. "Hand me the binoculars, will you?"

This pup was about two feet long, round and robust, its speckled fur camouflaged against the rocky beach. He was breathing regularly, with no yellow discharge from mouth or nose—all good signs. We didn't see any wounds, such as orca bites, propeller gashes, or bullet holes. But he could have suffered some internal injuries. Only careful observation and time would reveal his fate. If the pup is injured or doesn't leave the beach after forty-eight hours, we call our marine mammal stranding expert, Kristin Wilkinson, at NOAA (National Oceanic and Atmospheric Administration), who may authorize someone to remove the seal to a rehab shelter for treatment. Though Washington State has a thriving seal population, 50 percent of juveniles do not survive their first year, and every seal season we neighbors witness seal pup deaths.

George and I were sitting second shift, studying the pup's body language: can he lift flippers and head in the agile "banana position" to scan for predators and mother? Our most important job as seal-sitters is to shoo dogs and overly curious people politely away from the pup, partly because diseases are communicable among the three species. We also chat with other neighbors and passersby and educate them in seal etiquette. If the mother returns and finds her pup surrounded by too much human activity, she may abandon her baby.

"This pup looks plump and healthy, don't you think?" I asked George in a whisper.

"I sure hope so," he murmured.

Violet mists floated just above the waves like ghost ships. Suddenly, a foghorn moaned in baritone blasts, and the seal pup shuddered. He lifted his head, his black eyes huge, his tiny ear slits opened wide, listening.

"That's how it'll happen, you know," George said quietly. There was a note of triumph in his tone. "The trumpets will sound, and we'll be lifted up far away from here."

For a moment I considered not engaging in this loopy, no-exit dialogue. But because this was my neighbor, not my family, I simply smiled. George and I had a lot of time and a seal pup on our hands. No way out. "Listen, George," I began. "Why are you so . . . well . . . cheerful about the end of the earth?"

This gave him a moment's pause. Then he said, with some chagrin, "You can't blame us born-agains for wanting at last to get our heavenly rewards. We've waited thousands of years."

His dark eyes flashed a familiar fire I'd seen in preachers' faces during my Southern Baptist childhood. As I watched the seal pup settle back into his vigilant scanning of the waves, his belly rising and falling in those deep drafts of breath that only the very young of any species seem to enjoy, I persisted. "Why would you want this world to end, George? What's the hurry?"

I could see that my neighbor was now studying me as if I were the seal pup, as if he had already passed me in the slow sinner's lane on the freeway to the Apocalypse. "The hurry is that right now we see signs and wonders proving that the End Times are upon us," George insisted. "We've got holy wars, world financial markets crashing, Israel's military power, Islamic terrorists, and even global warming." This last sign he pronounced brightly, as if our global climate was gleefully graduating into a hot time in the old world.

I wanted out of the conversation. I felt claustrophobic in the tight grip of my neighbor's End Times intensity. Oddly, I wondered if my restlessness was like the anxiety fundamentalists seem to feel about the whole world, as if they are trapped by the original gravity of their sins. Or perhaps to the Rapture hopefuls, the earth's fall into global warming signals that our world has become what they always suspected—hell, the "fire next time." Perhaps their Rapture prophecy is a kind of biblical lullaby to calm their environmental terrors. As one relative assured me, "There are no drowning polar bears and melting ice caps where I'm going."

It struck me that being "raptured" out of this world trumps the insecurity of living and the surrender of dying. No bodily indignity. No suffering. One will simply be whisked off with the fellowship of the believers, the Rapture gang, to a heavenly and just reward. In the twinkling of an eye, they say, the righteous will ascend, dropping golden dental work, nightgowns, and perhaps some spouses. Unless you count losing the earth and billions of unfortunate sinners who cling to it, getting raptured is a blast. Who wouldn't want to escape the prophesied plagues of locusts, frogs, and killer viruses, an earth overwhelmed by tsunamis, volcanoes, and nomadic legions of the unsaved?

"Sandwich, George?" I rummaged in my backpack for a pimento cheese sandwich. Though I've backslid from my mother's Southern Baptist religion, I still carry on her fabulous food rituals.

My neighbor shook his head. His hunger was spiritual. Not to be put off, he told me, "I'm afraid you'll have a rough time of it here during the Tribulations."

"Don't you love any of us who will suffer in those Tribulations?" I asked. "Those of us you leave behind?"

George took my arm a little too tightly. "But you could come with us to meet Jesus midair in the Rapture. You could escape all the Tribulations—and wait for the Second Coming to return here. Then Christ will defeat the Anti-Christ and establish His kingdom. Then the earth will be pure again."

George was closing in, just as surely as the tide was rising, surf coming closer to the seal pup's small, whiskered snout. I politely disengaged. It was enough that I had to contend with some friends who calculate that by the end of the Mayan calendar in 2012 all civilizations will either be spiritually transformed or destroyed. And, of course, some of my most extreme green comrades are convinced the earth will be a more pristine place without people. Given this Greek chorus of apocalypse, what was one more vision of the Last Days?

I hid behind my huge binoculars. But I really was a little worried. It had been twelve hours since the discovery of this pup. In a few more hours it would be high tide again. Where was the mother?

Not to be put off, George rummaged in his backpack and pulled out his laptop. He often brings his home office to the beach while seal sitting. We can tap into dozens of wireless haloes shimmering unseen around nearby apartments. "I'm sending you this link," George said. "It's the home page for the non-raptured."

Squinting in the morning marine light, I could barely make out the computer screen, which read: "Inheriting from the Raptured." A very official last will and testament followed: "Contact your saintly friends now. Offer to let them use the convenient form below to keep their fiscal assets from slipping into the hands of Satan's One World Government agents."

"But, George," I protested. "This site isn't serious."

"It doesn't matter if it's joking," George insisted. "It will still work."

I saw that the will had blank signature lines marked "Infidel Witness #1" and "Infidel Witness #2." "Well, I suppose," I suggested with a smile, "that we can ask some of the other seal-sitters to witness this for us."

"Yeah, we can do this together."

Then I remembered I had seen his car boasting a new bumper sticker: IN CASE OF RAPTURE, THIS CAR WILL BE UNMANNED. I had wanted to tell him that I was going to get a new bumper sticker too: IN CASE OF RAPTURE, CAN I HAVE YOUR CAR?

Now here he was, my dear neighbor, actually signing me up to inherit his worldly possessions—his world.

I was strangely touched.

With a pang I realized that while some End-Timers may not have the stamina and constancy for compassion, for "suffering with," many, like George and my family, feel real concern for the infidel loved ones they will abandon. And watching George's expectant face, I reminded myself that his spiritual stewardship, like that of some other evangelicals, did include other species and the natural world. Not long before, George had built a floating platform for an injured pup so she could find sanctuary offshore while saltwater and sun healed a gash she received from a boat propeller. Anchored by another neighbor's boat buoy, this "life raft" became a refuge for many other resting and nursing seals. One of the seal-sitters, Susan, actually witnessed a pup's birth on that raft. An eagle swooped down, taking up the placenta and afterbirth in her talons. But the newborn and mother seal floated safely below.

George has also helped me bury the pups who don't survive each season. We are trained to bury them deep under beach sand so their bodies can nourish the whole ecosystem. Once we seal-sitters had the sorrowful task of burying a pup as the mother swam back and forth in the surf, calling and cooing to her newborn to come back to her. The mother's moans stay in my mind these many months later.

"Oh, look," George exclaimed in a whisper and snapped shut his laptop. "He's up!"

Our pup intently scanned the waves for his mother and the beach for predators. For the first time, he fixed his full attention on us. Through the detached intimacy of binoculars, I could see that his breathing had steadied and he was actually rolling over on his side into a more relaxed and natural position. As he lifted his front flipper up to scratch his whiskers, his huge eyes held mine with that unblinking gaze that is at once wild and very familiar. After all, seals are our mammal kin. In coastal cultures all over the world, they are said to be shape-shifters, selkies, shedding their seal skins onshore to become human, if only for a night, a nuptial, a haunting reverie.

George and I tracked the seal pup's every move—and now there were many. Repeatedly, he lifted his head and hind flippers to scan the waves and beach, then scratched, scooted, rolled over, and gave a long, leisurely yawn.

If, over the hours spent hauled out, seals are protected, we've actually seen their initial wariness relax into deep naps. The seals know we are near, and because we do not approach they find some peace. And so do we. How often are we humans privileged to watch an animal dream beside us? Even when a seagull nipped at his tail flukes, the pup barely stirred. Fast asleep, he was dreaming through the late-afternoon dissonance of commuter traffic, rap music, some school-boys' Frisbee contest. Was the pup certain his mother would return? Was George this sure of the Rapture?

"George," I suggested, "why don't you take a break? Go join your family for supper."

"Anytime now," George murmured, "the mother will return. That's my favorite part."

And then I understood something about my neighbor and about myself. All of us know what it feels like to wait for someone to call, finally to come home, to recognize our love, to reunite with those of us who long for something more, something greater than ourselves. Maybe it will come in the night, in that twinkling of an eye. Maybe it will save us from a lonely beach.

As if in answer to our longing, a glossy head popped up far out in the waves. The seal pirouetted to find her pup on the beach. George and I sat absolutely still, hardly breathing. A soft cooing call from the mother. The pup fairly leapt up, flippers unfurling like wings. Flop, flop, flop, and then an undulant body-hop along beach stones as the pup inched toward the surf.

"Ah, you're safe now, buddy," George sighed, as the seal pup slipped into the waves and swam as fast as his tiny flippers could carry him back to his mother. There was tranquillity in George's face, a sweet calm that often comes from sitting on the beach all day with nothing to do but watch over a fellow creature. From our driftwood seat, we saw the two seals dive and disappear. Nearby, comic black-and-white harlequin ducks popped up in the waves. Even though our seal sitting was over, we didn't move. A great blue heron swooped in with the caw of a dinosaur bird. How could this ancient bird fly with such huge wings? How did she escape extinction? Somehow the great blue had adapted beautifully.

The driftwood creaked slightly under our weight. It was a madrone log, its soft ruby bark peeling from years lost at sea. I surprised myself by going back to the subject I had worked so hard to avoid. I asked George, "What if we're sitting here to make sure that there will be something left for our kids?"

He seemed to ponder this for a while. "You're a really good neighbor, George," I told him. "We would all miss you so much if you zipped up to heaven. We'd all say, 'Well, there goes the neighborhood!'"

George took the compliment in stride. Along with seal sitting, he also participates in our neighborhood block watch. He is someone I might call upon in an emergency, unless, of course, that emergency was the Rapture.

"I'll miss you," George admitted, "and . . . and all this too."

"You know, George," I said softly, "I really want to be left behind."

My neighbor looked at me thoughtfully and then fell quiet as we watched another harlequin float past, bright beak dripping a tiny fish. Happy, so happy in this moment. The great blue cawed hoarsely and stood on one leg in a fishing meditation. Wave after bright wave lapped the beach, and the summer sunset glowed on our faces. We sat in silence, listening to waves more ancient than our young, hasty species, more forgiving than our religions, more enduring. Rapture.

part one

My Old Testament

Shall We Gather at the River?
(Baptist hymn)

THE FOREST GOT TO ME FIRST—BEFORE THE FAITHFUL.

On the High Sierra lookout station of my birth, I was a baby in diapers stained green from crawling after my ranger father. Way up in the mountains, there were more wild animals than people. We lived in a tiny cabin populated with my parents, me, and a crowd of benevolent deer-head trophies I believed doted upon me in my crib. When I remember that first forest, I hear the crackle of great Ponderosa burning and small animals screeching through the woods trying to escape a forest fire my father battled with just a shovel, like Smokey Bear. I smell the rising pine sap of spring, the pungency of elk scat and leaf rot as I explore the forest floor. I trace my first letters on the ancient bark of the old-growth elders that circle our cabin like grandparents. Echoing nearby, a spring river sings its arpeggio rapids of clear and chill snowmelt. Who would not bond with the earth, given such a childhood primer?

But how did this ancient forest remain sacred within me when our Southern Baptist religion—so often at odds with nature—was all that was called holy?

I also remember this: I'm eleven years old and in Vacation Bible School, a summer day camp in northern Virginia, where my nomadic father has landed us, having left the West and "the field," as the U.S. Forest Service calls its forests, for the South. This Bible camp is complete with quasi-military Christian marching songs, extravagant potlucks, and serious biblical scholarship made into children's games. The Southern Baptist church was my family's constant in shifting landscapes. It was also my childhood career, since I was there almost every night of the week, just as I was in school every day. Prayer meetings, choir practice, and Bible studies dominated our weeknights, bookended by traditional morning and evening Sunday services.

Only one year, when I was seven and my father moved us from California for his fellowship at Harvard, had we ever taken a sabbatical from so much churchgoing. My siblings and I had prowled the tide pools and sands of Revere Beach, where we lived in a quaint tenement right across the street from the Atlantic Ocean. The ocean kept us from realizing that we were poor; we believed ourselves rich in time and tides.

Our father loved his university library as much as we did the beach. But Boston was a "wandering in the wilderness" for my mother. Not only were we surrounded by the "secular" unsaved—as my mother suspiciously eyed the Cambridge university crowd—but there were no Southern Baptist churches to be found. Mother had to settle for "those cold fish," American Baptists. They met only on Sundays, sang dirgelike hymns, and held potlucks that paled next to my mother's culinary imagination. "They're not real Baptists," my mother shrugged. She barely endured that year. What else could you expect from Yankees?

After Harvard we had veered off for a year to Missoula, Montana, where my parents had to make their own church in a garage where hunting trophies hung on the rough walls as if to join our congregation. Mid–school year, my father was promoted, and he planted his family in woodsy Fairfax, Virginia. Now in fifth grade, I had attended four different elementary schools.

Back in the fold with multitudes of Southern Baptists, summer vacation meant only more time for Vacation Bible School. Fortunately, my teacher, Mrs. Eula Shepherd, was a marvelous storyteller. Unlike my mother, who read us King James Bible stories every night, but at warp speed, Mrs. Eula was almost Shakespearean in her portrayals of prophets, holy wars, and a cast of fascinating sinners. Mrs. Eula was particularly interested in miracles, and so was I.

"Today we are studying the miracle of bringing forth water from stone," Mrs. Eula began one hot July morning with her usual enthusiasm. Her hair was bright red and had the static electricity halo of a home perm. *Howdy Doody hair,* I thought of it rather fondly. "Turn to Exodus 17, children."

Raptly I listened to her describe the weary and very thirsty Israelites wandering in the desert of Rephidim. "They were so thirsty," Mrs. Eula said, "and they deeply doubted their prophet, Moses, and a God who could keep them so lost all these years in the desert. But God made them wander as we sinners must, before we find redemption."

As an unwilling wanderer myself, following my father's dizzying rise through the ranks, I well understood those homeless Israelites.

"Oh," Mrs. Eula sighed and theatrically threw up her hands. "How they did long for the Promised Land, the way we always long for heaven."

And how I did long for a home. Would it finally be Virginia? With its luxuriant hardwood forests, hurricane-carved coasts, and foggy, blue Shenandoah Mountains, Virginia seemed like heaven on earth. But any night my father could come home from work to announce we would be moving again, wandering.

"Can anyone tell me what that Promised Land was called?" Mrs. Eula asked.

Canaan. I wanted to shout it out, but had to sit on my right hand for fear I might raise it again and alienate the other Bible School campers. If I answered too often, they would shun me at recess.

I looked around. No one else was really listening. It was midsummer, after all, and we were sweating even in our pedal pushers and bright flip-flops. There was the temptation of sprinklers chigg-chigging away on the church lawn and the waft of fried chicken and blackberry cobbler.

Mrs. Eula was too excited to wait for us. "Ah, children, it's called Canaan!" she sang out the holy name with the deep-throated desire of a blues singer. Surely she had missed her calling, spending humid days with children in Bible School instead of some sultry speakeasy where her rich contralto could make people slow dance all night. "But before the Israelites could enter the promised land they had to be tested. And their faith was sorely tried when thirst and fear made them question God's plan for them. Do you ever feel lost like that?"

Mrs. Eula glanced around. Except for me, leaning forward in a folding lawn chair, she had lost her audience, who were transfixed watching the women setting up for lunch.

"I do," I mumbled, in a confession that I hoped would not make me pathetic or, worse, unpopular. "I feel lost. Sometimes."

Eagerly, Mrs. Eula seized upon me. She knew I was already officially "saved." At seven, I had made the penitent trip up the aisle during the postsermon Invitation and accepted Jesus Christ as my personal savior. As revered deacon and pianist, my father and mother were pillars of the church. But perhaps I was being tempted by Satan, only going through the motions, while secretly planning to give up my faith? If so, I must be brought back into the "fellowship of the believers."

"Don't you believe that God has a plan for you?" Mrs. Eula's dark green eyes held mine intently. "Don't you look around every day for signs and wonders and God's miracles?"

I certainly did. And every day I saw them in our garden and running wild through our vast backyard woods. Even at the "apex of childhood," as my father called it, my temperament leaned much more toward the mystical than the dogmatic.

As a passionate student of earth science, I was developing my own theory that many biblical miracles were really natural events. Moses parting the Red Sea might have coincided with a tsunami, I reasoned; Job's insect plagues might have been drought-related; the burning bush that was not consumed might have been a lightning strike, more electromagnetic than fire. Once in a Montana pasture I had been lifted off my feet by a lightning bolt that galvanized a nearby tree. The tree burned to bare ashes, but I was just jolted, hair standing straight up on my head, and then my skin hummed for a while. To me, nature's language was God's way of engaging the earth to speak for Him to us—since most people had stopped conversing with animals, trees, rocks, and rivers.

I hadn't stopped. Nor, did I suspect, had my father, who murmured all the time to his horses and in soft whispers encouraged his gigantic vegetable garden to give us good harvests. He would not have admitted this to other U.S. Forest Service employees or his hunting buddies. My father even said prayers of thanks when he knelt over a great-hearted buck he brought down with his rifle to feed his family. Then, as his own French Canadian, Cherokee, dark Swede, and Seminole ancestors had taught him, he would place a slice of apple and green twig in the deer's mouth as a sign of respect.

My theories about miracles as God's speaking through nature were also kept to myself, especially in Bible School. But today was different. It was too humid not to tell the truth. Like sweat, some things just slip out.

"Yesterday I witnessed a miracle," I confided in a small voice to Mrs. Eula, who was still leaning hopefully near me. "I saw a squirrel flying between two trees . . . and I realized that God was giving me a sign, but I don't quite yet know what it means. Do you?"

For a moment Mrs. Eula's eyes also shifted toward the lunch preparations, especially the abundant dessert table.

"I do not think God is speaking to you through some flying squirrel," she sighed and shook her dazzling head.

Mrs. Eula gave me a long, direct look that I recognized. I'd seen this puzzled scrutiny before and had interpreted it to myself so that it didn't hurt so much. I didn't realize that I was an odd, rather wild, and unknowingly subversive child. I was so used to being an outsider, a "new kid," that I was in a permanent state of culture shock, much like an alien. I often reasoned—as I did now with Mrs. Eula—that I was bewildering because I was "just not from around here," as many had concluded with raised eyebrows.

With an indulgent smile, Mrs. Eula told me, "What you witnessed was *not* a miracle. I'm sorry to say this, dear, but that is kind of silly."

Now all the other Bible School students tuned in, giggling. Nothing like being made a fool in public to attract the hunger of a pecking order.

In her way, Mrs. Eula tried to lessen my humiliation. "I'm not saying that God wouldn't ever use a squirrel to teach us a lesson. Nothing is too humble for Him to notice. But God is pure spirit. That means He does not dwell in earthly form. So He is never tainted by our world—or by us. And you know, God is very busy."

"But God became us, and He came to live on earth," I protested.

"That was God the Father's divine mercy and God the Son's suffering," Mrs. Eula reminded me. "Remember, Christ didn't stay very long. Some of us are still waiting for Him to come back after He left us behind."

"So God the Father never comes here—ever?" I asked, truly bewildered. How could this be when I saw the divine everywhere I looked—a flock of geese lifting off the lake, a horse nudging her foal to walk, a thunderstorm rising over the hill like a cumulus revelation.

"God is in heaven watching over us," Mrs. Eula explained. "*Super* means 'above.' God is super-natural. He is superior over all nature—and above us."

Oh, He's over and out, I wanted to say, but didn't. So God was out of the world, separate from nature, even though it was His creation.

Was he like a landlord or an overseer who never visited or repaired what was not working?

Mrs. Eula concluded, "I know this is difficult for a child to grasp but . . . oh, no!" Mrs. Eula startled us by falling to her knees on the grass.

I wondered if she might speak in tongues to continue our conversation and then I would have to find another adult who could translate for me. But then she cried out in clear English, "Oh, I've lost it. I've lost it!" Squinting, she called us to get down on our knees around her. "Children," she cried, "pray with me that God will help us find my contact lens. It just popped out and will be so hard to find in this grass. Look for something shiny or reflecting the sunlight."

I didn't move, though being the oldest sibling, I was usually quite a helpful child. Instead, I contemplated the scene before me as if I were over and out of it all. I'd long had the ability to step back and watch as if I were not even there. I have many memories of flying around that first forest lookout cabin and studying everything from the point of view of the wooden rafters. Maybe it was because my parents were always hoisting me aloft as if to practice ascension. No one had ever seemed to notice, so I assumed that maybe during these moments of intense observation I was indeed invisible.

I refused to kneel down and search for my Bible School teacher's contact lens. If God so loved the world, as the Bible said, but wasn't even courteous or curious enough to show up on this earth, why should I pray to Him to find what was lost here? My Catholic school chums seemed to have a much more practical division of labor worked out for God by praying to everyday and useful saints, such as Saint Anthony, the patron saint of lost things. In my mind, that flying squirrel was a kind of saint who was in this world along with me. Maybe to spare God my time-consuming prayers I could supplicate animal saints?

"God doesn't have time to help us look for your contact lens," I said very quietly. I had to say this, even though I hoped Mrs. Eula in her panicked search wouldn't hear me.

"What?" she glanced up sharply. "What are you saying?"

"God is too busy to be here," I repeated sadly. "He's above it all."

I shivered with the dread of punishment there in my summer lawn chair. And I felt real regret in breaking my earlier scholarly communion with Mrs. Eula. Surely she would dismiss me from her class.

She did. The Bible class never did find Mrs. Eula's contact lens, though they looked so long they almost missed lunch. I left them kneeling there and ran over to eat my fill of the sumptuous Southern Baptist feast. But I had lost my appetite.

When Mrs. Eula told my parents of my sacrilege and desertion, I was grounded, which meant I was not allowed out in the woods all day. I had to stay inside doing house chores and studying my Bible. I decided to study all the miracles—water to wine at a wedding feast, the Tower of Babel, and Lazarus up and raised from the dead. I took great comfort in knowing that my house arrest was temporary because in a few weeks we would be off to my grandfather's farm in the Ozarks. I had no idea that word of my Bible School scandal would precede me or that in the Ozarks my original sin would appear so grave that my southern sheriff grandfather would have to take me down to the river to meet God.

* * *

MANY SUMMERS my parents left us with my grandfather and Jessie, his second wife. We grandchildren all adored Jessie because when she was not in the farm kitchen fixing her famous hush puppies, butter beans, and a sinfully delicious blueberry cobbler, she was in town at her garage beauty studio, Chez Jessie. Most thrilling of all, she also moonlighted as a hairstylist in the small-town morgue, offering the residents her "beautification," as she called it.

The "ladies" in Jessie's hair salon took great comfort in knowing that Jessie would dramatically sculpt their hair for the biggest dress formal of their lives—their funerals. I'd heard some church folk joke that

Southern Baptist weddings seemed as dutiful as funerals and Baptist funerals were the real weddings. After all, what woman wouldn't want to be a Bride of Christ with no housework or endless chores, lazing about in the Father's many mansions? For their posthumous debut Jessie promised her clients a perm that was a "primp for eternity." Her clients would go to their glory and meet their Maker in style. Some of them looked even more radiant and well-dressed dead than alive, since no expense was spared at Southern Baptist funerals and people saved up over decades for this big show—when they would receive their heavenly reward. Jessie often adorned her late ladies with shiny barrettes and rhinestone baubles as symbolic of the "stars in their crowns."

I always wondered what souls actually did in heaven, besides sing and praise God. I imagined that maybe everyone was still in school, an eternal afterlife of study with recess anytime we wanted to stretch our wings. Once in fourth grade, I had a vivid dream. In my little wooden desk with the folding top carved in hieroglyphics, I saw that I was surrounded by others who all happened to be very studious snakes. Our teacher was a luminous King Cobra raised up in her full, hooded glory. But she did not strike; she swayed and danced. On the blackboard behind her were listed possible classes:

Understanding
Forgiveness
Helpfulness
Stillness
Mercy
Hopefulness
Loving Kindness

I decided on "Forgiveness" and "Loving Kindness" but was told, not unkindly by the teacher, that this was too heavy a class load for one life. I must choose. I looked down, disappointed in myself, and only then casually noticed that I too was a snake, but not poisonous. I was a little garter snake like the slippery ones that my father taught us not to kill because they were good for the garden. That significant sign helped me decide my course of study. I chose the "Loving Kindness" curriculum, which seemed really to please the white cobra teacher because she hissed, "That is a most difficult class."

At that age, I knew nothing of Buddhism or any other religion that assumed reincarnation. It would not be until high school and world history that I would hear of other spiritual traditions and their beliefs in many lives. For now, all I knew was that my dreams were as real as daily life. My dreams were as much a home to me as a parallel universe. The Bible and its fantastic stories also seemed an alternate universe. Otherwise, how could someone living in northern Virginia in the early sixties amid segregation riots and a suspiciously Catholic president also be living in her spiritual imagination in places like Canaan or Jerusalem or, better yet, the astonishing visions of Revelation? In that last book of the Bible, John's dreams of End Times were so full of magical animals, they rivaled any bestiary.

What many don't understand about the most fundamentalist Christians is that the feral quality of their imaginations is bred on a Bible that is not read as symbolic but as the absolute Word of God. Miracles, dreams, and the afterlife enliven a daily reality often prescribed and rigid. My parents are not extreme fundamentalists. As "moderate evangelists," they have not followed their Southern Baptist Convention into its far-right rigidity. They are not as conservative as others in the family. But they still firmly believe in a Rapture interpretation of End Times. They dream of another world nearby where God dwells and where they hope to be lifted up to meet Him midair.

God often talked to prophets like Daniel and directed their lives and an entire kingdom through dreams. But any magic in the real world, or especially in nature, is suspect—or worse, of the Devil.

Didn't Satan often use animals, such as the serpent, to beguile us? Anyone paying too much attention to trees or animals might be accused of communing not with nature but with evil. As a dreamy child, often distracted by the radiant world outside the high church windows, I was often chided for not listening. It was not my intention to be disrespectful. I could listen as well as look.

In this context, my dream that I was studying in a seminary school for snakes was not all that strange. Revelations and End Times prophecies made my little dreams look tame. Nevertheless, I knew enough about the bad rep that snakes had gotten in the Bible never to tell the dream to anyone. I really liked snakes and was intrigued that the subtle serpent had once been a favorite angel. If snakes were good for our earthly gardens, why was the Satan serpent so bad for the Garden of Eden? Scientifically, this Bible story had never made much sense to me. I also liked trees so much that the Tree of Knowledge being off-limits always bothered me. And why, if Paradise was once here on earth, could we not rediscover it again, like a lost world, by becoming explorers as in *National Geographic*, my favorite magazine?

If I were ever going to confide some of my true beliefs or dreams, it would be to Jessie. She loved and gossiped with her huge garden like a family. In that Ozarkian backwoods she was what was called a "yarb" doctor who used plants and herbs for healing. With these herbs, her beauty parlor potions, and her quick wit, Jessie was more pagan than even she knew. But I didn't realize that; I only knew that my patriarch of a grandfather, who seemed the very fearful image of God the Father, was devoted to Jessie and so was I. Since I was still smarting from being bounced from Vacation Bible School this summer, I was looking for a role model upon whom to model my religious life. Jessie seemed a fine candidate. Jessie told me that God was in her garden and by tending her green world she was being a faithful servant. She didn't kill snakes either.

By planting God firmly in her garden, and so in this lush world, Jessie gave me a grounded sense of hope about being here. She was a good Christian, though not a fundamentalist. Even today, my step-grandmother will make a distinction that many of the faithful do: science should pay more attention to wonders and miracles—for God is everywhere suffused in nature. When science strips away the spiritual dimensions, even many moderate Christians, like Jessie, feel secular scientists are godless and perhaps not to be believed.

Jessie was stunningly beautiful. Black-blue hair curled in a French coif, perfect Modigliani face and olive skin with the brightest fuchsia lipstick in the county. Her elegance was the unspoken envy of many townswomen. To me, she was more enthralling than any movie star.

Jessie's birthday gift to me that summer of my Vacation Bible School shame was a permanent. While I sat in her beauty parlor chair, I asked her if she thought God had a wife or mother or daughter, since women seemed strangely absent in the Old and New Testaments.

"You're the scripture gal," Jessie teased me, just as she was teasing my thin hair into a storm of dark blond ringlets held in a beehive by blue goo called Dippity-Do and a steady mist of hair spray so foul-smelling I had a choking fit. "Any mention of God's kinswomen in the Bible?"

"Not many," I admitted. "I've looked for them everywhere, but except for Eve and Ruth and Naomi, and maybe Deborah, the Jewish judge, and Mary Magdalene. . . . " I paused, and looked at her meaningfully in the mirror. "Of course, there *was* Jezebel."

"Now," Jessie laughed and slapped my knee, "I bet that gal was a lot of fun, don't you? Probably just having too good a time for her own good."

Squinting through the haze of hair spray Jessie aimed at me, I had an epiphany: I believed that she would have made a very good wife of God. Or maybe just a misunderstood, high-spirited Jezebel. Yes, I decided, Jessie would be my spiritual role model.

"Don't know if God is really a woman," Jessie concluded, appreciatively eyeing my new perm. "But I do believe he needs to find hisself a better half."

God the Father definitely needed the civilizing and kindly helpmate of a wife and mother, I agreed. Noah had one; so did Abraham, the patriarch who would obediently almost slay his own son; unforgiving Lot and long-suffering Job and, of course, Adam—the man my grandfather believed was "henpecked."

For all his bluster, we all knew that Grandfather was beholden to Jessie. He loved her desperately, still acting, even after decades together, like a suitor. Years younger than my grandfather, Jessie would sometimes cajole him as he lounged idly on the porch swing, "See that old thang? That *used* to be your grandfather!"

I wanted so much to be like Jessie that when she spun me around to look at my birthday coif in the mirror I did not gasp out loud. My crimped curls looked like Shirley Temple on the electric chair. Swallowing hard, I told Jessie this perm was just what I needed to start sixth grade. Secretly, I knew I would be relentlessly ridiculed.

That very night, hoping to loosen the curls, I hung from the rafters in the farmhouse attic sleeping room I shared with my cousins. That was how I jostled a wasps' nest and got stung sixty-seven times, enough venom to kill some people, said Jessie. But she heated water over her wood-burning stove and gave me a warm sponge bath with baking soda, then dotted each wasp sting with her own herbal salve of aloe vera, comfrey, and calendula.

The next morning I was a little sore and distracted by the red welts, but well enough to play dolls with my grandfather's newborn hound puppies. I dressed them in Barbie clothes and set the snuffling pups in a woven basket under a protective cottonwood tree. Then my cousins called me to ride bareback through the woods on Grandfather's old mares. We returned for lunch with ticks studding our scalps. By the time Jessie had extracted all the swollen ticks with tweezers and turpentine, I felt like a little Job with my skin plagues. Then I remembered—the pups!

I found them perfectly still in their doll's clothes with flies abuzz around them. Dead from sunstroke. How could I have forgotten that shade changes with the angle of the sun? How could I have murdered such innocents? Even with my wasp welts, tick bites, and pinched perm, I believed my suffering was too slight. As I awaited my grandfather on the porch, I yearned for his righteous punishment. When Jessie whispered to Grandfather my crime, he stood completely still. I will always remember the exact slant of light across his battered ranch hat, the stubble of gray beard, and his dark eyes when he glanced across at me where I sat, breathless, on the porch swing. It didn't creak one bit.

Grandfather astonished me by clenching his teeth and not yelling. Instead, he walked right past me and out to the edge of the lake he had bulldozed to stock catfish. He took up his whittling knife and slashed at a piece of lodgepole pine. Why didn't he take the strap to me? Why didn't he ease my horror at what I had done with a well-deserved thrashing? Why would Grandfather as biblical patriarch spare the rod? I was sure that Yahweh or Moses wouldn't. Maybe he would strike me and I would be turned to stone or water.

Grandfather whittled for a long while. Then, at last, with a sigh and a significant glance at Jessie, Grandfather came back over to stand above me with his knife. This was a man whom I'd seen once casually lean over at the picnic table and castrate a juvenile pup with his pocket knife. "Ifn' I was you," he growled, "I'd be down on my knees 'bout now."

I slid down to the wooden porch floor, welcoming the splinters. "I'm so sorry, Grandfather," I sobbed. "I never would hurt . . ."

"But you did, didn't you?" he asked in that low voice that rumbled menacingly like heat lightning before a storm.

"Yessir." I could hardly catch my breath. "I did."

"Well, the god and the river don't give God's mercy," Grandfather said. "Not unless you ask."

Surely I needed some mercy. But how was I to ask for it from both my grandfather and a river? It did not occur to me at the time that here was someone who, like me and Jessie, actually believed that God was still here on earth, dwelling in a river.

"Git her ready, sugar," my grandfather told Jessie, and his voice changed into a baritone purr when he spoke to his wife. "I'm taking this chile down."

Very seriously, Jessie nodded and said, "I'll be right along after, Rory."

Current River runs through my fire-and-brimstone childhood like a balm. Boasting one of America's fastest-flowing currents, this river flows from the southern Missouri Ozarks all the way down to the hardscrabble hills of Arkansas. Its spring-fed water rarely freezes. Many summers, the river carried my family on our daylong float trips. In a flotilla of giant inner tubes strung together with rope and long, idling legs, we cousins, aunts, and uncles rode downriver, gossiping about each other all the way.

My wayward Uncle Ira, the only one who drank alcohol, would sprawl in his inner tube like a river god, smoking Lucky Strikes and greeting other floaters. Uncle Ira could bum Budweiser and smokes all the way down the wide waterway.

Now, on the porch as I still knelt before his judgment, Grandfather spat a wad of tobacco ominously near my bare foot. "Why do you think we get baptized in the river?" He fixed me with his black eyes, stroking his beard stubble. He was used to reckoning with criminals.

Grandfather was the town's sheriff, and we used to play checkers in his small jail with his prisoners—usually repentant drunks or "disorderlies." He also often gathered us cousins into his battered pickup to cruise the backwoods roads, rounding up votes for his anti-drinking campaign. He'd park outside a speakeasy or moonshine still and deliver righteous campaign speeches that sounded like sermons. To his grandchildren, he was the closest thing to a biblical god we could imagine. When he talked to us, we listened up.

"Because the river can cleanse our sins?" I asked hopefully, not daring to look at him.

I knew only too well that it was water that Yahweh once used to destroy the whole world. I had never been afraid of Current River, but we were all frightened of our grandfather. And I was so guilty and repentant, I half-hoped Grandfather might just drown me in the river.

"Into the back of my pickup now, gal. Git!"

I got. As Grandfather roared along dirt roads down to Current River, I almost flew out of the truck bed.

When we arrived at last at the wide, rapid river, he muttered, "You just sit here on the riverbank and maybe it'll all come clear to you."

He strode off to find another whittling stick, leaving me alone for the first time since I had discovered my beloved pups dead. The river was loud, but not loud enough to drown out my thoughts. How often had I nuzzled those hound pups, sung them lullabies, cuddled them? They were my babies. Because of me, they were dead. I could hardly stand to be around myself. Surely Grandfather would now give me the most terrible punishment of my life. He could drown me here and nobody would notice.

I sat there on the riverbank in complete silence. Closing my eyes, I listened to the voice of the rapids, the singing leaves of the thirsty cottonwoods, the drone of mosquitoes and dipping of dragonflies.

At last my grandfather sat back down beside me, silent, except for his whittling. I don't ever remember another time when I was alone with my grandfather. "What am I waiting for, Grandpa?" I finally broke our reverie in a small voice.

"Well, young'un, what we're all waitin' for." Though he usually didn't chew tobacco, Grandfather surprised me by spitting a medicinal wad onto his hand, and then he leaned over and smeared spittle on the wasp stings along my skinny arms.

I stared at my grandfather in surprise. His high-boned face held mysterious power. I was surprised by my grandfather's seeming patience with me now. His less gruff manner was usually reserved for his animals and his fishing. Maybe it was Jessie who had hinted to Grandfather to take his granddaughter to Current River alone.

"Where's . . . where's Jessie?" I asked in a trembling voice.

"She'll be right along," Grandfather answered. "She's got business here with the river—like everybody else."

The business, I soon realized to my great relief, was baptismal. One of Jessie's kinsfolk had been saved and was here for baptism in the river. A small gathering of church people began joining us on the riverbank. They were all clothed in homemade choir robes flapping like fresh laundry on the summer breeze.

Someone pulled a rough baptismal gown made out of a burlap bag over my shorts and T-shirt, and it scratched my wasp stings. But I did not cry out, accepting the painful sack like a penitent.

"Don't go torturing her no more!" Jessie appeared out of the crowd and in an instant rid me of my burlap gown.

She wore her fancy face—skillfully etched eyebrows, Loretta Young lips, and an artfully twirled French twist. Her high heels did not even sink in the mud. "Rory"—she turned to my grandfather— "this young'un's all swolled up with wasp venom, and she's in her own hell from killing your pups. No more meanness in the family now!"

Grandfather shrugged and then did something shocking and wonderful. He winked down at me. Never in his life had my grandfather winked at anybody but Jessie. I considered this akin to a biblical sign.

"Thank you, ma'am." I hugged Jessie.

"Nevermine," Jessie told me. "Lord knows, you've seen some small suffering this summer. So, let the river show you her real miracles."

Her. Jessie had called this river female. The power of naming rivers and mountains was usually given to men, patriarchs of Bible and family. Men in my family used female names when referring to their boats, their cars, and the prey they shot for supper. But no one to my knowledge had given the feminine pronoun to a body of water. Maybe this was a holy place where the Father God in heaven met and mingled with his wifely waters here on earth? Maybe this was a little oasis of the Garden of Eden that I had discovered again.

I settled myself on the riverbank, and Jessie leaned forward in a lawn chair my grandfather had set up for her. "In my beautifications at the morgue, I can make over most anything," Jessie confided as we watched the baptismal procession—all the sinners in their burlap robes floating toward the river bank. "Except for meanness and stinginess. I just can't ease meanness from a face, not with all the makeup in this world."

To Jessie, God wanted folks to get "beautified," both body and soul. The way she talked about God, you'd think He'd also gone to beauty school and had His own shop to help sinners with their spiritual makeovers. Jessie didn't dwell on the crucifixion of His Son, like most other adults. Instead, Jessie liked to tell the story of Mother Mary helping to take her broken-down son off the cross. "It's always the women do death chores," Jessie would often say, "washing the poor old bodies, primping them to be angels in heaven."

"Do you . . . ," I hesitated as I watched an old man sinner splash out of the river after his baptismal. "Do you think I'm still going to heaven . . . after what I did to those little pups?"

Jessie said nothing for a long time. "It's not right what you did, young'un." She laid a large hand on my shoulder. "Those little pups died because you didn't pay them no mind. Most evil is like that. It's forgetting 'bout anybody but yourself."

Tears again streamed down my chin, flowing onto the riverbank. This serious talking-to from Jessie was worse than Grandfather's anger. I had disappointed the grandmother whom I so loved. I was worse than any sinner here. Even Current River could never truly wash away my shame.

"But," Jessie lifted my face to hers, "you didn't do this terrible thing on purpose. That's the really big sin, sister. *Wanting* to hurt somebody."

Now on the muddy riverbank as a procession of penitents paraded past us to the very edge of the Current River, Jessie began a rousing chorus of "Shall We Gather at the River?"

> *Yes, we'll gather at the river,*
> *The beautiful, the beautiful river.*

I could see the world more clearly now. The stream of believers floated into the river, their pale gowns flowing up around them like the flotsam of their sins, while they fell trustingly backward into the currents, embraced by the preacher. A miracle happened right then and there—I forgot my own misery.

"Now, honey," Jessie whispered and took my arm. "Looks like you need some savin'."

I let Jessie take my hand. To my surprise, she did not deliver me to my grandfather or the white-robed minister. She walked me away from the baptismal gathering and down to a favorite "putting-in" place for our family float trips.

From her large tapestry bag, Jessie took out my red swimsuit, a bottle of Coca-Cola, and my battered red Keds. She kissed me on the forehead, her scent of Chanel No. 5 and hair spray clinging like sweet humidity. Then Jessie stepped back from me. "Now, child," she said, "*float.*"

As soon as I stepped into the river, the current knocked me down. But I was a strong swimmer. Jessie waved me on and called out, "We'll fetch you down at the bridge."

Floating fast, I stared at the blue sky, trusting the river to carry me as always. As she rocked me along, my body unclenched and rested on the warm water. For hours it seemed I floated, watching the summer clouds above. I swear some of them were shaped like little hound pups, still in this world and watching over me.

When at last I reached the covered bridge, my grandfather waded into Current River to snatch my relaxed body from the fast-moving water.

"Good," he said, noting that I still held my empty Coca-Cola bottle in one hand. "You didn't litter the river none."

As I shivered in the pickup's front seat between my grandfather and Jessie riding back to their farm, Jessie took up humming the chorus, *The beautiful, the beautiful river.* . . . Grandfather joined in with his rough bass, and I listened to them singing together like two old angels—their voices a little wobbly and off-key. Grandfather slid his arm around me, probably reaching for Jessie, and she reached out to rest her arm on top of his so that I was encircled by them. Forgiven. Loving Kindness.

two

Helmet of Salvation, Sword of Spirit

(Ephesians 6:17)

HOLY BIBLE IN HAND, I STOOD IN OUR FAMILY RECREATION ROOM IN Virginia, a skinny and serious twelve-year-old student of earth science, literature, and music. It was 1962, and I was happily still in summer school; homework was my refuge from the many weeknights of churchgoing. In the southern woods bordering our small brick bungalow I had found another haven that I dared not call heaven. The neighbor boys—who included our pastor's juvenile delinquent son, Blair—and I had built a three-story tree fort. When we were not in school, we were in lush forests fleeing from acorns hurled from slingshots, or snowballs.

The parallel universe of electronics had barely been invented. No cell phones. No computers or tiny "pilots" in our palms; television had no hold on us yet, since we were allowed only one show a week. Our companion was the forest. And we were not afraid to dwell there all day until dark. There were no missing children on milk cartons or day planners with playdates scribbled in for every hour. Sunning ourselves on the roof of our tree fort, we were wily and free and, like my father's new filly, unbroken.

It was only when we came inside to eat and sleep and study that we were domesticated. That is why I was "champing at the bit," as my father chided me, practicing for the next Sword Drill at the semi-final state level. Southern Baptist Sword Drills are like spelling bees for true believers. The Holy Bible was my sword, scripture memorization was the drill, and manual dexterity made the winner. It was a dance of rote memory and fast fingers shuffling through the onionskin pages of the Holy Scripture. This afternoon I was missing out on a first for our tree fort. Blair was installing stolen shag rug carpet in the spacious fort's first-floor library and lounge. So I was surly as I practiced my scripture.

"Stand up straighter," my mother scolded. "They judge for posture, you know. And smile. They don't want a sourpuss at the competition."

I scowled, determined to keep my mouth shut. But even as I resisted my mother's tutelage—she was thrilled that I had made it this far in the cutthroat church competitions—I was torn between my ambition to win and my growing fear that I was turning into a kind of scriptural automaton.

"Attention!" my mother commanded like a biblical drill instructor.

Bible clenched at my right side, I snapped up to my full beanpole height, eyes straight ahead as if scanning for a sniper.

"Draw swords!"

With an audible smack of leather binding between my palms, I lifted the Bible to chest level and presented it for inspection—my perfectly oiled and cleaned weapon, the Word.

"Ephesians 6:17!" my mother screamed, unable to contain herself. Her exhilaration eclipsed her duty. She was no longer a trainer but a zealous fan. "Go!" she shouted. "Go!"

Everything had to be calibrated—body and memory. My brain scanned to remember the scripture, at the same time my fingers expertly gripped the Bible, thumbing for the verse. The instant I alighted on Ephesians 6 my forefinger pointed to verse 17, and I stepped forward with bold righteousness, eyes straight ahead, enunciating each word, "And take the helmet of salvation, and the sword of the Spirit, which is the word of God."

"Correct!" my mother exulted, and before I had time to snap back to full attention, she fired off another verse. "Romans 8:28," she said. It was one of her favorites.

Like the finely honed biblical machine that I was, I stepped forward and barked out, "And we know that all things work together for good to them that love God, to them who are called according to *His* purpose."

"Hooray," Mother jumped up and down. "I'm sure you'll take State!"

I doubted it. In fact, as I ran through the military motions of the Sword Drill, I realized I doubted everything. I knew scripture. I knew what my parents and everyone around me in this southern hamlet believed, but not what I believed. I was an increasingly mutinous mystic who chafed at the simple answers and formulas of Southern Baptist dogma. Most of all, I was appalled by the hellfire— like the devouring flames I well remembered from a childhood in the national forests—that my family so cheerfully imagined dispatching sinners and heathens. What was worse, our Sunday school teacher had just declared that Southern Baptists believed animals were not allowed an afterlife. She was an ardent breeder of basset hounds, so she was benevolent enough to reserve a kind of sweet limbo for pets. But her lessons of heavenly bliss were populated only with humans, specifically Christians.

This Southern Baptist doctrine was especially troubling because our beloved cat, Snookums, had just delivered herself of her first batch of black-and-white tuxedo kittens. Like little pagans, we kids worshiped her blind, mewling litter. I serenaded the kittens with my clarinet, discovering they preferred Mozart and Tchaikovsky. Brahms lulled them to sleep, and Chopin inspired them to suckle. My siblings and I sang four-part harmonies, mostly gospel songs and musicals to them. "Amazing Grace" and "I'm Going to Wash That Man Right Outa My Hair" were all-time feline favorites.

Even as I practiced the Sword Drill with my mother, my mind was distracted by the symphony of the kittens' snuffling piccolo. *How could God give us such trusting, companionable animals and then simply throw them away into darkness when they died? Why whisk only humans off to heaven? What kind of Rapture was that?* I wondered if heaven had forests and oceans, maybe as old as God. Who cared about mansions in a Father's house? I wanted an afterlife with animals, and a wilderness I could wander for eternity.

I knew this was heresy, but I also knew that somehow I had an unconscious ally in my father's devotion to this earth. I had watched him navigate the world of wildlife as a forester with an unwavering belief in Southern Baptist doctrine. Though he was always a pillar of every church, my father's work was a subtext of his spirituality. In my family, it was possible to love God *and* not forsake all his creations; it was possible to love this earth and still long to leave it. That paradox called forth in me a crisis of faith.

I dreaded Sunday school, just as I feared I would disappoint my more dogmatic mother by failing to win the Sword Drill. It didn't help that my mother was now drilling me in a popular variation of our scripture competition called Animal Sword Drill, which was more a children's learning game than what would be required of me, a middle-schooler, especially at a semi-final competition. Upon locating the verse, one had to sing out the animal sound. This usually made the training more playful and cheered me on. But not today.

"Sparrow!" mother chirped.

Mind scanning, fingers shuffling—ah, there it was. I stepped out, Bible sword raised, "Luke 12:6. . . . Are not five sparrows sold for two farthings, and not one of them is forgotten before God?" And then I raised my head way back and whistled a warbling bird song as any woodland child would do.

"You aced it!" Mother, rushed up to embrace me. "Let's go treat ourselves to some of my homemade ice cream."

I braced for her hug as we kids always did. "Locomotive" was how we described her launches toward us at full tilt. Often she knocked us down.

Mother was a woman who could never contain herself, whether it was playing piano at church so passionately and with such a boogie-woogie bass hand that the choir director had to line up potted plants to hide her performance from the more staid churchgoers; or whether it was expressing emotion. We thought of our mother as a wild animal, say a leopard, who didn't know her own speed or strength.

Her ice cream was another story. Hand-churned for hours by my dutiful father, it used so much real cream that she wouldn't divulge the amount. Into this rich, sugared coolness she folded fresh-picked strawberries and black walnuts that she cracked by putting them in a burlap sack and repeatedly running over them in our station wagon.

Ice cream in our family exerted a mystical pull on my three other siblings and even my father home early from his office work in the U.S. Forest Service. Since he had moved us to Boston for his fellowship to Harvard when I was seven, he was "in training for Big Things," as my mother told us. Supper talk about those Big Things paled next to the promise of luscious peach-pecan or Rocky Road homemade ice cream.

That night at the dinner table, my heresy was discovered. Our tables were scenes of great debates, mostly political, with my father presiding. He didn't enjoy philosophical dialogue, preferring the practical and reasonable—and a damn good story. His favorite style was the lecture format in which he gave his children, like his employees, the Ten Commandments according to his pragmatic experience of the world. My family spoke four languages: animals, religion, politics, and music.

That night my father shocked me by turning my way mid-lecture and asking, with real curiosity, "What's on your mind?"

I was so surprised by his inquiry that I simply told him the truth. "Well," I began, "you know my earth science project?"

"Ant farm, right?" a sibling piped up.

"Yeah, she spends all her time staring at those boring ants like some kind of TV," another sibling explained, as if I were developmentally slow. Today they would call it "reality TV."

All I knew to say was, "It's not boring! I've been watching very closely and taking field notes, like my earth science teacher taught us." I paused and looked around the table, giddy with my rare audience. "And sometimes the ants just stop what they're carrying and look out at me through the glass. Like they really see me." I hesitated, and then advanced my theory. "Maybe the ants think I'm a planet that rises and sets over their world?"

I stopped abruptly. I had never seen my father's dark blue, hooded eyes so bewildered. He gazed at me as if I had just announced that I was from another planet—something I routinely confided to my siblings at night. I could see my father struggling between true concern and the more convenient banishment from the dinner table to "get my head on straight." I could plainly see that he was appalled.

He shook his head, without saying a word. At last he murmured, "Well, I don't think I'll ever ask you that question again, honey. You can just keep those things to yourself. And you might not want to tell your teachers either."

I stopped myself from announcing to the dinner table another of my science theories. Not only did I believe that animals were always watching us, but I also believed that humans were simply other animals. Often at school and church, even with my family, I just listened and watched people, imagining I was an animal researcher in the field, like Jane Goodall. I observed human-animal behaviors, noting them with what I hoped was scientific detachment.

A sibling snitched on me. "But she already told our Sunday school teacher something." "What?" my father demanded. "Told her what?"

"That she believes animals have souls, too. That they die and go to heaven, just like us."

For a moment, my father seemed to consider really engaging in this spiritual dialogue. But my mother jumped up, declaring, "You are certainly *not* a planet being gawked at by ants. And Snookums is just our cat. She doesn't have a soul."

We knew that Mother wanted to get rid of the kittens as soon as they were weaned, and we were lobbying hard to keep just one.

"Snookums does . . . "—my youngest sibling stood up to our mother—". . . Snookums has a soul. She's told me she is my guardian angel."

"That's silly," Mother said and tried to sweeten her argument by serving up a perfect peach pie with a cross-lattice of bubbling, brown crust. It was a perfect match for her ice cream.

For the moment, the pie distracted us, since we were more dessert fans than Great Debaters. But then my mother made the crucial miscalculation of assuming my father was completely aligned with her in this dinner table exchange.

"And we certainly won't have to feed your father's horses every night in heaven," she declared.

I was heartened in my heresy by the fact that my father winced at Mother's sanguine exclusion of his Tennessee Walkers from heaven. I would hear my father openly weep only twice in my life: when his mother died, and when he had to put his favorite horse down. For a moment I thought he might take on Mother and the Southern Baptist doctrine, but he quickly recovered his patriarchal composure to conclude, "This is not a subject that children can debate." Then he added, with a fond rustling of my hair, "Now, let's see those kittens. How are they doing today?"

It was a bit of a reprieve from my doubting, but I was still secretly troubled by my loss of faith. My father supposed my spiritual malaise was stubborn world-weariness.

In the following months, my father often lectured, "Boredom is a sign of a small mind." Finally he broke down and bought me a microscope and chemistry set. Perhaps he hoped biology might settle me down, or at least balance the hormonal impairment of female puberty.

Biology did ground me during junior high and at a tumultuous time. In 1962 the South was still two years away from the Civil Rights Act that would finally end segregation. Our school was not yet integrated. There were rumors and growing street protests, some even led by Baptist ministers, like Martin Luther King Jr. On his famous road to integration, the Reverend King had been arrested on trumped-up charges, such as driving without a license or attempting to desegregate public buildings. The next year, in 1963, Dr. King would deliver his transcendent "I Have a Dream" speech on the steps of the Lincoln Memorial to a jubilant, racially mixed crowd of 400,000 people.

But in 1962 our junior high was still teaching from a gray tome with a Confederate flag on the cover. "Virginia History" was a required course for seventh-graders. It was divided into three sections: the first, which was the bulk of the book, was dotingly devoted to Virginia's glorious Confederate period. There was a slim section entitled "The Present," and for the future there was a ten-page epilogue that no one, not even our teacher, ever discussed. But we were relentlessly tested on every battle and engagement of the Civil War. And to my shock, there were regular test questions that even I at twelve years old could see were obviously racist. One question haunts me still: "Negroes are best adapted for work as: (a) minstrels (b) laborers (c) statesmen." When I answered (c) I was scored down because the "correct" answer was "laborers." I protested, and the teacher promptly failed me for the whole test.

Nevertheless, we still paradoxically played "Rebel and Yankee" in our forest tree-fort wars, each of us vying to be a Rebel. I was considered an outsider with only a slight southern accent, a suspicious transplant born in California. I had lived in Virginia only since fifth grade, and who knows how long I would be rooted here? My parents, though southerners, had taught their children to believe in equality between the races. My father's travels as a young man in the Navy during World War II and his Native American heritage—though he rarely spoke about it—had taught him to be more open-minded than our Virginia neighbors. Still, there were no black people in our church. While some of the faithful quietly discussed integration, most often our worship services and Bible studies were resoundingly white and dull.

As the only introvert in the family, I often retreated to my own room to read and daydream. If someone knocked on my door I told them I was praying. This was the best "Do Not Disturb" signal I had ever discovered. I also endured our endless churchgoing by seeking the eccentric company of Old Man Bode. He went to church not to repent, sing, or socialize, but simply to whittle. Mr. Bode was a scrawny screech-owl with a shock of reddish-white hair that today would be called punk because it stood straight up like Woody Wood-pecker's. Bent over a plug of pine or balsa wood, Mr. Bode was en-gaged in his masterwork: he was making a replica of Noah's Ark. I'd already watched him carve sea serpents, rhinos, and dragons, the really big creatures, but now he'd moved on to my favorite—mammals. I was studying marine mammals in earth science and brought my biology books to church to show Mr. Bode. Sometimes he'd sketch from them.

Together we would sit in the back pew, bent over as if devoutly praying, but instead I watched him whittle away. Sometimes his ani-mals were fantastical, a bestiary captured mid-metamorphosis be-tween species: there was a lion with wings I later would discover was a chimera, and a unicorn, and a teradactyl-like dinosaur bird with wolves' teeth. He painted the animals in his tool shed, and every Sun-day he would reveal his latest handiwork. He inspired in me a keen sense of animal extinction, as well as an obsession with dinosaurs, many of whom he loved to carve, especially Tyrannosaurus Rex and Brontosaurus.

Far from the forests of my birth, I sometimes believed that most of the forest animals I knew were indeed going extinct, so I began studying dinosaurs with the passion of one who is witnessing history. My intensity led my father often to conclude that I would grow up to be an archaeologist diligently at work on far-flung digs for dinosaur bones. He teasingly called dinosaurs my "imaginary friends" and explained my sketchbooks full of brontosaurus and ichthyosaurus, the ancient ancestor to dolphins, as the product of a "young scientist at work."

Had I ever confided my real plan for the dinosaurs, my rational-minded father would have again been dismayed. Secretly, I imagined that the dinosaurs, even though they were dead on earth, were still alive in spirit form somewhere, if only my prayers could reach them. In 1962 the escalating Cold War tensions triggered the Bay of Pigs crisis, and the nation became obsessed with a nuclear bomb. At twelve years old, I'd been plotting my own civil defense plans. I reasoned that if the world was going to end with a big bang, as happened when the fiery comets destroyed the dinosaurs' world, then why not turn to dinosaur logic to try to survive? All the sermons predicted there would be the Armageddon of fire next time. I had a plan.

It was to Mr. Bode alone that I confided my survival plans for the looming World War III. "We have to get back to the sea, that's all," I told him in what I hoped he would believe was a sensible, scientific voice. But at my first confidence, I could see I didn't have to stick to the facts. Unlike any adult I'd ever encountered, Mr. Bode had an active imagination, and one that also embraced other animals.

"Will the sea really save us from nuclear fire?" Mr. Bode asked, quite intrigued.

"You know, our planet is 80 percent ocean." I quoted the statistic with the fervor my mother usually reserved for scripture. "And I don't believe ichthyosaurus has ever gone extinct. He's just evolved into a dolphin. They are so smart that even scientists can't figure out their language."

"So the dolphins will rescue you from land just like they do drowning men at sea?" Mr. Bode smiled.

"Yes!" How wonderful that for once an adult could grasp my reasoning. "So here's my plan. We'll survive the first nuclear blast in my mom's fallout shelter. As soon as that's over, I'll take my family to Virginia Beach. We'll call on the dolphins to carry us out to sea where we'll be safe. We'll learn to float on the waves and go ashore only to sleep on the beaches."

Mr. Bode nodded, considering this. "You mean, we'll become amphibious?"

"That's it, yes!"

What I did not tell Mr. Bode was that I had already drowned once and this near-death experience was one of the highlights of my life so far. As a toddler, my parents had brought me down out of the primal forest for the first time to see our relatives and the Pacific Ocean. At the sight of the mesmerizing surf, I'd flung open my arms and run straight into the waves. No one noticed that an undertow took me, swirling me around like so much flotsam. I did not struggle. When the wave lifted me back up onto the beach, my father flapped my limp arms, thumped my tiny chest, and breathed for me. From then on, I believed myself half sea-creature. And ever since drowning, I was dedicated to the oceans; I dreamed of one day becoming a scientist-sailor who wrote seafaring stories.

Mr. Bode dazzled me now by leaning over and slowly unlacing his leather boots. He took off his shoe and red-plaid sock to reveal a wonder: there between his second and third toes was the most delicate, pale webbing.

In one of my more arcane science texts I'd read that of 1,000 schoolchildren examined in a 1926 study, 9 percent of the boys and

6.6 percent of the girls had webbing between their toes. But I had never seen this marvelous phenomenon. Here was the proof. For just a moment I thought I might burst into tears as I examined this missing link between Mr. Bode's ancient toes. I reached down and tenderly touched the pale webbing as if it were a biblical miracle.

"When the world ends," I told Mr. Bode, "I'd like you to come with my family back to the sea, where the fire can't follow."

"When they drop the Big One," Mr. Bode amiably agreed, "I'll be coming along right behind you." Then he pulled back on his sock and boot.

That same morning he whittled a beautiful balsam ichthyosaurus for me, a wink toward our secret Armageddon survival plan. I let myself lean against the old man's wizened shoulder. Who knew what the preacher was saying anymore? All he did was preach about the Rapture, when righteous folks would be lifted up on a divine cloud and all those left behind would perish in fires and pestilences below. When I compared this exclusive and mean-spirited Rapture with my own scientifically inspired civil defense plan for surviving nuclear End Times, mine seemed much more reasonable and open-hearted.

In our back pew, Old Man Bode and I were in our animal communion, even as the congregation cheerfully sang cherished hymns, such as "I Was Sinking Deep in Sin." As long as I was in church, no one paid much attention to what I was actually doing or thinking. I knew enough not to tell anyone about my spiritual discourse with Mr. Bode. I never even told my younger siblings, who still believed in almost anything. I guarded my friendship with Mr. Bode the way my father kept his animal skins and trophies for himself. Some churchgoers claimed Mr. Bode was senile or crazy, especially when he'd drop one of his Noah's Ark carved animals into the offering plate as his monthly tithe. But I knew he was a man full of the Holy Spirit—a modern-day Noah.

Here was someone in whom I could confide my spiritual misgivings and my private longings to leave the church, even though my parents expected my faithful attendance, if not my daily faith. But I felt no spiritual connection with the continual Southern Baptist story line of sin, suffering, separatism. When the congregation sang, *This world is not my home, I'm just passing through / If heaven's not my home, then, Lord, what will I do?* I bowed my head in consternation. How could they happily jettison the entire world for an afterlife that seemed thinly conceived and lonely for all I most loved? Another thing: if God so loved this world, why didn't Christians take better care of it?

Once I dared to ask my Sunday school teacher, "What does it matter who we worship or if we save all the people, if we don't have a home?" I was growing troubled by all the stories my earth science teacher was telling us about a "silent spring" from pesticides.

"Oh, but some people will always be here." My teacher pounced on my question with a fervor I found vaguely menacing. "Unbelievers will be left behind."

I was about to tune out when the teacher said something that to this day explains why the most fundamentalist Christians can detach from their earthly home and their own bodies.

"Remember, dear, we are *in* this world," the teacher intoned, "but not *of* it."

"You mean," I asked, my twelve-year-old mind wrestling with this, "that we don't belong here? . . . Not at all?"

"Never did," the teacher said with satisfaction, "never will."

From Mrs. Eula in Vacation Bible School I had learned that God didn't dwell in the earth but was in spirit above us all. Now they were telling me that we didn't belong on earth either.

"Are we . . . are we, well, aliens from some other planet?" I had to ask.

"Heavens, no!" The teacher eyed me suspiciously. "Have you been reading science fiction instead of your scripture? And don't you have a big Sword Drill to prepare for?"

I barely heard the teacher's question. If we didn't belong here, if we were just waiting around for a savior the way a loyal dog awaits her master, then, I wondered, what was the point of being here at all? *How could I ever find a place in this world?* Perhaps, as I feared, I would never belong anywhere.

This deepening doubt plagued my performance at the Sword Drill semi-final championships. The following week, my fingers were nimble as ever, but my rote memory was interrupted by the true enemy of dogma—questions.

The moment I lost my spiritual way—my Waterloo in this biblical battlefield—was when the judge called out 2 Timothy 2:15.

"Study to shew thyself approved unto God, a workman that needeth not to be ashamed, rightly dividing the word of Truth." The judge spoke each word of scripture like a drill instructor in biblical boot camp. Standing there on the stage with other earnest competitors, I asked myself: Do I want to be a Christian soldier in this army? Do I really want to divide the word of Truth by packing and presenting my Bible like a rifle? Do I belong to this fellowship of the believers—or was I just passing through their ranks like a visitor who could one day leave them behind?

In my sharpshooter peripheral vision, I glanced up and down the line of other adolescents bent over their Bibles scrambling for the verse that I had already fingered. My training told me to step out and be counted among the believers. Take my place on the fast train to heaven. Claim some prize, some star in my crown.

But I didn't move. I looked down at the verse and did something completely wrongheaded. I pondered. *Why would God's workman ever need to be ashamed? If God, the Father, didn't approve of me, would I be forever banished from the ark of heaven, like all the other animals? Would God really send a twelve-year-old to hell?*

While I was engaging in my inner battle, I looked out in the audience and saw my mother's face. She knew I had the right answer. Mother clearly saw that I had found the verse first. Her expression demanded, *Why aren't you leaping out to be counted among the blessed, the winners?*

I stood still, realizing how separate I felt from this fearsome God, from my family and mother, from everyone on the stage. A spotlight was shining down on me, isolating and exposing me to enemy fire. Almost a teenager, I felt trapped in this faith. But one day, I decided, I would run away.

My mother's face was a revelation. Though I was her "spitting image," as people always marveled, having inherited her wildcat eyes and unruly hair, I would not be her mirror. From that moment on, she would no longer see herself in me. Mother looked at me, her eldest daughter, as if I was now Top Ten on her daily prayer list. At twelve, I was already a lost soul. Just as I was beginning to feel like a little Israelite wandering in the wilderness, it occurred to me—in a moment I hoped was divine inspiration—that my first mother was the forest, and I was most at home wandering that wilderness.

As if throwing off a demon, my mother shook her head, scowling. She made an impatient gesture with her hands, a sign language I recognized: *You know this! We've practiced. Now snap out of it—and win!*

I don't remember what position I placed in the Sword Drill. I'm sure it was a disappointing score because Mother never mentioned it again, except to say, "She who hesitates is lost!" That loss ended my brilliant career as a biblical scholar.

Today, as a backslid yet devoted earth science student, I might have found both my grief and my passion meeting in an ecology class. I might have been reassured that my embrace of the nonhuman world was in a tradition as recent as John Muir and as ancient as the Celtic Christians, who believed that the popular Saint Jerome shared his study with dogs, deer, doves, peacocks, parrots, cats, and even a majestic lion. Saint Jerome had once tenderly removed a thorn from this lion's forepaw, thus inspiring the kingly beast's companionable loyalty—so much so that Saint Jerome and his scribes were said to have drawn blood from his lion for bright ink to use in writing his holy texts. Scripture written in the blood of the sacred animal.

If I were a child of today, I might have been lulled to sleep at night with the loving lessons of E. O. Wilson's modern-day "biophilia" or "innately emotional affiliation of human beings to other living organisms"—in other words, a love of all that is alive. Wilson's erudition and compassion might have explained to me that my rapt attention to other animals was natural; in fact, it was what he termed "a naturalist's trance" of being not only witness to but also participant in the lives of other animals.

I barely regretted the end of the Sword Drill competitions. What I mourned was losing Old Man Bode. My last memory of Mr. Bode alive was sitting beside him as he whittled his masterwork: a large, pinewood ark for all the animals he had accumulated over the many sermons we endured together. Carefully positioning the elephants, eagles, baboons, horses, and, yes, ichthyosauruses in their tiny stalls, the eternally taciturn Mr. Bode delivered himself of his own sermon.

"Animals know things that people don't," he said. His breath smelled like horehound cough drops, chicory coffee, and tobacco. "Things that we forget."

Then he looked at me fondly and held up a duck-billed platypus. I had just read in earth science that, like the dodo, the oddly comic platypus was now extinct.

"Animals never forget who they are." Mr. Bode tenderly set the lost animal into his ark. "A duck is always a duck. He doesn't think he is an eagle or hawk. It's only people who go false on themselves."

Mr. Bode never did go false on himself or me. When he died, his rural relatives knew enough about him to carefully position those hundreds of beautifully carved animals in his coffin. The whole church marveled as congregants filed by his casket. My mother at the piano played a marching tempo of "I'll Leave It All Behind," but people still lingered to gaze in at the old man and his carvings.

"What next?" Mother fumed after the funeral. "Toy cars and rifles in the caskets? We're not Neanderthals burying our belongings with the dead."

"Lay not up for yourselves treasures on earth," I quoted, hoping this scripture might appease her. Then I had to ask, "But if you could put something in your casket, what would it be?"

"Well," she considered a moment, then pronounced brightly, "my Bible for sure, maybe some of my favorite sheet music. Also a Scrabble set and some good spy thrillers. Maybe even a jar of my mother's apple butter."

My mother's casket was beginning to resemble our fallout shelter.

As she named a few more eternal keepsakes, I had to smile, but without showing it. Mr. Bode's coffin had inspired in her a fanciful flight. As she gazed in at the brontosaurus, the gorillas, the graceful giraffes, my mother's face changed from derision to delight.

three

Render to Them Their Desserts
(Psalm 28:4)

AS ONE WHO BACKSLID FROM THE SOUTHERN BAPTIST FOLD, THERE are only a few fundamentals I still miss: the food, the music, and Pastor Joe Strother and his wife, Sue, at Sunset Hills Church in Virginia. Today, when I visit my parents' Virginia home from the far-flung Northwest Coast, I still carry on some traditions of the faithful: eating and singing. And I still carry on a meditative inner dialogue with Pastor Joe and a real conversation with Sue, who survives him. Joe is one Christian who would have been called "green" today. His sermons were about compassion more than conquest. During my adolescent years of doubt, it was Pastor Joe and Sue, an ex-parole officer, who taught me that my love of the earth was a devotion to the divine, and that Rapture was possible right here on earth. There are so many reasons to be left behind.

In the fervent circles of my childhood, food was love. As one of my Jewish friends, who has tasted my mother's black walnut divinity, says, "Isn't food one of the primary reasons to be here on earth? Maybe that's what Eve and the apple were all about—nothing to do with good and evil, or knowledge, but food, glorious food."

Perhaps because many Southern Baptists don't drink or smoke or dance, the sensuality of food is a powerful persuasion to keep coming to church. Who could resist the temptation of wild blackberry cobbler, the creamy manna of my mother's homemade wild blackberry ice cream, or the church ladies' triple-fudge brownies studded with glazed pecans? Southern Baptist women, often called "refreshment committees," are wizards at starches—olive-macaroni salads, butternut squash casseroles, and delicate pie crusts that a French pastry chef would envy. Around food, Southern Baptists surrender to culinary pleasures and family-style warmth like Italians. Like Russians, southern believers share a passion for pickling—mushrooms, cucumbers, sweet beets. Mother always made us Russian tea at Christmas, a grudging nod to the Soviets, whom the Rapture folk call "Gog," for the sinister part they believe Russia will supposedly play as conquerors of Israel and harbingers of End Times.

Russian tea, a concoction of citrus Tang and Lipton's black tea, served with salty sausage cookies, was our traditional Christmas Eve present before our yearly excursion to see a "live" Nativity scene on the freezing front lawn of Sunset Hills Church. Our thermoses were filled with spicy hot chocolate and our pockets still stuffed with the sausage cookies that drew the attention of dogs, who often stood in as Christmas camels or lowly cows tethered around the manger. I was always so happy to see the newborn savior attended by animals, right next to the Wise Men. A barn full of animals for a church—now that was my idea of worship.

My mother always taught us that no one should be alone at Christmas and that we must expect miracles and mysteries. The madeleines of her Christmas were her peanut-butter fruitcake, cherry and pineapple fudge, and virgin eggnog. When I was fourteen, a heathen coworker from my father's field survey, office brought bourbon balls to our home as a gift. The hapless man was newly divorced— quite scandalous in those days—and Mother hoped to do some matchmaking with one of the widowed women in the choir. If this "match made in heaven" took, Mother would have accomplished two

Southern Baptist goals: marriage and saving a lost soul. But the bourbon balls determined that the guest must remain single. Before Mother had a chance to deliver his sweets over to the fate of all liquor in our house—down the drain—we kids had gobbled up half a dozen balls apiece. As the remaining bourbon balls gurgled in our newfangled garbage disposal, we spun around the Christmas tree tipsy, stringing cranberries.

Later that same evening when we bundled up for the crystal cold of that Christmas Eve to witness the Nativity live, the scene did not surprise us a bit. In fact, it seemed quite in keeping with the spirit of that evening and the bourbon balls that the girl who played the part of Virgin Mary was a teenager and she was actually pregnant. Oh, sinner that she was, this tableau was her redemption. The girlish Mary approached the makeshift barn astride a real donkey, her eyes downcast, an upstanding, albeit nervous Joseph in false beard beside her. The holy couple was awaited by a shivering gaggle of children, Wise Men who were really church deacons, and shepherds who were local farmers. One had even brought several sheep, which the dog-camels kept in line more or less near the manger.

This Mary struck awe in all of us because we knew her backstory. She was a runaway from "pillars of the church" parents; prodigal, she had returned home eight months pregnant, unmarried. Our kindly Pastor Joe put out the word that her story was not unlike that of the real Mother of God, who had to leave her home and, to some, might have seemed suspect when she told her story of an angel and divine conception.

We were strangely moved by this modern Mary who calmed herself in her starring role by blowing incandescent pink veils with each breath and her bubble gum. After that Christmas pageant, bubble gum became a staple of our stockings, a little ritual that my Catholic friends—who usually cornered the market on Mother Mary, miracles, and their all-purpose saints—had to envy. It had never occurred to us before seeing that particular live Nativity that the mother of such an important baby might have been frightened or felt alone. But this knocked-up Mary evoked in us a quality that Southern Baptists are not known for: mercy. I'd never met an unwed mother. As I watched this young girl shiver and drop her eyes in shame, I thought, *So many mothers in the world must bring children into the world alone—children who are equally divine, even if they are not born Baptist.*

Anybody frightened or alone at Christmas seemed incongruous to my family, though the adults were always hauling us off to progressive holiday dinners with the "shut-ins" or the "backslid," as we heard them described. These were people who were either too sick or too sinful to come to church. What the wayward often did attend with gusto were the progressive dinners, which were basically pious pig-outs. These eating marathons proceeded from house to house, from hors d'oeuvres to salads to side dishes to main course, completed by a Roman debauch of desserts. In my adolescent diary I was so astonished by one progressive dinner that I wrote down the menu:

> *Salads—First House:* Waldorf salad, red cabbage slaw, Heavenly Hash, hot, wilted lettuce with ham hock, honeyed pears and blue cheese, strawberry Jello-rings with celery and cottage cheese. *Appetizers:* pickle chow-chow and corn relish, home-cured beef jerky, Vienna sausages and Ritz crackers, Swedish meatballs on colored toothpicks.

> *Side dishes—Second House:* Barbequed butter beans, cornmeal-fried okra, homemade hominy, sweet potatoes with candied ginger and pecans, mustard greens and braised kale, green bean casserole with onion rings, corn and lima bean succotash, parsnips in brown sugar, German potato salad with sausage, cornbread, grits, and cream gravy.

Main course—Third House: Roasted wild turkey with walnut stuffing, beer-batter fried chicken, pork roast with dried apricots, Mother's mooseghetti (from my father's recent hunting trip to Montana), bratwurst with dill sauerkraut, and salt-encrusted Smithfield ham.

Desserts—Final House: Chocolate cream pie with coconut, strawberry rhubarb tarts, sour cherry cobbler with brown sugar crumble, vanilla custard cream puffs, double-fudge brownies with caramel sauce, Mother's peach ice cream.

After a progressive holiday dinner, we always had to lie down in the back of our blue Buick station wagon, groaning all the way home. Unlike Catholics, who must suffer Lent, no meat on Fridays, and the sin of gluttony, we Baptists could eat without any spiritual worries until doomsday. Gluttony is no sin.

When I was fifteen and enjoying the stratosphere of a high school sophomore, our church youth choir even got so bold as to take our Christmas treats and our singing to the prestigious and widely revered St. Elizabeth's mental institution in Washington, D.C. The complex cantata we had practiced all fall was called "Night of Miracles," and in addition to my mother's piano accompaniment, our performance would be bolstered by the choir's diva, Mrs. Elana Simmer. Her rich, dark mezzo-soprano voice was reason enough to go to church. Mrs. Simmer had sung professionally before succumbing to the fate of many a Southern Baptist wife—motherhood, under what I was beginning to think of as "house arrest."

When she sang, this rather odd-looking woman with her bouffant black hair and a distracting wart on her lip was transformed into a guardian archangel. With each high note, Mrs. Simmer held on to the choir loft and practically levitated; with each vibrato low note, her dark eyes smoldered. I marveled that any man, especially just a husband, could keep her housebound. Mrs. Simmer's singing was so heartfelt, so full of longing and sensuality, that everybody, even little children, leaned toward her vibrato. It was acoustic light, full of unseen overtones and mysterious resonance.

We were bewitched. Some bowed their heads and wept openly. Mrs. Simmer's voice was rumored to cure high fevers and help the dying pass to their reward. Most of all, Mrs. Simmer called forth a kind of musical rapture in us. This world was not so heavy, not so hard, when Mrs. Simmer sang.

Her solo, I was firmly convinced, would also heal some of the mentally ill incarcerated at St. Elizabeth's. In the same way that Christ had cast out demons like so many pigs tumbling over a cliff, perhaps Mrs. Simmer's singing would ease psychosis. In any case, those who could not be cured with singing could enjoy our special dessert: Gift of the Magi cupcakes. This was my mother's special recipe: a trinity of chocolate on chocolate on chocolate. It was like the original sin of chocolates—why else would it be called "devil's food"?

Some of us in the youth choir had sampled the cupcakes en route to St. Elizabeth's and sang out with lips stained dark. Once we arrived, the patients gathered around us in a circle, all dolled up for our visit. When we sang, they nodded and tapped feet like normal folk, and we decided they weren't crazy at all. I suppose we had expected to see people foaming at the mouth or even worse, naked. But the inmates all ate their cupcakes and clapped, just like the polite go-to-church audience.

All that is, except a very small old lady with two bright splotches of rouge on her cheeks that endeared her to me. She peeled her Gift of the Magi cupcake with delicate white lace gloves and then, smiling, as we belted out the rousing chorus of "Night of Miracles," smashed her cupcake right atop her head.

No one moved. We stopped singing, shocked. And then Mrs. Simmer did something that was so simple. She left the choir and crossed over to the old woman with the cupcake smeared over her silver head. Singing ever so softly, as if they were the only two people in the whole world, Mrs. Simmer began her solo, all the while disentangling the gooey chocolate cupcake from the old lady's hair.

Sleep, holy child, for thou art safe, in heaven's keeping, Mrs. Simmer cooed.

The old woman looked up trustingly at Mrs. Simmer. She was not crazy, I saw, she was a child. Someone had dumped her at St. Elizabeth's because they didn't want to see her return to the incontinence, incoherence, and helplessness of an ancient infant. But was this old woman just being born again, like all the Baptists talked about? *Maybe old people have to become babies again to be reborn.*

Mrs. Simmer smiled and stroked the old woman's shoulder. She raised her voice to a reassuring mezzo-forte. The old lady now gazed up at Mrs. Simmer. What did she see? I wondered. Her long life, her heavenly afterlife? Or did the woman simply hear radiance showering her and see a mother who never stops loving, who will never leave her child? That was the first time I understood why Catholics worshiped a Madonna, even said prayers to "Mary, full of grace," which my mother claimed was a sure sacrilege.

That Christmas I pondered these St. Elizabeth mysteries and miracles. I was in need of miracles in my own daily life. Our high school was huge, with several thousand students, and its societies were highly stratified. I suspected that I would not be pledged into any of the illegal, but thriving, sororities with any of the popular girls. This did not trouble me so much because hardly a week passed without some hapless student suffering indignities during hazes. One frat boy wannabe was forced to swallow a slimy tadpole tied to a string, and when it was pulled back up his throat, still squiggling and barely alive, the boy's esophagus was damaged.

A girl in my earth science class invited me to her slumber party to scout me for her sorority. Because I had no acne, the other girls tried out a face mask makeover on me. But someone put plaster of Paris in the green goo, and it cemented to my skin so painfully that I had to be rushed to the emergency room. When the doctor peeled off the green mask, I lost several layers of skin in some places, especially under my eyes—scars of sorority trials gone awry. My father said I looked like a little raccoon.

The only high school cliques I really cared about were the girls' basketball team and the symphony—one of the finest in Virginia—in which I played clarinet. It was in the symphony that I discovered a beautiful antidote for religious monotones: harmony. Even when I was intently focused on playing my own third clarinet part, I had to keep an ear out for the whole symphony.

Our director, Mr. Dunmar, was fond of saying, "If one instrument is out of tune, you will drag the entire symphony off-pitch. If I catch you listening only to yourself—no matter how pure your tone—you'll be dismissed. I don't care how good you are, you can't just blare out your own part. Toot your own horn, as they say. We play *ensemble* or we don't play."

Mr. Dunmar taught us that there was really no one way to play an instrument. No perfect technique or right position. Inspired music, like prayer, was all about rapt attention. Inflexibility and too narrow a focus, Mr. Dunmar said, showed a sad lack of talent. Sometimes Mr. Dunmar insisted we play one another's parts so we could better recognize how we all flowed together. It was a holistic and nuanced approach to symphonic art. While it didn't lessen the competition between chairs in sections, it did force us to attune to each other with a passionate openness particularly rare in high school, where peer groups—like some religions—are often focused on exclusion.

"Music was our first language," Mr. Dunmar would lecture us from his podium, his precise plastic baton raised like an antenna. "Even animals understand octaves, counterpoint, crescendos. They've got more rhythm and tone than we do," Mr. Dunmar emphasized as he cast a critical eye over the erratic percussion section. Then his all-seeing eyes swept each of us. Mr. Dunmar listened as much with his eyes as his perfectly pitched ears. He continued in his distinctive baritone. "Animals also make music, and that's probably how early humans learned the art."

When a first violinist smirked at what she obviously believed was a lowly comparison, Mr. Dunmar set his baton on his music stand—a bad sign—and turned his unnervingly green eyes on the girl.

"You don't know that Mozart often listened to birds before he wrote his music?"

Laughter from the symphony. I noticed that even our laughter held harmonies and overtones that might be hidden if one weren't listening for them. We had played together so intently, our voices intuitively sought to synch all our sounds.

Scanning the symphony from my third clarinet section, I had a revelation: everyone looked just like other animals. The first flautist, with her elegant, elongated neck, was a temperamental swan; the second oboe, with his twitching nose and eyebrows as he pursed his lips, was a rat; the trombone impresario who swung his instrument back and forth as he bellowed was a trumpeting elephant. And what animal was our imposing director? I studied Mr. Dunmar's wide face, his wavy crest of silky red hair, his all-seeing eyes, and his long arms: Mr. Dunmar was a regal orangutan.

Mr. Dunmar stepped down from his podium and began pacing before us, swinging his lean arms as if to accompany his own thoughts. "Think of birdsong as an art song, a courtship ritual," he said, nodding to himself, "or wolves howling together in a pack as a symphony that is all about bonding together to survive." He stopped, cocked his head as if listening to some complicated music, and then suddenly strode over to the first flautist and plucked up her expensive instrument. He held it aloft like a baton. "Did you know the first musical instruments were made from the bones of a swan?"

I was thrilled. Mr. Dunmar, too, had seen how birdlike the first flautist was. Then our director strolled over to the trumpet and

French horns, who always smelled of sweat and spittle. Many of us dainty woodwinds were appalled at the brassy boys always flapping open their horns to dribble their spit on the wooden floor. It was as disgusting to us as the wrestling coach who also taught sex education; he kept his spittoon on his desk and would splurt out tobacco juice to punctuate his creepy anatomical descriptions.

"If we just listen, the whole world is in resonance," Mr. Dunmar concluded and stepped back up to his podium. He picked up his baton and pointed toward the clarinet section. "What do I mean by that word?"

I knew the answer from earth science, but I was so intimidated by our maestro that I never spoke, I only played my clarinet. As Mr. Dunmar eyed our section, my heart thudded in 6/8 time and I felt faint. When his baton singled out a second clarinet sitting right in front of me, I let out a long withheld breath that might have been impressive had I been using my instrument.

"Resonance," repeated the science geek with greasy hair, "in physics is an oscillation at the same frequency . . . a sympathetic vibration."

"Very good, Albert," said Mr. Dunmar, eyeing the boy as if for the first time. Later that month, Albert would find himself a chair higher in his section.

Mr. Dunmar picked up two of the tuning forks he always kept on his music stand. Sometimes if one of us was repeatedly off-pitch, Mr. Dunmar would go over, strike his tuning fork, and set it vibrating atop the offender's skull. "If I strike one tuning fork like so"—Mr. Dunmar struck one tuning fork against his music stand, setting off an echoing ding—"what happens?"

We did not have to answer. The other tuning fork Mr. Dunmar held in his hand, without being struck, thrummed and hummed at the same exact pitch.

"The miracle of resonance," Mr. Dunmar concluded. "It is a mystery, isn't it?"

We all nodded heads, our instruments bobbing. How we longed to be part of any miracle Mr. Dunmar could call forth from our young hands and hearts and lungs. How we yearned to see him cock his head and listen to us with that dreamy and surprised smile on his face when by some miracle we played together in perfect resonance.

Between my ardent studies in earth science and symphony, I learned that, as in nature, there are no absolutes in music—only ever-changing tones and colors. A fine musician has to adapt herself constantly to other voices, dissonant sounds. "Blend" it is called in singing and symphonizing. The ability to blend is much like that of a chameleon that changes colors according to the environment. It is a survival skill. The symphony was the first time I was part of a collective that was not based in religion, that did not depend on a group of people all believing the same thing. Was the trombone player in favor of the Vietnam War? Did the first violinist believe in God? Did Mr. Dunmar think the burgeoning environmental movement was based in science? I didn't know. This exhilarated me. Nobody tried to force his or her part on others. We had our own crescendos and diminuendos—and all we cared about was finding a way to play together.

Sometimes on weeknights, when my family was in various church meetings, I would secretly take along my symphony scores. While other people were reading the Bible, I also intently bowed my head, but I was studying my clarinet part, my fingers silently practicing the notes. The symphony was competing in a statewide extravaganza with a concert on the grassy mall of the Washington Monument. We would be playing Tchaikovsky's *1812 Overture*. Momentarily, I had considered boycotting this concert because of my stance against the Vietnam War, but I decided that music was beyond politics. And I did not want to impose my beliefs on others or lose the bonding that music brought my symphony mates—as Mr. Dunmar said it did other animals. I was glad I had forsworn politics for music when I discovered that our director was a fervent birder. He could whistle and warble to mimic mockingbirds and call robins and red-wing blackbirds. Even if one of the reasons birds sang was to defend their territory, the beauty of birdsong transcended aggression.

My fascination with earth science and music reached its zenith in my first attempt to write a novel—a saga passed around the symphony stealthily, like Russian samizdat. In my weekly soap opera, the musicians were characterized as animals. I took my inspiration for this parody from George Orwell's *Animal Farm*. My favorite chapter of this soap opera was entitled "Some Pigs Are More Equal Than Others."

If I had identified myself as the author of this mimeographed opus, I would have been wildly popular. But anonymity allowed me so much more freedom of expression. I took secret pleasure in watching and writing about my symphony mates and their romantic liaisons. Adolescent hormones have a rhythm all their own. Add in the emotional depths of great composers and the brew was even more exciting.

Our first flautist was a Scandinavian beauty with ash-blond curls and Rubenesque curves that were the envy of all of us developing girls. At fifteen, I was what my siblings called a "stick figure," which made me a whiz in basketball, but too tall for most boys. I didn't like loud noise or parties, preferring one-on-one encounters—and not of the sweaty backseat sort, but those found in more tender discussions about literature or music. My romantic career, however, had begun early. In third grade, on the beach in Boston, I had been taught by a French boy how to kiss in exchange for tutoring him in English. And I had also diligently practiced with the Harper boys, our neighborhood pals—the preacher's kids—in our tree fort. Dennis Harper was athletic and an expert at piling up autumn leaves over us so that we could kiss while rolling around embraced by a must-perfumed blanket. He was devoted, and he looked just like Dennis the Menace. I preferred to pine away for Mr. Dunmar, whose marriage to a very prim woman seemed to me to lack resonance.

Our music, like the times, was changing. The Civil Rights Act of 1964 turned the Old Dominion's social bias upside down. The soundtrack to the sudden integration of Virginia schools was boisterous. Buses of black kids from nearby neighborhoods arrived each morning with transistor radios blasting the anthems of 1965 hits: Otis Redding crooning "I've Been Loving You Too Long"; the Temptations' close harmonies on "My Girl"; the gorgeous girl group the Supremes commanding us to "Stop, in the Name of Love"; and the haunting "A Change Is Gonna Come" from Sam Cooke, who had been mysteriously shot the year before. We blacks and whites might have been separated in our schools, but we sang the same sixties songs.

Our high school symphony swelled with new talent. When a black trumpet player and the first flautist flirted, they created the complicated and clandestine music of an interracial couple. Mr. Dunmar addressed their romance obliquely in a brief lecture.

"Integration," he said softly before we rehearsed one morning, "is like music. It is natural. Now we hear all the parts we've been missing."

Our girls' basketball team was now almost all-black. The star forward passed me copies of Gwendolyn Brooks, James Baldwin, and Malcolm X. But I was not allowed to do a book report on these because, as my English teacher, Miss Edna Reeves, said, "It would incite a riot." She was a doddering Daughter of the American Revolution; sometimes when lecturing she would trip over the wastebasket.

There were riots anyway—in the classroom, in the cafeteria, and especially on the basketball court. I learned to perfect my long-shot, standing far away from the fray, because the jolt of black and white elbows under the basket often had more to do with skin than scoring. My closest ally on the team, who protected me from any reverse racism, was a black girl named Marian. Her nickname was Jump Start. I was called Baboon Arms. Jump Start was my bodyguard when the basketball games moved into a fast-motion, up-and-down-the-court race riot.

In one playoff game we were warming up with a rival school, a still all-white team known for its rough-and-tumble attitudes, which thinly disguised their rage over integrated teams. Since I was one of only three white girls on the team, we were also the butt of slurs, uttered with a jab of the opponent's elbow to the ribs. With Jump Start always at my side, I rarely received a rib-jolt, yet the game was different this time. Whenever we started to leap up for a basket, players from the opposite team would stomp on our feet at the moment of flight, nailing us to the wooden gym floor.

"Goddamn animals!" someone on the other team yelled and jammed an elbow into my abdomen so hard I doubled over and collapsed on the floor, fumbling for the ball.

Suddenly, several teammates protectively piled on top of me.

"Foul! Foul!" Marian called out to the referee as many hands reached in to lift me up from the melee. "Ref, you've got to call it foul."

"You don't belong here, jungle bunny," the referee snarled, jerking his thumb backward. "You're outta the game!" And then the official let loose a string of muttered epithets.

As one body, our basketball team walked off the court in protest. Our coach was locked in a long, hot argument with the ref. They were joined by other adults, all waving their arms and yelling. At last the ref blew three sharp blasts on his whistle.

"I call a foul on number 32. The charge is blocking!"

Shocked, we all looked at Jump Start. At least she was back in the game. But who had she been blocking? I realized that the move was Marian's attempt to defend me after the opponent punched me in the stomach. The ref's call was so obviously unfair. Marian's body-check was nothing compared to the guard's jab in my guts.

Everyone in that gymnasium knew it was a false call. The white ref made a call against a black girl who had dared to stand in the way of an all-white opposing team. That team would soon belong to what my father called the "Waste Bin of History." We went on to win that game, to make a new history. This was the first time I remember feeling part of a world we might one day change.

In our church, there was also a big change. Our more traditional, aging preacher, Mr. Harper, was called to a country church. With him went his sons, the sweet gang of boys who had taught me everything from kissing to baseball. Our new pastor, Joe Strother and his wife, Sue, were young and educated, qualities some congregants greeted with skepticism. Pastor Joe and Sue had slipped beneath the Southern Baptist radar, a bastion of Republicanism. Having descended from generations of teetotaling Republicans on each side, I had never met a Democrat in my life, except perhaps Mr. Dunmar. But he talked mostly about music. The new preacher and his wife allowed even teenagers to discuss current events—not just what happened in an ancient Bible world. It was shocking. I was the designated babysitter for their three charming children, who, though very young, were still encouraged to think for themselves and ask questions.

I asked a zillion questions of Sue and Joe. Sue's sense of humor was darkly comic and irreverent, while Joe's kindly scholarship translated into sermons full of real-life stories that navigated a complex moral compass instead of the single plotline of hellfire. He was more a man of spirit than religion—a mystic and a devoted teacher. They had a refreshing take on End Times. "This Rapture nonsense is just not biblically based," Sue declared one night as we sat around her kitchen table after my babysitting stint. I drank root beer and dove into a plate of Sue's homemade walnut fudge while she continued. "Listen, Jesus said even he didn't know when the end was coming."

A slender blonde, Sue's style belied her beauty every time she let out a raucous belly laugh. She actually snorted with pleasure when she was skewering some self-proclaimed saint in our congregation. I could see why the criminals on parole had such affection for their witty parole officer. Under her vigilance, few ex-cons ever returned to prison. And very few churchgoers assumed Sue was the submissive pastor's wife.

Sue's words rekindled in me the lapsed scriptural scholar. "What about the Book of Revelation?"

"The End Times is not widely accepted biblical scholarship," Pastor Joe noted, joining the conversation. With his movie-star black hair, pale skin, and patrician face, he always inspired respect, even in those members of his congregation who found his liberal politics suspect. "It's really just one pretty far-out interpretation by some nineteenth-century preachers of the Books of Daniel, Thessalonians, Matthew, and Revelation."

Joe went on to explain that Christians were perennially preparing for the Apocalypse. "If you study biblical history," he said, "believers have been anticipating the end of this world quite zealously for two thousand years."

"Apocalypticism," as Pastor Joe called it, surged or ebbed depending on the political and religious tides of the times.

"But what about our duck-and-cover drills and nuclear war?" I asked. "Doesn't that sound like the end of the world to you?" Then I confided in Pastor Joe and Sue that I didn't think I would live past the age of thirty because the world would surely be over by then. And besides, I might be too decrepit to want to continue on.

Pastor Joe gave me a meaningful look. "You know that sacred texts are stories, right? And even the best religious scholars always know that they are interpreting the divine, not speaking for Him."

"These Rapture types think they have all the answers," Sue added with her great, robust laugh. "And woe to those of us who don't believe what they do! We're left behind with the Mark of the Beast tattooed on our foreheads and Horsemen of the Apocalypse trampling us down!"

"The point is," Joe continued mildly, "the end is supposed to be a mystery, a true revelation, not a pitiless evacuation plan for believers."

"If Christians spent more time simply *being* here, instead of planning their one-way vacations in heaven," Sue concluded, "we'd have a kinder world."

Then Joe reached over for his worn leather Bible and looked up a verse with a speed and grace that impressed the old Sword Drill contestant in me. "Here it is," he said with satisfaction. "Revelation 11:18 . . . this is the verse all the End Times folks miss when they're going on about horsemen and plagues." He read aloud with his most resonant baritone preacher's voice:

> Give reward unto thy servants the prophets,
> and to the saints, and them that fear thy
> name, small and great; and shouldest destroy
> them which destroy the earth.

Sipping my root beer, I marveled at these words. Pastor Joe was saying that to plot and happily plan the destruction of our earth was to risk God's destruction—not of this planet but of those who so zealously jettisoned it. This little known Revelation passage seemed to be telling believers that if we anticipate the end of our world (through war or environmental destruction), moving that end nearer, we are guilty of a great sin against God's creation. The real reward is given to prophets and saints, like Pastor Joe and Sue, who, like God, "so loved the world. . . . "

*   *   *

ON THE NIGHT of this enlightening discussion I did not realize that the "end times" of my family's own sojourn in Virginia was upon us. Only days later, my father announced that in six weeks we would pack up and move to California. We might as well have been told we would be undertaking our own moon walk.

In 1965 Berkeley was heating up with antiwar protests and what my mother called "pagan cults"—people who ritually ran around half-naked in the streets. Even though I wondered if I might fit in better with that freethinking coast, I was still fiercely rooted in the South and had scrawled across my high school sophomore class photo, "Virginia Forever!"

My mother tried to soften the blow. Of course, she would do it with her cooking. "I know you're not a popular girl in school," she told me bluntly. "But let's send you off with a bang. They'll really miss you when you're gone."

"Why will they miss me?" I asked morosely, already sinking deep into the sin of depression.

Another cross-continent move. Another loss of school, friends, homeland, and even church. I had finally managed to make first chair, third clarinet; and my antiwar short story, "A Time of War and a Time of Peace," which Miss Reeves had flunked in my English class, had gone on to win first place in the high school literary magazine. It didn't change my grade, but it completely revitalized my career hopes, even though my father said that my plan to support my writing as a concert clarinetist was like "supporting your starving by starving."

"They'll miss you," Mother exulted, "because we're going to throw a slumber party with the best food those kids have ever tasted."

"Yeah, the last supper," I grumbled.

"Just make up your guest list and let me get started." Mother's enthusiasm almost snapped me out of my miasma. I invited Jump Start and some other black girls from my basketball team, but they told me that since they were bussed into our suburb, it was probably best we only got together in school.

In 1965 in Virginia, none of my friends had ever heard of tacos. There were no Taco Bells on every street corner or the scrumptious street vendors of the western border states. Special delivery, Mother ordered spices from my aunts in southern California whose homes were near the Mexican border and delicate tortillas from a tiny Latino tortilla factory squirreled away near Washington, D.C. She thawed my father's best cuts of lean moose meat and visited the local farmers' market for the fleshiest avocados. Mother whipped out her recipe for homemade salsa saved from our early years in California. She chopped, grated, browned, and plotted her culinary conversion of these bland eaters to her exotic foreign food. She hoped it would be a religious experience.

Closing my eyes as I helped Mother create her Mexican master-piece, I listened to the music of her cooking: the spicy sizzle of sweet moose meat smothered in chili powder; the percussive chop-chop of avocado, onions, cilantro, and ripe peaches; and the spatter of frying tortillas. Mother and I sang a fast-tempo duet of "On the Jericho Road"," and then slipped easily into Tennessee Ernie Ford's classic "Sixteen Tons, What D'ya Get?"

By the time other sophomore girls arrived for the Friday night slumber party, Mother had been cooking for hours in between pack-ing cardboard moving boxes. With their perfectly pressed Villager blouses, their loafers, their pageboy hairdos and paisley skirts—our school had a dress code that disallowed jeans or pants for girls—my schoolmates stepped into what they feared might be little Tijuana. Their expressions suggested they might be white-slaved any minute by my whirling dervish of a mother in her strange-smelling kitchen.

This was the era of Cheez Whiz and Cool Whip. While I didn't keep company with any religious kids at school, preferring the com-pany of musicians, my basketball teammates, and literature geeks, I'd have to say my friends' taste in food was still parochial: meat and po-tatoes, maybe some risqué barbecued chips. Once a new girl from Appalachia who brought fried pigskins for lunch had been plunged into obscurity when her "lower-class" transgression came to the at-tention of the tight, sorority-ridden strata of this aristocratic south-ern high school.

When my mother merrily announced that we would be feasting on moose meat tacos, there was an almost biblical exodus for the door. Half of those invited to my party didn't stay to eat or slumber. Those who stayed—loyal friends who took pity on me because they knew I was moving away and they could always throw up if the tacos were too terrible—braved the taco buffet. Timidly, they filled their fried tortillas with spicy moose meat, shredded cheese, tomato slices, sour cream, and a suspiciously green dish called "guacamole," all topped with "salsa picante."

As if facing the firing squad, my friends grasped the taco concoctions and took their first frightened nibbles. Talk about revelation! I have never seen diet-conscious teenage girls gorge with such abandon as that night of my slumber party. Mother's tacos were a triumph, and she was suddenly a culinary prophet. One of my friends, the first French horn player, proclaimed, "If I had money, I would invest in a restaurant that sold only tacos!" Had she followed her commercial inspiration instead of her music, she would be a millionaire today.

Though short-lived, these were my glory days at school. Word of the South of the Border slumber party got around, and I was invited to more parties in the last three weeks than in the previous two years of high school. But, perhaps because my mother so possessed her kitchen, I could never replicate her success when asked to bring a potluck dish to other parties. I was reduced to bringing chips and a chili con queso dip I learned to make. It paled, however, when compared with my mother's tacos, now the subject of culinary gossip.

When I had received my $25 check for winning first prize for fiction in the high school literary magazine contest, I made the mistake of emulating my hero, Virginia Woolf. My image of a successful novelist was someone who, if lucky enough to escape a suicidal walk into a lake, sat around brilliantly drinking wine and smoking elegant, slim cigars. In those days, all alcohol in Virginia was imprisoned in squat, concrete Alcoholic Beverage Control stores. There were certainly no convenience stores with racks of beer or wine, no gaudy loan and liquor stores on derelict streets. But having never seen anyone actually purchase alcohol, I assumed it was readily available at any grocery store.

So I rode my bicycle to the local grocery store and cruised the aisles until I found a lovely wine-shaped bottle in a woven straw basket; I purchased cigarillos from a distracted grocery clerk and happily rode home to the tree fort. There, atop the spacious, carpeted third floor, I could survey my forest realm with pride. I tacked up my first-place fiction award on the wall along with a rather glum photo of Woolf. And I took my first gulp of the forbidden wine that would tell the world—or at least all the tall trees around me—that I was at last a published writer.

Oh, the wine was vile. How could anybody ever become an alcoholic? I spat out the first taste and lit a black cigarette. That, too, was hideous—the smoke made spasms in my chest. No wonder Virginia Woolf looked so morose if she was drinking and smoking this stuff. No wonder my evangelical family preached against the sins of alcohol and smoking. Were worldly pleasures all so sour-tasting and harsh? I had to consider that maybe the church people were right. To the chosen, these worldly delights were devastating, like kryptonite to Superman. Too many generations of clean-living churchgoers had not prepared me or my body for literary dissipation.

Nevertheless, I forced myself to drink all of the wine in that deceptively lovely bottle and to smoke every last one of the cigarillos until my stomach and brain were swirling. Sin had never felt so nauseating, I was sure, as I unsteadily climbed down from the tree fort. I was not drunk, but I was vomiting and staggering just like those bums I'd seen on Washington, D.C., backstreets. When I reached the house, my mother was shocked at the pale sinner who spent several hours retching in the bathroom. When she put me to bed, she had diagnosed that I had the stomach flu and kept the other siblings away. But she kept shaking her head in bewilderment and saying, "You smell just like a salad."

After consuming that entire bottle of red wine vinegar, I swore off alcohol forever. To this day my body cannot tolerate wine, which is a shame because I so hoped to grow up to be someone who sits around late-night dinner tables and talks about the great questions of life, or like Virginia Woolf walks on water with words. I did smoke briefly in my early twenties while working at *The New Yorker*, where every writer's head, like a mountain peak, was hidden in a gauzy tobacco cloud. But my family's heritage of weak bronchial tubes kept me from continuing to blacken my lungs or my image.

After my unexpected success as a slumber party hostess and descent into ersatz alcohol and tobacco, I was determined to protest my parents' move back to California. So I simply ran away from home, even though our house was all packed up and empty anyway. I ran to Pastor Joe and Sue's house, where I had some faint hope that I would find sanctuary.

And to my shock, I did. In a turnabout of gender roles, Sue gently lectured my father about the harm she had seen in her ex-cons from losing too much too fast, from broken homes, and too much stress. Pastor Joe must have given a hell of a sermon to convince my folks that I needed to stay with them and not be whisked away into the sunny paradise of far-off California. I was granted a stay of the whole summer living with our pastor and his wife. I could continue in summer school and symphony. All that summer I sang the haunting Appalachian song of the nearby river and mountains, "Shenandoah."

Oh, Shenandoah, I'm bound to leave you, I'd sing to solace myself, and I vowed I would return to Virginia the first chance I got to run away from California.

There is a black-and-white photo that endures to this day: I'm standing, my face smeared with tears. Pastor Joe and Sue are on either side of me, each resting their protective hands on my narrow shoulders. My father must have taken the photo, for it is a quick, nonchalant shot, as if he did not want to see or preserve the inconsolable sadness that his daughter betrayed. I was not happy to be carried away on the ascending wings of his promotion; I did not believe in this heavenly West Coast afterlife that would so destroy my adolescent earthly plans; I was determined, body and soul, to stay.

four

Spirit of the Beasts

(Ephesians 3:18–21)

AS IT TURNED OUT, MY HIGH SCHOOL TACO SLUMBER PARTY HERALDED the beginning of what would become my mother's home career as an evangelical cook. This was a ministry that would soon find its believers in the foreign students of the University of California at Berkeley, who needed home cooking from someone willing to try their far-flung recipes. In this new and pagan land, my mother took a volunteer job working alongside a fascinating missionary from the Home Missions Board. This erudite PhD had the auspicious name of Evelyn St. John. Evelyn was a six-foot-tall Texan, an unmarried Southern Baptist, and a brilliant scholar of world religions.

My mother was a devoted disciple of this learned lady, who ended up living with us in a platonic ménage à trois that irritated my father. No longer was he the only lecturer at the dinner table. Even though Evelyn was a believer, she was also a world traveler, and that disqualified her as a true fundamentalist. She was a bit of a feminist at a time when women were demanding equal rights. Berkeley in those days hosted daily demonstrations. Two years later, Governor Ronald Reagan would permit police to use tear gas on protesting university students in the streets and at the UC library and on protesters in People's Park. In 1967 Berkeley was still more about Flower Power and "beatniks," as my mother dismissed them. Everybody at my new high school seemed to be against the Vietnam War, especially the male students, who were all potential draftees.

Away from the staid hierarchies of Virginia, I was in profound culture shock, but I was also vaguely aware that this open land was my birthright, if I could reclaim it. At last, in a place where free speech abounded, I fit in politically. But there was one big problem— I had stopped speaking, both at home and in school. Though I wrote notes to my parents telling them that my silence was to protest our family's nomadic traumas—we were living in a motel near Berkeley for the first months while my parents searched for a house—the more compelling reason for keeping my lips tightly shut was that I still had a slight southern accent. It wasn't deep, but more lilting, with almost British intonations of Virginia. But my accent was different enough in the pecking order of my peers to get me laughed at when I stood up at a high school football game and screamed, "C'mon, y'all!" After that incident, I began to stutter, not terribly, but enough to make me keep my mouth firmly shut.

Even mute, I found a few friends who allowed me to eat lunch with them. Every high school girl wants a good listener. That first year, 1967, as a junior, I finally found a true friend in Kip Lowenstein, an exhilaratingly smart schoolmate who was devoted to the mystical Kabala roots of her Jewish ancestry as well as studying Buddhism. Kip was the first to frame my silence as "Zen practice." She had no idea I was simply listening intently to everyone around me to learn how to speak Californian again. She had never heard my embarrassing stutter. And when she intuited that I was unhappy, she explained it to me by saying, "Buddha taught us that suffering is a truth."

Because I would not speak and because the school authorities noted my F in literature—courtesy of Miss Edna Reeves's pro-war politics—I was put in a remedial English class with another stutterer, an epileptic, a boy who only spoke Hungarian, and a girl who nowadays would be diagnosed as autistic. All we did was memorize and repeat out loud a tongue-twisting soliloquy:

> An Austrian army awfully arrayed, bolding by battery besieged Belgrade, Cossack commanders cannonading came, dealing destruction, devastating doom. . . .

It was a nightmare for my sibilant stutter. Uttering this rhythmic precursor of rap and singing in the church choir were the only times I actually made a sound. My family and teachers said I was in my own world; Kip said, "Pretend you're in a silent retreat, except everybody else is still hanging around. Silence is a very high state."

I didn't quite know how to interpret her words. It seemed to me that everybody in Berkeley was in a "high state." Or did she mean "high" as in spiritual elevation? I was intent on trying LSD, though marijuana had simply put me to sleep. Then something happened to detour me from drugs and instead to simply open my mouth.

I was given a routine IQ test and performed as I always did with multiple-choice questions: (a), (b), (c), and (d) all seemed to have some validity, if one looked hard enough. I was unaware of the literary theory of forced relationships, in which the author consciously brings together seemingly unrelated elements. All I knew was that I could not choose between multiple answers and I spent all the test time considering each choice.

My father despaired. "You have such an open mind, it's just one big hole in your head," he declared. "It's bad enough that you tend to listen to just about everything anyone tells you—like that Buddhist friend of yours." Father fixed me with those hooded eyes and shook his head sadly. "You just don't seem to have inherited *any* sense of logic."

Logic was one of my father's fortes; to have a child so devoid of this clarity was a blow indeed. My mother remarked, "If you'd stuck with your Sword Drills, you could ace these multiple-choice tests. There's always a right answer!"

On the IQ tests I had resorted to a routine: I filled in the little black dots and made patterns of trees so that at the end I could hold up the paper and see a little forest of number-two pencil stumps. It looked kind of like a clear cut—something that was going on in the great forests of my birth. Later these would become an old-growth holocaust when then-Governor Reagan was elected president. In time, President Reagan would give his Secretary of the Interior, the born-again Pentecostal James Watt, stewardship over American wildlands. Watt would one day be well known for his End Times pronouncements. He would tell Congress, "I do not know how many future generations we can count on before the Lord returns."

Back then, Reagan was just a governor whose rapacious use of natural resources was no more than statewide. My science teacher disdainfully referred to our movie-star-rancher-governor as "Ray-gun" and his cronies as "Captains of Industry who don't realize they'll go down with the Mother Ship." This little sailing ship was our own planet, he said. This sea-blue sphere suddenly seemed so small in black space, so fragile and sublime, when the early space program declassified and released photographs of earth.

All this was thrilling for me to hear, though I still said not a word. The high school guidance counselor called my parents in to tell them the grave news that my IQ tests recorded the intelligence of a mere 80—or "only that of a dolphin." I was secretly honored to be among such an intelligent species, but my parents were deeply concerned. This "silent treatment," as my mother called my muteness, had gone on long enough. There was one bright glimmer in my test scores—the essay sections. The counselor said she was taking the unprecedented action of adding a Great Books class to my remedial English curriculum. This didn't mightily impress my parents, but it redeemed me.

Our Great Books teacher, Mrs. Sylvia Costarella, was a Berkeley psychotherapist when she was not teaching Shakespeare, Plato, or

Eliot. With her Brooklyn accent and dark, blazing eyes, Mrs. Costarella was fiercely popular. She made a deal with me: I didn't have to speak at all in class. All I had to do was write for her. Happily, I agreed and took my place in the very back of the classroom full of frighteningly brilliant students with no betraying southern accents.

"Ego," she lectured us, "is what separates man from animals—and sadly so! Look at an animal like a lion or gazelle. They live without ego. Survival, society, and nurturing the next generation—that's what drives an animal. Can we not do as well?"

With her Russian Jewish background, her union-organizing ex-Wobbly heritage, and her dazzling red necklaces made with seeds, coins, and beads from Third World countries, Sylvia Costarella had the air of an Artemis. "In animals," she taught us, "aggression is always limited. You don't see mass killings in the animal kingdom, like you do in humans. Look at Vietnam."

And we were off—our jungle war and Tolstoy's *War and Peace*, George Eliot's *Middlemarch* informing our feminist struggles against Reverend Casaubon dogmas, and Jane Austen's marital minuets. Literature was alive and relevant to us, even as high school students still living at home. We could protest, we could change the world. A socialist and agnostic who sat down to cozy, polemical dinners with the likes of the ex-longshoreman and radical philosopher Eric Hoffer, Mrs. Costarella was the only teacher who tempted me to break my long silence.

Firmly pronouncing that I must never take hallucinogenic drugs because "it would be redundant" for me, Mrs. Costarella sent me off to the impressive UC Berkeley library for books by Jane Goodall, Gerald Durrell, Konrad Lorenz, Aldo Leopold, Edward Abbey, and John Muir.

Mrs. Costarella often sighed when she gazed at me, sitting mutely in the back of the class. I was writing my first short stories about a fundamentalist sect that handled snakes to show their devotion to God. In discussing my fiction, she told me, "The good-hearted warmth of secular humanism can't really compete with the divine fire of your family's apocalypse, can it?"

In the back of the class, I flushed and stared hard at my desk at being so singled out. Mrs. Costarella laughed lightly. "Well, I have to admit that with all its holy wars and miracles, the Bible *is* still a damn good read. But it's literature, not literal truth."

I knew that if at home I ever quoted Mrs. Costarella's reference to the Bible using the word "damn," I would be removed from her class. My mother had already rigorously protested the use of the words "damn, damn, damn, I've grown accustomed to her face," in the school's production of the musical *My Fair Lady*. So I kept mum about what we were studying in Great Books, which was easy to do since I was not talking. My vow of silence had never been more convenient.

One day in Great Books class, Mrs. Costarella interrupted herself midthought while teaching us the story of Plato's cave to stride directly to the back and stand beside me. "I think we've all stared at shadows long enough, haven't we, class? It's time to leave the collective and climb up out of the cave to find whatever light awaits us." Laying her hand on my shoulder, Mrs. Costarella shook her curly head, earrings tinkling. "Remember, my dear," she whispered just to me, "you don't just belong to your family. You belong to the whole world."

It was a shocking idea. Even though we were so well traveled, my family was also insulated. Like immigrants, we had no real roots, except for one another. Being exiled from my close-knit family would be like losing my only home. Yet in my silent retreat from them, and amid such shifting cultures, I could also feel some mysterious core of self expanding within me. Maybe that was what Kip meant about Buddhists going on a wordless retreat to discover their inner world. Southern Baptist prayers were so chatty and demanding of God. *Do this. Give me that. Please help me find my contact lens.*

Kip lent me a book, *Gravity and Grace*, by the French Jewish-Catholic mystic Simone Weil, who said that prayer is "rapt attention" to the divine. I now considered my several months of silence in a much loftier light. I was paying attention to something greater than my family, my friends, even myself. I'd always been watchful. Many decades later, when one of my friends would ask my father what his eldest daughter was like as a child, he would frown, bewildered, as if trying to remember me. "She was, well, she was really very quiet."

Mrs. Costarella also framed my silence as "the contemplative life." She explained there was a long history of retreat and contemplation in many religious traditions. And all artists, she said, need quiet time to observe, understand, and create. She also quoted Plato's Socrates: "The unreflected life is not worth living." She gave the entire class the assignment of joining me in one day of silence—so better to truly perceive the world around us. Suddenly, instead of being a freak in class, I was a model. Other students, even some seniors, took note of me for the first time. It was as exhilarating as it was uncomfortable. I was so used to being the hidden observer.

After reading an essay in which I compared Edward Albee's *Who's Afraid of Virginia Woolf?* to a wetlands bog, full of lotus blossoms and quicksand, Mrs. Costarella mused, "I suspect, my dear, you are a bit of a Taoist. Do you know what that means?"

Probably that I was going to hell. I had never heard of Taoism. It sounded vaguely communist, certainly sacrilegious. "No," I answered before I forgot I was not speaking. "Bbbbbut I can aaaaaaask my mother's friend at Berkeley who understands world religions."

"You do that research," Mrs. Costarella said. She smiled her trademark crooked grin, her brilliant lipstick a little smeared at the edges, and looked me directly in the eye. I was not used to such focused attention from adults. "Do the reading, and then you write for me. Talk to me about your soul."

Talk about my soul? With someone who wanted to listen, even if I said heretical things? It was an invitation that transcended my humiliating stutter and accent. Besides, Mrs. Costarella had a foreign

Yankee accent, the Hungarian boy in the remedial speech class was braving his first baby English words, and the epileptic was speaking, so why not me?

That very night after my talk with Mrs. Costarella, I gazed around the dinner table, preparing myself to join the verbal fray. No one had much noticed my not talking since family dinners were always so lively; added to that, we had the two lecturers, Father and Professor Evelyn St. John, and often foreign students dining with us to be converted by my mother's culinary evangelism. Mother had fixed a favorite, East Indian chicken, with seasonings so hot we teased that "even untouchables" wouldn't touch it. But we dove into the spicy red curry with rice that in California was always a nutty brown. We also had saffron potatoes and pineapple-carrot coleslaw. And homemade strawberry-pecan ice cream was waiting for dessert.

Our two Buddhist foreign student guests that night were Gutpa and Salim, Indian engineering students who politely enjoyed my father's lectures but were clearly there for the food and the pubescent females. Speaking to them as fellow engineers, my father intoned, "We have to look at everything we value with a double vision and ask: does it have the twin virtues of beauty *and* utility?"

Then he went on to expound on multiple use in forest management and the beautiful and very useful Golden Gate suspension bridge, over which he commuted every day to his job in the San Francisco office of the U.S. Forest Service. Salim and Gutpa both nodded, shoveling food into their mouths as if they had starved ever since coming to this country to study.

"Yes, beauty," Salim said and bobbled his head.

"Yes, utility," Gutpa echoed.

Father continued his speech, but there was a lot else going on. My siblings were giggling and engaged in a subtle food war, pelting each other with minuscule rice pellets, and my mother at the end of the table was proselytizing Salim in a low, fervent whisper.

Into this complicated mix, I decided to speak up for the first time in six weeks. "My Ggggrrrrrr . . . ," I began in a somewhat rusty voice, "Grrreat Books teacher thinks I might be . . . a sttttttttt . . . student of Taoism."

"What?" my father asked.

Had anyone noticed that I was breaking my vow of silence? I could not repeat the name without stuttering, so I turned to Evelyn St. John. "Whhhhat . . . is a Taoist?"

Before Evelyn could answer, my father said with a sigh, "Don't do your homework at the dinner table, honey. You are dismissed, if you need to go study."

I glanced plaintively at Evelyn, hoping she might stay my exile from the dinner table by delivering one of her fascinating lectures on world religions. This rawboned and beautifully plain professor did not fail me. Unlike most people in Berkeley who heard Evelyn's Texas drawl as a blight on her erudition, I listened to her explanation as a faithful student.

"I can certainly see, honey, how your teacher might believe the Eastern spiritual tradition of Taoism is a good fit for you," Professor Evelyn began, settling into her subject with the same appetite she applied to Mother's international cooking. "It's a philosophy of nature and humor and it's so . . . well, do you know the word 'ineffable'?"

I did not, but I was ready to bolt to the study to look it up when my father interjected.

"Those Asian religions don't have a personal God, like we do. It's all very esoteric and primitive, if you ask me."

"That's right," Evelyn agreed amiably, but then she went on to make her point. "In Taoism, the idea of a Supreme Being is replaced by the notion of a supreme state of being. It's really quite an elegant contrast." Seeing my father's scowl, Evelyn softened her scholarship. After all, she was eating his food, at his table, and there were foreign students and possible converts listening. Quickly, she added, "Of course, we Baptists believe that God is engaged with our every act and everything we do is of interest to Him. It gives one's life more a sense of purpose to feel that He is intimately watching over us."

"His eye is on the spppparrow so I know he wwwaaaatches me," I rummaged through my adolescent brain for a scripture that might help me stay at the dinner table. I was fascinated by the idea that my many heresies might actually have some tradition, some meaning.

If Evelyn was right, that meant my days spent sliding down blond, grassy hills on cardboard sleds, skipping class to go sailing with my high school friends in Golden Gate Bay, and hiking along the wild creeks and cottonwoods behind our brand-new house above Berkeley were also a form of worship. Or at least these activities qualified as what Kip called "spiritual practice."

It was not unusual that our dinner table was the scene—especially when adorned with heathen foreign students—of intense religious dialogues. I was always astonished when I visited my friends' homes and found their families talking about what they did at school or work or chatting about issues like fashion or movies—trivial pursuits to God. It was common to hear how one of my siblings defeated Satan that very day at school by not cheating on a test or called in God's guidance in basketball by choosing not to jab a hostile opponent in the ribs after an obvious foul. The idea of an impersonal deity who created humans as a part of divine nature was something I'd already encountered in Mrs. Costarella's Great Books lectures. She had particularly inspired me when lecturing on how Thomas Hardy and Gerard Manley Hopkins both sought supernatural signs in nature—from birdsong to river rapids. Mrs. Costarella had commanded complete reverence in her Great Books class when she quoted her favorite Hopkins poem, "God's Grandeur," from memory, finishing with a flourish:

> The world is charged with the grandeur of God.
> It will flame out, like shining from shook foil.

I had sat at my desk and trembled in a way that no sermon had ever moved me. The poem stirred me like great music. Somehow I shimmered; I shook with each word. I longed to tell my family at the dinner table about how there were other Great Books besides the Bible, how literature was alive and still being written with spirit and revelation. Since I had been born and bred among Southern Baptist brethren who believed that God often spoke through burning bushes and whirlwinds, it was comforting to me to hear of great writers who also looked for miracles and divine handiwork in the natural world. I had been earnestly working on a paper for Mrs. Costarella comparing biblical signs and wonders—from the parting of the Red Sea to bringing forth water from stone—to the mystical nature writing of Hardy and Hopkins. It was the kind of far-flung comparisons she particularly admired.

Back at our dinner table, I took mental notes on Professor Evelyn's religious scholarship. Maybe I would write an essay on Taoism for Mrs. Costarella. The prospect thrilled me.

"Yes, exactly," Professor Evelyn continued enthusiastically, winking just at me. "His eye *is* on the sparrow and us. But if you were a Taoist, the sparrow itself would be a very mysterious way to the divine without a God-the-Father directly watching over you."

"There is no mystery," my mother said, though she was obviously loath to contradict her heroine. "The Bible makes it very clear what we must do to be saved—and to save others." She glanced meaningfully at Salim and Gutpa.

"We Hindus believe that some animals are sacred," Salim replied. "In my country, we worship the cow-head god Krishna and make a practice of *ahimsa*."

Professor Evelyn was smiling broadly. How she relished the compare-and-contrast of world religions. She almost seemed to forget at times that she was here to evangelize, not engage with the foreign students. "Yes," she said, "*ahimsa* means non-injury to sentient creatures."

"So we must not harm life in any form, human or animal," Salim finished, "because all life is sacred to us."

This explained why Salim had politely refused mother's East Indian chicken piled high on his plate, preferring to polish off several helpings of her potatoes and pineapple slaw. He was the first vegetarian I'd ever met. And even though my family ran anemic, I was pondering giving up meat, a direct rebuttal of my father's pleasure in putting wild game on our table.

Gutpa now joined in the conversation. He launched into a lively description of *pinjrapoles*, which were animal hospitals in India, and *goshalas*, which were animal refuges, especially for sacred cattle. "We revere the cow as a symbol of motherhood," he finished triumphantly, with a special nod to my mother, who was just then presenting her strawberry ice cream to the table. Gutpa's delight suggested that Mother might be on the verge of converting him with this sumptuous revelation. "The cow gives us all life," Gutpa explained. "And in another life, if we are kind to animals, then we, too, will find kindness whenever we are again human."

Mother almost dropped her dessert; she was scandalized by talk of reincarnation at her dinner table. She was about to launch into an evangelical ambush when, wisely and without warning, Gutpa changed tack. He turned back to my father. "Yes, yes," he said and held up his plate for Mother's dessert. "Beauty and utility, like your excellent dessert. It is the way we engineers look at a bridge, correct? Very, very beautiful, your Golden Gate Bridge with its steel and high suspension spans. And very, very useful. How else would your citizens go back and forth between such different worlds?"

We didn't yet know at that dinner table that Gutpa would go on to marry a grateful spinster in our church choir. She would paste a red caste dot on her forehead and treat everyone else like untouchables. But before her first marriage anniversary, she would be found dead, having fallen from the balcony of their high-rise apartment.

But the interesting part of the dinner-table dialogue was over for me. There should be no more talk of sacred cows since my father was a hunter and my mother had already told me that my Buddhist friend Kip, who believed in divine white elephants, was going straight to hell. Even Evelyn was outmatched by the men talking steel and engineering marvels that seemed next to godliness.

I closed my eyes as my father and Gutpa continued their praise of the particular steel used in building the Golden Gate Bridge. But instead of those graceful arches, all I could see was my own living room, and all I could think about was how strange I often felt now at home. It was getting harder and harder to keep my freakishness under wraps. I was already the only one at the dinner table who obviously disagreed with my father over the Vietnam War, and I was so backslid at our Baptist church that I read my Great Books in the back pews. I was college-bound to the University of California, but my father was again hoping to deploy the family back to Virginia whenever a promotion came along back to the Southland. He'd announced to me that if he got a promotion and moved, I might not be able to go to college in California.

"More dessert?" Mother asked brightly, and everyone but me dove into seconds.

I found myself staring at the massive moose rack dominating our fireplace mantle in what I hoped was a kind of one-pointed Buddhist meditation technique for dealing with stress that Kip had taught me. The dark, winglike moose antlers were mesmerizing, so much so that Mother had tried to diminish their dominance by hanging trinkets from them. Yet even adorned with two Hawaiian coconut smiling faces, a green Woodsey Owl, and some petrified-wood ornaments, the moose was still a conversation stopper at our supper table. Next to the antlers was a life-size velvet painting of Smokey Bear with my father's face, holding a shovel in one hand and a Bible in the other, with the caption Only You.

"Are you stoned or something?" my little brother asked, nudging me out of my bewildered contemplation. At twelve, he had friends who were dropping LSD and mescaline.

"I ddddo have homework," I announced in a small voice and stood up so quickly from the dinner table I almost knocked my ice cream to the floor. "May I bbbbbeeeee excused?"

Was there relief in my father's face when his eldest daughter exited? Was there disappointment in Professor Evelyn's expression when the only one who ever asked her questions was excused from the table? I didn't look back to see.

*   *   *

I DIDN'T LOOK BACK much at all the turbulent summer of 1968 after my high school graduation. Instead, I looked forward as I prepared to leave home for the University of California. It was a very good time to take my leave. Our dinner table debates grew as hot as my mother's East Indian food, especially since I was talking more. To my great surprise, in my senior year I had been released from the remedial speech class because my stutter had all but disappeared. Mrs. Costarella had advised me to enroll in a public speaking class with the theater teacher. She also invited me to literary and political soirees in her Berkeley home, which I considered a great honor.

"Don't be afraid to speak up," Mrs. Costarella advised me, the therapist in her informing the high school teacher. "Everybody is doing it these days."

Martin Luther King Jr. had just been assassinated that spring, and U.S. inner cities were aflame with riots. Berkeley roiled with antiwar protesters and draft dodgers. Democratic presidential politicians, such as Eugene McCarthy and Robert Kennedy, were decrying President Lyndon Johnson's foreign policy. Feminists and environmentalists took on 1950's sexism and consumption. A radical new generation was rising up, believing we would transform the world.

My father and I now openly argued about everything, from Vietnam to acid rain in the national forests. The arguments could have their playful moments. When I announced to my father, "Everyone in my class, including me, is going to vote for Eugene McCarthy for president," he responded with a grin and a wink.

"Maybe we should rethink giving eighteen-year-olds the vote."

Because I was the one who usually disagreed with my father during the dinner debates, our meals were often exhausting for me. I suspect he was exhilarated by them. Once, when I asked him about the downside of his increasing professional power within the U.S. Forest Service, my father answered, "No one argues with me anymore. People don't tend to tell the truth to their bosses."

In his professional life, my father often asked colleagues to purposely take the opposing argument to better suss out all solutions to a problem. This was the best of him. But in his family, my father valued a united front over individual expression. Our nomadic childhood had left us more of a tribe than a family, and our Southern Baptist religion strongly reinforced this one-way-or-the-highway bonding. To a Southern Baptist, you were either in or out, with them or against them, saved or unsaved. Had I been the eldest son instead of daughter, I probably would have left not only my church and family that year but also my country over the Vietnam War and the draft, which was sending my older friends off to die in far-off jungles.

While our dinner table never lacked for Mother's luscious and inventive food, I was losing my appetite—along with every argument. But knowing that I was college-bound made me bold. A high school classmate, Daniel, and I were chosen by the theater teacher to give the high school graduation speech. While we practiced a completely acceptable speech with the public speaking coach, Daniel and I secretly prepared an antiwar, anti-establishment speech duet.

On a balmy June afternoon, Daniel and I stood on a stage set on the high school football field. At separate microphones, we began our dramatic dialogue based on the Beatles song "She's Leaving Home." We didn't sing the words. We didn't have to. Every graduate standing behind us on their tiers in dark robes knew the lyrics by heart.

When I intoned into the microphone, I was shocked by the sound of my own voice, echoing out over the huge crowd on the bleachers. It was so huge. What if I suddenly reverted to my old stutter? Hesitantly, I began. "Many of our generation no longer believe what we were taught. We question everything."

Daniel spoke of not only leaving home but letting go of the Establishment's ethics and this devastating war in Vietnam, which was drafting and killing so many of our friends. His rich baritone steadied me, though I could see from across the stage that his hands were shaking as he held up the onionskin pages of our secretly rehearsed speech. No adult had advised us; we had written our speech all on our own to protest what we perceived as our parents' preference for commerce over conscience. Our subversive zeal had made us forget the first rule of public speaking: remember your audience. Daniel's glasses were slipping down on his scholarly nose as the crowd murmured and programs fluttered, though there was no wind.

There was a commotion in the stands, as several parents, offended by the implications of the song, by all that might have been "always denied" for so many years, bolted up from their bleachers. Shaking their heads in dismay, they climbed over many feet and knees to leave the ceremony. I was shocked that they were so upset by our speech when there were always protests in the Berkeley streets. I guess the difference was that this protest was personal and we were their children.

She is leaving home. Bye, bye. I wanted to sing the words because, after all, they came next in the song. I felt a flush of sadness and shame. I wondered if singing might ease the tension, as it always did in my own family. We could be arguing intently, and without missing a beat, we would switch to mellifluous four-part harmony. All was resolved—for a song.

But instead, I skipped to a part of our dialogue about not knowing what was wrong "for so many years." I hoped that I might be more mediating from the parents' points of view.

Daniel had to finish our song-speech, because we had programmed the public-address system to end with the Beatles song. Neither of us was experienced enough to ad-lib to stop the dozens of parents now exiting. Oddly enough, my own parents dutifully kept their seats. I suppose they were not surprised by my rabble-rousing.

I finished speaking before my voice was drowned out by the Beatles singing this anthem for our graduating class.

Why was I surprised and even hurt when many parents in the audience simply walked out of our speech? Probably because I was so focused on my own great escape and opinions that I didn't really think parents could have the same option: to protest in public. I remember standing there at the podium as scowling people exited the bleachers and thinking: *Maybe Mrs. Costarella is wrong and the whole world will be just like my family. I will always be the odd one out.*

Yet even as we watched parents abandon us, I could feel the collective energy of my fellow graduates. It was a chinook, a warm wind at my back. We held the stage now, however briefly. I felt the wooden platform beneath my feet reverberate with hundreds of stamping feet showing their support. I glanced behind me and saw smiles and approving nods. The graduates of the class of 1968 were not allowed to clap, but they sure could stomp.

It was the first time I ever remember feeling aligned with, instead of against, the collective. It was like finding the main stream after trickling around in one's own little backwater. I'd never been popular, which I blamed on never staying long enough in any one school. Just by the time I was being accepted into any pecking order, I would be whisked away. Suddenly to be applauded and celebrated by my peers was exhilarating. Too bad it was the last time I would ever see most of these people.

My mother, surprisingly, saved the program from that graduation for my baby book. The family was strangely silent on the audience exodus. Perhaps they even felt a little protective in the face of what they considered their daughter's public humiliation. Before I could make good my exodus from my parents' guiding hand, they packed me off for the summer to work in a Southern Baptist camp near Santa Fe, New Mexico, called Glorietta. Since I was responsible for saving toward my college tuition, this escape from home, even if it was into the "fellowship of the believers," seemed a sensible arrangement. I think my Glorietta stint might have been mandatory, but my memory is that I translated it into an opportunity to travel. My parents could hope that I might abandon my Berkeley hippie ways in this boot camp for Southern Baptists. I could hope to find happiness in New Mexico's glorious mountains. As I was fond of telling my Berkeley friends, "I was born high." Nine thousand feet, to be exact.

My pals always laughed at this, and it went a long way in excusing me from joining them in smoking marijuana or dropping acid. Having been forewarned by Mrs. Costarella against taking any unnecessary hallucinogens, I was usually the designated driver for other people's acid trips. I didn't confide in my hip high school friends that I was glory-bound to a church camp; these bohemians, poets, antiwar protesters, passionate sailors, and honor students would have endlessly teased me about working as a servant to Christians seeking a "mountaintop experience" and gathering together to "speak with one religious voice and promote one religious message consistent with the published views of the Southern Baptist Convention," as the camp still advertises today. The Devil was in the diversity.

When I did confide my apprehensions about going to "Glory Land," my code word for Glorietta, to my meditative friend Kip, she advised me, "You can be Zen about this and just think of it as a spiritual retreat. You can practice mindful silence." Kip added kindly, "But those mountains are stunning, so if it gets really bad, take lots of hikes."

"Well, I'll try," I promised. However, it didn't inspire confidence to learn these mountains were called Sangre de Cristo, which is Spanish for "the blood of Christ."

* * *

"WHAT ARE THE MOUNTAINS LIKE in New Mexico?" I asked my father before leaving home.

"Well, Glorietta is near our Cibola National Forest," he answered. "You'll recognize some of the evergreen trees and aspens from growing up in the Sierra Nevada." He took out his favorite pipe and tamped down the sweet cherry wood tobacco, looking professorial. "Do you know why these trees are called *quaking* aspen?"

"No, but I'm sure you'll tell me," I smiled, softening and delighted to find something we could still share. His natural history lectures were a resting place between us. I trusted his knowledge of the forest.

"They quake, honey, because each leaf is rounded and attached to a flat leaf stem. So when the wind comes up, the leaves can twist and tremble and bend. They're stronger that way, and more protected in severe winds. The one thing that is really hard on aspen trees is shade. They need cool summers and strong sunlight to grow."

My father fell silent, little smoke puffs rising up from his pipe. He always seemed to be considering some mystery when he fell into his pipe ritual. And rather than be impatient, I cherished this self-reflective moment. He seemed so wise when talking about the woods. This was one place in our father-daughter relationship where I found myself listening earnestly, not reacting or hiding or readying my next argument. My defenses were at ease when my father was teaching me about nature. We found our first forest again, we trusted each other, and we made a truce.

"Aspen root systems are really amazing," he said with a nod. "You think you're looking at individual trees, but that's an illusion above-ground because underground each tree is related to roots that come from the parent tree and one single seed. They call a stand of aspen a 'colony.' Aspen can live together thousands of years, even though each individual tree only lasts about fifty to one hundred and fifty years aboveground. But its roots live on in the shared system." He paused to look at me meaningfully. "It's like a family."

"Family tree," I echoed and was surprised at the sharp and true sorrow I at last felt over leaving them.

five

I've Got a Home in Glory Land
(Baptist hymn)

GLORIETTA DID SEEM A PARADISE, SET AT TEN THOUSAND FEET IN COOL, arid mountains of evergreen and golden aspen. With its adobe architecture and a lake echoing the grand spires of the chapel, the church camp seemed to fit respectfully into its spacious natural surroundings. Hiking trails led right off from the employee barracks, and my snug room boasted a window with the Sangre de Cristo Mountains all but embracing the top bunk bed. I immediately set up my home base in the ramshackle dorm called Yucca Lodge with my hiking boots, my EUGENE MCCARTHY IN 1968 bumper sticker, my pet frog Frodo in his tiny terrarium, and my bookshelf with Tolkien's trilogy and the college-prep *Norton Book of English Literature*. With my sanctuary, I figured I could survive this Shangri-la for Southern Baptists no matter how hard they worked me.

The guests came in multitudes, arriving in buses draped with GEORGE WALLACE FOR PRESIDENT banners. Since over half of the world's Southern Baptists live in five southern states, license plates from Texas, Georgia, North Carolina, Tennessee, and Alabama crowded Glorietta's gravel parking lots. I quickly learned that the believers were always hungry. That meant we waitresses and kitchen staffers were on duty almost all day. No time then for hiking, for reflection,

for religious or political debates. Dressed in our faux–Native American pink crepe dresses fringed with silver embroidery trim, we dashed
from the sweltering kitchen to long family-style tables carrying trays
so heavy-laden with food that I nearly crumpled. Plates heaped with
hash browns, ham, corn on the cob, apple cobbler, coleslaw, and
brownies big as toasters—guests ate their fill three times a day, plus
snack times. When guests were not eating, they were in Bible study,
prayer meetings, and worship services. Glorietta was one gigantic
Baptist church social.

The other staffers, already college kids, eyed Glorietta as a star in
their résumé crown. They were training for missionary work or professional careers in Southern Baptist churches as youth or choir di-
rectors or ministers; most had already chosen Christian colleges.
Quickly I realized I was hopelessly trapped here with no escape, except perhaps hitchhiking home. I did consider running away to one
of the nearby pueblos to find spiritual refuge in sun-dried adobe
houses set humbly on mesas beneath a clear sky. But when I was visiting Santa Fe's famous Indian Market, I witnessed so much poverty
and heard that some of the nearby tribes were starving. They could
hardly take me in. Would I still even have a home or a family if I ran
away from this Baptist heaven?

I've got a home in glory land that outshines the sun! The echoes of this
old Baptist song were always ricocheting off the rafters of the
nearby chapel. And the chorus: *Do, Lord, oh, do Lord, oh, do you remember me?* When some of the worship services focused on the Rapture
and a favorite subject of the "Last Days," I felt the collective fervor
even more, like a Red Sea parted wide against me.

Towering over the man-made lake was the imposing Holcomb
Auditorium, with its theatrically high wooden arches and stained-
glass windows. While stuck listening to another sermon on Revelation, I scrawled these impressive figures in my Bible study notebook.

Worship at Glorietta—2,000-plus seats in church auditorium,
2,000 guest capacities, 2,000 acres:
An acre for each person!

How I longed to be outside on my own little acre of God's creation instead of attending mandatory worship services for staff. I
hunkered down, often taking notes for what I hoped one day would
become my first novel. My family always teased me that I took notes
even at family funerals. If I could observe and write it all down, I believed I had some sort of protection—or at least a hiding place.

The preacher wore a wide-lapel suit, a narrow tie, a clean-shaven
jaw, and a crew-cut. With an expression of perpetual mourning, he
could have been a funeral director. Even from the very back pews—
my favorite place to sit—I could see that his eyes were overly bright
and how he clasped his well-thumbed Bible like a blunt instrument.

The minute the Glorietta preacher grasped the microphone, he tore
it from its staid silver stand like a rock star. Then he shouted so loud the
PA system let out a piercing, ultrasonic scream: "Is *your* name written in
the Book of Life?" The heavy-set preacher roared his question, and his
voice ricocheted around the wooden columns that held up this majestic
church. "If you are saved, sisters and brothers, say *hallelujah!*"

"Hallelujah!" the congregation hollered back, clapping.

It was not the raucous cry of a sporting event crowd; it was more
zealous and triumphant. The voices were a clarion call to collective
communion. But to me it felt like a mob. The sound of righteousness
had always frightened me. To this day I distrust crowds—those who
celebrate or believe the same thing, whether at a football game, political rally, or religious gathering. I always look for the red Exit signs.

The preacher launched into the familiar End Times story. Called
"pre-millennialists," these Christians believe that after being swept up
with God in the Rapture—or first resurrection of the saints—those

left behind will endure seven years of Tribulations. Then Christ will return to earth to bind Satan and establish a literal kingdom to reign in peace for one thousand years. After that, Satan will be "loosed a little" to deceive and gather his great army of nations aligned against Israel in the final Armageddon battle.

The preacher seemed himself on the verge of ascending to the high rafters of the church. "Revelation, chapter 20, tells us sinners that fire comes down out of heaven to devour the evil nations of Gog and Magog as their armies launch their fateful End Times attack on Israel."

In Rapture prophecy, "Gog" is widely interpreted as the Soviet Union and "Magog" as China. Since we were in the throes of a late-sixties Cold War, these villains of Mao's Cultural Revolution and the Soviet Union's pre-détente nuclear threats came in handy. In 1968 the Soviet Union was on the verge of invading Czechoslovakia in what would be called "Prague Spring" later that summer. The Soviet Union's menacing response to that small European country's liberal-izations—as well as the ongoing superpower battle between the United States and the Soviet Union in guerrilla proxy wars like Viet-nam—gave preachers much ammunition for their vision of a world ending imminently in nuclear fire.

In Glorietta's great chapel—what would today be called a "mega-church"—a thousand upturned faces listened to the preacher. Using his baritone voice like a bellows and pumping his arms, he raised his Bible in his fist. "Brothers and sisters, in the final battle Revelation says that Satan is cast into 'the lake of fire and brimstone—where the beast and the false prophet are—and shall be tormented day and night forever and ever.'"

"Forever and ever!" the throng took up the chant. "Ever and ever more!"

I would have snuck out about this time, except my kitchen boss was sitting in the same pew with me. How I longed for a minister like

Pastor Joe with his subtle stories and soft voice, his thoughtful questions, and the way he listened, even to people of other faiths. Pastor Joe was as much a seeker as a teacher. And his wife Sue had devoted her seminary thesis to Revelation. Sue believed that this last book of the Bible had nothing to do with the end of the world but was written while the disciple John, probably a Jewish Christian and not John the Apostle, was imprisoned and writing his symbolic visions to guide his persecuted friends and fellow believers.

The majority of Protestants and most Catholics do not interpret Revelation literally, as do the fundamentalists and some conservative evangelicals. This last book of the Bible is instead interpreted historically: John of Patmos never claims to have known Jesus and was writing one hundred years after the crucifixion. The apocalyptic style of Revelation is typical of the first-century Jewish and Christian writers who fully expected a cataclysmic release from persecution in their lifetimes. They were probably not thinking about centuries hence. In this interpretation, John of Revelation was not Nostradamus. He was perhaps not so much a prophet as a witness and a poet.

Today many more moderate Christians believe that it was actually Christ's resurrection, three days after his crucifixion, that truly signaled the beginning of the "new heaven and new earth"—and that our responsibility right now and here on earth is to take care of this divine creation. But these more mild-mannered believers are often too unorganized and introspective about their faith, considering it a personal rather than a political path. Often their voices are drowned out by evangelical extremists demanding a literal and "inerrant" interpretation of scripture.

At the massive pulpit, the preacher wound up his body, with his Bible clenched like a knuckleball and hurled out his fast pitch. "Brothers and sisters gathered here today," he cried, sweat or tears streaming down his face. "I tell you that we can change the world! Do you believe it to be so? Say amen!"

"Amen!" The church rocked with one voice, except mine.

"We Christians do not change the world by marching against our own government. We Christians do not tear down college buildings or dodge the draft. We do our job as Christian soldiers. We bring democracy to those dying in sin. Say amen!"

"Amen, brother!"

I sank down in the pew, my heart pounding. There were no Exit signs in this great church. Psychologists might have called it a panic attack or claustrophobia, but I knew I had every right to be afraid. And deep in my throat I felt the return of my old stutter. Maybe to survive Glorietta, I'd have to return to silent Zen survival practice.

"We can change this evil world with our faith," the pastor boomed now, pumping his arms up and down like a marathon runner. "We can change the world with our votes! Say amen!"

The preacher stopped short of endorsing George Wallace. But looking out over the crowd of white faces, a majority with southern accents, there was no need to state the obvious. Much of the South had defected from the Democratic Party after the recent 1964 Civil Rights Act, which put an official end to segregation. Just because the government insisted on integrating didn't mean the Southern Baptist Convention (SBC) had to follow suit.

A survey by the SBC's Home Mission Board in 1968 showed that only 11 percent of Southern Baptist churches would admit African Americans. There had certainly not been blacks in our Southern Baptist church in Virginia, though the schools were fully integrated by the time I left Virginia in 1966. Here in Glorietta I had noticed that the response to Martin Luther King Jr.'s recent assassination was muted. Hardly anyone spoke of it—even though the Reverend King was a Baptist preacher. When Robert Kennedy was also gunned down in early June, I was struck at how little mourning there seemed to be among these guests at church camp. Kennedy was, after all, a fellow Christian, even if he was a Catholic and a Democrat.

This glaring lack of grief among the true believers at first bewildered me. But as I eavesdropped on dinner-table conversations—a perk of waitressing—I realized that the emotional tenor at Glorietta after those assassinations was really shock and fear. The White Throne of Judgment sermon that balmy night in church camp was the first time I remember registering how fear, for these faithful, could be translated into outrage. And fundamental resistance to change.

All this made me want to escape or go underground. "Going dark" I'd heard my mother call it, from years of reading all her spy thrillers. She always vowed that one day—if we could ever move back to Virginia—she would find a job at the CIA. Right then and there, I decided that for the rest of the summer I would fly just below the radar. If I didn't bleep on Glorietta's radar, they would not target me as someone who must be converted, or worse. I imagined a headline on a *Reader's Digest* "First-Person" story, most of which were about surviving shark bites. Mine would read: "Attacked by Killer Fundamentalists."

I sank way down in the pew, watching the preacher mop his face with a huge, white handkerchief. For the moment I was grateful for my fake-Indian waitress disguise. I remembered that my friend Kip had always said to me, "If you looked on the outside the way you are on the inside, you would have been stoned to death before you were five years old."

The preacher's voice boomed out again like cannon shot: "Only by acting together, only by joining hands and hearts as one body, can we join those chosen few who will be lifted up to meet God. Hallelujah! Say amen!"

"Amen!" everyone cheered.

"So I ask you one last time, brothers and sisters. . . . " The preacher bounded away from his pulpit and stripped off his jacket. He rolled up his shirtsleeves and held out his hands to the huge crowd. "Is your name truly written in the Book of Life?" Hungrily, his eyes scanned the crowd.

I really doubted there were many sinners who were vacationing in a church camp, but the preacher had anticipated my mutinous thought.

"Now, you may think you are saved," the preacher wagged his finger, "but maybe you need tonight to rededicate your life. Maybe you are sinning in secret and you believe nobody else sees it. Well, God sees you. There is no hiding place from God—not even here in God's refuge!"

I slouched lower in my seat and scribbled a few notes. But what I wrote down was: *Jesus Christ had dirty fingernails.*

I didn't know what I meant by this phrase that kept circling in my mind, except that my idea of Christ had nothing to do with this raging preacher. Christ was a man of humble means, neither warrior nor politician; he lived close to the earth and sought followers for thoughtful discourse. He was not a demagogue. He reserved his rare anger for the Pharisees of his own faith. It seemed to me that those bent on Judgment Day had blissfully zipped past most of Christ's more philosophical sermons to the carpool lane of Armageddon.

"I say to you gathered here today, brethren," the preacher wound up, sweat dripping down his face, "that you must be ready for a holy city, a new Jerusalem, coming down from God out of heaven . . . for He will come again for us and sit in judgment over us on a great white throne. As the prophet John tells us clearly here in Revelation 20, verse 14, 'Whosoever was not found written in the Book of Life was cast into the lake of fire!' Say amen!"

A massive "amen" rose up from the crowded pews. I closed my notebook and looked out at the lake. It was so calm and still. No wind tonight. Only the hurricane of hallelujahs inside this church.

Watching the water, I reflected on the fact that in just a few months I could make a choice to leave the Southern Baptist fold forever. I would be free to find my own spiritual way in the world. It might be a lonely journey, but I was truly weary of the fervent crowds.

I looked forward to finding the "still, small voice" that Christ taught was the individual conscience. I hoped to study world religions whose more mystical sets all seemed to be saying that the "kingdom of God is within you." I looked forward to being one of the meek who might inherit the earth.

Working long hours as a waitress, I kept to myself and was quiet during off-hours; I even worked double shifts for those who wanted to attend extra worship services so I did not have to go. No one seemed to miss me.

The searchlights scouring the sprawling Glorietta campus every night felt like prison. Every chance I got, I fled into the woods with my thermos and backpack and just sat quietly in a stand of aspen. Listening to wind fluttering the delicate aspen leaves, I would ponder what my father had taught me about the colony of aspen trees.

One evening on my break between waitressing shifts, I perched on my favorite aerie at sunset overlooking Glorietta. Closing my eyes, I listened to aspen. Leaf music. Would I ever really belong anywhere? What was my tribe, my collective, beyond my family? My father had said that the aspen's lateral roots could stretch far in many directions, sending identical sucker shoots over as many as one hundred acres, creating colonies, some of which were over eighty thousand years old. Even though I was far away from my family, I was still connected to them. Would I always be so? Would they recognize me, even if I was going to grow up completely different from them?

It was a little too early for the searchlights, and there was still some pale purple and red radiance from the mountaintop sunset. Glorietta was bathed in the beautiful, abundant light of high elevation. I knew these Baptists came to Glorietta to be reborn in their faith. But I couldn't understand why they didn't connect their spiritual life with the earth here so vividly embracing them. Weren't these astonishing mountains, these rivers, these deep-rooted families of aspen also God's creation?

A group of guests on the path below my perch were rushing off to the imposing chapel for evening worship service. They toted their backpack-size Bibles and their faces were intent, expectant. Who knew what further revelation or miracle awaited them in that mega-church with its arched ceilings and soldierly rows of pews? I sighed, suspecting the believers were off to do battle with the Devil who was lurking always, close as a shadow.

And then I realized something that I should have understood long before this mountaintop moment—the Devil was kept at bay outside the church. As long as the faithful were inside the holy taber-nacle, they were safe. They came to church to rest up from worldly and daily struggles with Satan. In church they could celebrate their stronghold, their mutual righteousness; their One Way. Church—not the tempting beauty of the natural world—was their Garden of Eden. Because they had primarily located God in their man-made fort, and not in His own creation, nature herself was separated from spirit. Why should Southern Baptists care if acid rain was falling over the forests or species were going extinct? Church, like the afterlife waiting in heaven, was where they and God could be together. Na-ture was just an ungodly backdrop against which to strut and fret their lives away until they were lifted up from this weary world into God's heavenly arms. God had thrown sinners out of His garden, so why become gardeners?

That mountain-high summer at Glorietta I resigned myself to be-ing a stranger in a strange land. I knew I did not want to become a Southern Baptist missionary. But what would I be? My savior came in an unexpected form. After weeks of fundamentalist guests, there was the happy shock of "Student Week" at Glorietta—a thousand-strong stampede of college kids. The worship services were suddenly full of lively discussions of the Southern Baptists' controversial "Crisis State-ment," which originally included a "confession" of racism and apol-

ogy to African Americans for segregation. Most of the students lobbied for the statement; others still supported segregationist George
Wallace and his denunciation of "sissy-britches intellectual morons."

One of the speakers that Student Week at Glorietta was the Reverend Ron C. Willis. Unlike the students in striped madras shorts and
plaid pedal pushers, Reverend Ron wore an old corduroy jacket and a
peace sign necklace. He was compact and energetic, with curly dark
hair that was longer than that of any other young men in camp,
though it wasn't shoulder-length. I calculated that he was only a
decade older than me.

In 1966, I learned, Reverend Ron, as a philosophy student at UC
Berkeley, had begun his "street ministry" working part-time in San
Francisco's Haight-Ashbury. In 1966 Haight-Ashbury was just a slum
where, as Reverend Ron said, "people were poor by chance, not by
choice." I had seen this sad side of the Golden Gate City when its
desperate streets were as forlorn as any urban ghetto. This was before
the influx of Flower Children and the counterculture movement that
in 1968 swelled the ranks of San Francisco's street people from 1,500
to 25,000. Reverend Ron had recently moved to take on a full-time
ministry at Golden Gate Baptist Church in Oakland—an African
American neighborhood dominated by generations of poverty and
the original home to the Black Panthers. The day after Dr. King was
murdered, this Oakland ghetto was roiling, and the public-school
kindergarten class of Reverend Ron's daughter was under lockdown.

By the time Reverend Ron came to speak at Glorietta, he had also
expanded his street ministry to the psychedelic scene of nearby
Berkeley's Telegraph Avenue, where students, radicals, hippies, and
people my mother called "pagans" ran rampant. Reverend Ron told us
stories of busloads of tourists from the South and Midwest snapping
their Brownie cameras in this hippie Mecca—until one day a bus was
boarded by street people who began to snap photos of the tourists.

Reverend Ron was unlike evangelical street ministers who advocated what he called a militant "invasion for Christ." His role was simply to lend a "helping hand," to listen, to feed—and to remind anyone, no matter how burned-out or broken, that "God is love."

This was my kind of minister. What made Reverend Ron even more fascinating was that he wore a dark, tattered sweater and a white, plastic clerical collar; he had discovered that people on the streets instinctively trusted the priest's collar more than evangelical rants from the street preachers Reverend Ron called "pure King James and Richard Nixon." At Glorietta, his white collar was regarded as suspiciously Catholic. He often joked that "for many Southern Baptists, to be a Catholic priest is like being a Communist." I had often heard this fearmongering among Southern Baptists—the Pope was the Anti-Christ, Catholics practiced "idol worship," and their greatest sacrilege was praying to Mary.

For his talks at Glorietta, Reverend Ron was not granted the great pulpit in the high-spired church by the lake. His chapel was a modest, pueblo-style building with white adobe walls and simple, hand-hewn wooden pews. His service began not with the traditional Baptist hymns, such as "When We All Get to Heaven" or "In the Sweet By and By." Instead, Reverend Ron was joined by a few straggly-looking companions with their battered guitars slung over their army jackets. They were all long-haired and bearded.

A college student next to me with a distinct drawl whispered excitedly, as if we were at the zoo, "Those must be hippies."

"Yes," I nodded, grinning. "Must be."

The sight of street people tuning their guitars onstage at a Southern Baptist retreat was as frightening to her as it was exotic. She leaned forward slightly, as if tempted.

I felt some unexpected sympathy for all these southerners. After all, I was only two years away from our five-year stint in Virginia, the longest my family had ever lived anywhere. Though I was not a na-

tive southerner, my ancestors and parents were. And though I had by
now lost my slight Virginia lilt, the southern accent was as familiar as
family to me.

Eyeing my neighbor in the pew, I took in her pleated and pressed
flowered-print dress, her bouffant that Jessie might have permed, her
King James Bible with her name embossed in golden script on the
brown leather. Mary Jo Smithers. Her name was obviously written in
the Book of Life. I had a Bible just like it, given to me as a graduation
present.

I turned to Mary Jo, knowing that she allowed me this confidence because of my Glorietta staff uniform of crinkled Indian skirt
and blouse. As happened so many other times in my life, I could simply "pass" for one of them, though if I'd opened my mouth I might
have been cast out. This self-preservation instinct for passing I
thought of simply as my "invisible trick." The chameleon gifts of the
nomad.

"Where are you from?" I inquired of Mary Jo Smithers.

"Georgia," she said proudly. "A little town called Lilburn, just a
stone's throw from Atlanta. And I'm studying at Baptist Seminary in
Fort Worth."

I nodded pleasantly. I had no idea that two years later my father
would be transferred to Atlanta and would take up residence in that
same rural community. I had some inkling that I might be planted
again in Virginia if my father got promoted again as he hoped. But I
never expected we might end up in Georgia. So I didn't ask for any
details about her Deep South. All I asked was a polite "Are you having a good time here at Glorietta?"

"I was, until tonight," she said, still nervously eyeing the ragtag
folksinging group. "Good Lord, you'd think they'd dress up for
church."

They look a little like Jesus, don't you think? I wanted to say, but did not.
Instead, I smiled and listened.

"I've heard hippies practice free love," Mary Jo whispered to me conspiratorially. "With everyone. They don't care what sex!"

I glanced down and saw that Mary Jo was married. She could not have been more than nineteen. I was accustomed to southern girls getting married early. In our Virginia high school, I had noted sophomore girls eagerly raising their hands, even if they did not know the answers, to better show off their engagement rings. Since I was still a virgin at eighteen, I had to consider that Mary Jo might really be worldlier than me. Besides, she was already in college and I was just graduated from high school. So I met her eyes with a raised eyebrow of my own that I hoped was sophisticated. "Hmmmmmm," I said.

"I've seen photos of hippies," Mary Jo whispered, "in *Life* magazine."

I had to wonder: if I had stayed in Virginia, as I had begged my parents, instead of landing in the wilds of Berkeley, might I have looked a little more like this neighbor than I did at home in blue jeans and tie-dyed T-shirts, braids, and silver bracelets? Like Reverend Ron, I was also undercover here at Glorietta in my staff uniform. All the better to watch and wonder what these other people might really be feeling.

Mary Jo's discomfort was almost contagious. I felt it the way an animal picks up the scent of human fear. I tried to see the folk group and Reverend Ron through her eyes. Just as I wanted to escape home and seek my true tribe, so Mary Jo wanted to escape these disheveled strangers and return to her familiar seminary fold.

In our pew, I studied Mary Jo Smithers and decided to risk an outlying opinion. I ventured to her, "I actually think those folksingers up there onstage might be Christians."

Mary Jo looked at me in shock as the folk group launched into a vigorous version of "The Times They Are A-Changin'."

It was obvious from the tapping feet that a minority of the students had heard folk music and even allowed guitars into their youth services. This was a decade before the Christian music business would begin to boom. Those who disapproved of the motley folk trio as they swung into Bob Dylan's "I Shall Be Released" read their bulletins, fanned themselves, and watched politely. They were, after all, in church.

Mary Jo whispered to me, "You've heard people like them sing before?"

"Yes," I said softly, and then added, "in the streets of Berkeley."

To her credit, Mary Jo did not slide down the pew away from me. Instead, she looked me directly in the eye and said, "Oh, you're one of them." She now studied me openly, as if I took a considerable amount of concentration. "Excuse me for staring," she began in a soft voice, "but I just never met anybody like you before." She glanced at my ring finger. Empty.

I braced myself for conversion, or what would be worse, pity. Instead, Mary Jo Smithers asked me a difficult question. "Are you . . . are you happy?"

The folk trio wailed out the haunting refrain: *Any day now, any day now, I shall be released. . . .*

"Am I happy to be here?" I answered, shaking my head. "No."

I meant at Glorietta. But Mary Jo took me to be a spiritual ally. She leaned nearer and confided, "I really like this song." Nodding in rhythm to the wailing trio, she added, "It's all about longing—you know, to be free from this earth."

I sighed. We were so young, and yet she already wanted out of this evil world. Each of us, in our own minds, was in prison.

Reverend Ron looked out over his small crowd and began in a musing tone, "The people I work with on the streets—some of them have been thrown out of their families, or lost jobs. They are searching. Some of them are burned out on drugs or in despair. Others are just plain angry at the way the world has treated them. Many of them feel lost—not like sinners," he paused, "but like seekers. So the question is, do we believe they are as worthy as we are of divine love? Do we recognize street people and hippies and even radicals as our equals in the eyes of God?"

Taking as his text the parable of the sheep and goats in Matthew 25:31–40, Reverend Ron came out from behind the small pulpit to stand near us. "You all know this one. When Christ returns to sit on his throne of judgment to separate the nations, 'as a shepherd divideth the sheep from the goats.'" Reverend Ron's voice softened. "Let's not focus on the judgment. We've all had too much of that. Let's not get caught up in a debate over whether the sheep or the goats were the most righteous, the ones chosen to 'inherit the kingdom,' as the Gospel says."

His eyes scanned the crowd in silence. "You can all probably recite the most important verses in this passage by heart, so why don't you say them with me now: 'For when I was hungered, and ye gave me meat: I was thirsty, and ye gave me drink: I was a stranger, and ye took me in: Naked, and ye clothed me: I was sick, and ye visited me: I was in prison, and ye came unto me.'"

There was a shift in the crowd as people joined in reciting the familiar scripture. "What I am asking you tonight," Reverend Ron's voice rose slightly, "is to give life to these words. There are people on the streets you pass by every day in your cities, there are prisoners and people in hospitals who feel completely abandoned, who do not know human love, much less God's love. And what have we done for them? Have we judged them, have we dismissed them, have we decided that because they are not the same class, or color, or religion, that we owe them nothing?"

Murmuring now, and in deep discomfort, a few students walked out, but the majority stayed solidly in their seats. They were used to sermons.

Reverend Ron spread out his arms to include us all when he asked, "What did Christ say when people were arguing about who would sit on what side of His throne or who would inherit his kingdom? Christ said, 'Inasmuch as ye have done it unto one of the *least* of these my brethren, ye have done it unto me.'"

Mary Jo Smithers leaned right over and clasped my hands warmly. She was, I suppose, practicing what Reverend Ron had just preached. And while I was amused at the implication that I was "the least," I was really quite touched by her gesture. She did not try to save me. She simply patted my hand and said, "I'm glad I got to meet someone—well, like you."

Mary Jo's kindness and Reverend Ron's sermon gave me courage. I changed my survival strategy of just lying low at church camp. A few of the kitchen staffers hoped to become home missionaries, like Evelyn St. John back in Berkeley. We had bemoaned the fact that while there were abundant leftovers from dinners, the food was being sold to local pig farmers for slop. This seemed wrong when so close by some tribes were starving and in need of clothes. A few of us asked Reverend Ron why we couldn't siphon off some of the leftover food and drive it to the reservations at night. There was so much food. Who would notice? This surreptitious food delivery system could be our street ministry.

Reverend Ron cautioned us about being too obvious, and he did not organize the ministry himself, only advised us. Soon we were making nightly runs to drop off much-needed food for the nearby tribes. Another group of us began meeting to write an underground newspaper, which we mimeographed in office off-hours. One of the first headlines was the one I had scrawled in worship service: "Jesus Christ Had Dirty Fingernails," with my article and poem on Christ's life as a common man. We distributed the ink-smeared newspapers around Glorietta.

Guests complained. Someone outed our operation to the camp leaders and those of us who were running food to the tribes were told to report to the authority or face being fired. Instead, we held a meeting of staff and drew up a petition asking Glorietta to give its excess food to the reservations in need, not sell it for profit to pig farmers. Proudly, we posted our petition, signed by dozens of staff members, in the main office. It was met with a directive from above: we had twenty-four hours to cross our names off the petition. Those who did would be assured that they could still find future work in the Southern Baptist Convention. Those who did not, well, they would be cast out of glory land and never see a career in missions, home or foreign.

It was not a difficult choice for me. But I watched as many of my peers agonized over their decisions. One by one, names were crossed off, with sincere apologies.

"You have to understand," one of the other staff told me. "I've got a church job waiting for me in Georgia."

"I want to serve God," another said penitently, "but I grew up in the Southern Baptist church. It's all I know."

After twenty-four hours, there were only three or four names left. We unrepentant awaited our fate. In this limbo, I joined Reverend Ron for his seminars with several hundred students to discuss the "Crisis Statement," from which the SBC had deleted the official confession. *Newsweek* had just quoted one Southern Baptist author of the "Crisis Statement," Foy Valentine of the Christian Life Commission, as saying, "Southern Baptist officialdom is moving away from its old racist origins. The culture here is finally being rejected in favor of Christ."

The students and the few unrepentant worked to write up a petition of our own to include a strong confession of racism to be read aloud at the last worship service of Student Week. We planned a protest, a show of concern.

At the final worship service of Student Week, Reverend Ron and we few disciples took up positions in the great church. Even Reverend Ron admitted he was frightened about what we were about to do. Would it work? Reverend Ron said that he was more scared that night than when an escaped convict on the streets had at last handed over his loaded gun. I was also nervous because when the Glorietta preacher finally finished his sermon, one of the twelve students stood up to read aloud our statement of concern, our confession and petition. And then the trembling student read my poem very softly over the microphone.

Jesus Christ had dirty fingernails.

Absolute silence in the vast church. I expected another exodus like at my graduation speech ceremony. Then one of the students tore off his coat and laid it on the altar. Twelve of us came forward and took off sweaters, jackets, and shoes. As we did so, Reverend Ron stood up in the main aisle and spoke to the two thousand people gathered together.

"What we are asking you to do here tonight is not symbolic," Reverend Ron said, almost in a whisper. "It is real and simple. There are people nearby us tonight in need." His eyes swept the vast crowd. "We Christians, we understand suffering and sacrifice. We come from a spiritual tradition of persecution and imprisonment and being judged by worldly powers. You know very well that Christians have not always been in the mainstream." A murmur in the crowd. A memory. Reverend Ron continued, "Christ's own disciples were a raggedy lot. And yet they gave everything they had, because Christ also gave everything He had. His life."

Reverend Ron was asking them to do something rather unseemly—unless they were being baptized, Southern Baptists did not undress in God's house. They were much too modest. To divest themselves at that moment of their shoes, their jackets, what might be called in biblical terms their "fine raiment," seemed somehow uncouth. And Reverend Ron was asking them to do so without any tangible return on their spiritual investment. By giving rather blindly, locally, by giving simply because they could, the only reward was the gift itself.

Reverend Ron fell silent as he watched a few people come forward, not in the usual invitation to give their hearts to Christ, but in the humble offering of their sports jackets, their ties, even a few wingtips.

"Thank you," Reverend Ron said quietly. "Bless you," he nodded, his face wide open.

Reverend Ron looked very young to me at that moment, full of the radical hope that ignited his generation of Joan Baez, Bob Dylan, and Allen Ginsberg. We baby boomers would be carried on the shoulders of the visionaries of this so-called Silent Generation.

"I offer this to you tonight," Reverend Ron finished. "What Christ teaches is simple kindness. Love thy neighbor as thyself. That's it. That's everything."

Weeping now, more people left their pews, pulling out wallets and unbuckling expensive watches. A girl jiggled her small purse upside down, dollar bills and change falling into her lap like pennies from heaven. In front of me an entire family leaned forward, unlacing tennis shoes and sandals; a robust man neatly folded a cherished golf jacket and strode to the stage to lay it atop a growing pile of clothes. The church platform looked like a rummage sale as people surged forward with their offerings.

I had a Smokey Bear watch my father had given me that I dearly loved. Since I could not offer up my staff uniform, I took off my purple flip-flops and watch, taking my place in the line. By the time I reached the stage, there was a mountain of clothes and shoes. The folk group was smoothing dollar bills and corralling coins into offering plates. I noted that one of their guitars lay gingerly balanced atop a column of jackets.

"Thank you, brother." Reverend Ron was taking people's hands in his very gently. "Thank you, sister."

His words were a benediction. We did all seem like brothers and sisters. Not the chosen, not the insular saved, but the neighbor.

When it was my turn to lay my little offerings atop the mountain, Reverend Ron met my eyes. His expression was fierce and tender. I did not know that right before the worship service a Mississippi student had approached Reverend Ron and made a confession of his own: the student had plotted to kill a street minister because the boy had been raised by church and community to hate black people. He had pledged allegiance to the Christian flag in Bible schools and truly believed integration was wrong. But listening to Reverend Ron during the fray of Student Week at Glorietta, this southerner had realized his bigotry. He came to Reverend Ron and humbly asked for his forgiveness. This night in glory land was unlike any other. This night we had seen the power of the faithful when they were inspired not to exclude, but to embrace. That mountain of abandoned clothes sure looked a lot like the Rapture.

Perhaps we both suspected this might be my final night at Glorietta. Reverend Ron did not embrace me; all he did was nod and then placed his hands on my shoulders.

"Go with God," he said, "whenever you go."

Reverend Ronald C. Willis would go on to develop his street ministry programs in Southern Baptist churches from Maine to Texas. He would continue his antiwar efforts, serving as vice president of the Maine branch of Clergy and Layman Against the War. He would work in the U.S. House of Representatives as a senior staff associate on health and education. And he would work for many years at George Washington University as a liaison with Congress. His 1971 book *A View from the Streets* vividly describes his street ministries.

I knew even then that Reverend Ron would go far. But where was I going? The next day the three of us staff members who defiantly kept our names on the petition were called early to the main office.

"None of you will ever be a Southern Baptist missionary," a camp leader said, and one of us burst into tears. "You will all be escorted off the premises. Gather your things."

We were deposited at the Santa Fe train station to be packed home to horrified parents. All the way to Berkeley on the train, I gratefully took in the mountains and high deserts as one might do when just released from prison. I wondered what would become of the food runs to local reservations. Would the underground newspaper ever be mimeographed and stealthily distributed again? I would never know.

I had only wanted to escape the collective and to find my individual way that year I left home. But at Glorietta I had glimpsed what might happen if the power of the believers was harnessed to help others not at all like ourselves. I had seen the sheer power of benevolence—not to save our own souls in return, but because it is in our collective nature to care.

six

Then Are the Children Free

(Matthew 17:26)

HAVING PERCEIVED MYSELF AS THE LONE INFIDEL AMID CHRISTIAN soldiers for most of my eighteen years, and after my descent from Glorietta's mountaintop, I longed for peace and contemplation. My high school Zen silence had taught me there was an inner world as lush as the natural world around me. It was an interior wilderness I wanted to explore.

So I chose the most pastoral campus of the University of California state schools. UC Davis was an "aggie," or agricultural school, as it was called in those days, because at UC Berkeley in 1968 the main curriculum was "Protest 101." My friend Kip wrote me that few of her fellow UC Berkeley students actually showed up for lecture classes because there were so many lively street demonstrations. I had experienced enough protest, both at home and in the streets. I had also attended my first and last radical SDS (Students for a Democratic Society) meeting, where the fervor held alarmingly fundamentalist echoes. So I sought what I imagined would be a spiritual and intellectual retreat—something like Taoist monks in their solitary caves, meditating for the world while not having to bother with it day to day. *In* the world, as my Sunday school teacher Mrs. Eula had taught me, but not *of* it.

I wanted only to read, study, and understand world literature and biology. Riding my red bicycle along the rural flatlands and translucent irrigation ditches of UC Davis, I was finally free. Open to everything, with a sunny and warm wind at my back.

Mrs. Costarella had sent me off to college with a card inscribed with a quote from W. B. Yeats that I tacked on my college dorm wall next to my Only You poster of Smokey Bear and my glow-in-the-dark galaxy map of the night sky.

> When such as I cast out remorse,
> a sweetness flows so great into the breast.
> We must laugh and we must sing.
> We are blest by everything.
> Everything we look upon is blessed.

College friends noted that I did seem strangely blissful and mistakenly assumed I was taking hallucinogens. But it was just exhilaration. I was keenly aware that I had narrowly escaped the religious conservatism of my family. I was so happy to be here. UC Davis has the blessings of latitude akin to incandescent African savannahs. Blond grasslands, gentle hills, and green fields shimmered as if under a spell. Walking or cycling to class, I was often late because I would stop to savor the angle of sunlight slanting across an alfalfa field or dawdle under an ancient oak or the fragrant drape of eucalyptus trees.

"You have an unusual capacity for rapture," my anthropology professor, Mr. Raeburn, wrote on one of my research papers.

With my upbringing, I didn't take this as a compliment.

But then he added, "We could really use someone like you in the sciences. Wish you were better at math."

Math, like logic, always eluded me. And my Christmas-tree dot-to-dot strategy for filling in multiple-choice tests was no more effective in college than it had been in high school. Yet how I adored listening to Professor Raeburn's lectures.

"Why did the Neanderthals die out?" he asked us three hundred or so rapt anthropology students. "Well, mostly because they just couldn't adapt to a changing environment. Do you know any people like that?"

We sixties students of world revolution laughed, feeling as superior to any earlier generations as Homo sapiens might have felt over the dim, slack-jawed Neanderthals. Secretly, I was quite fond of Neanderthals, and I'd wept when Professor Raeburn told us they were the first of our species to bury their dead—a sign of spiritual development.

Now that I was free to study world religions openly, I was intently tracking other spiritual traditions. This was California, after all. Everyone around me was dabbling in meditation, yoga, Zen, and anything Far Eastern. Zen poet Gary Snyder, Harvard acid enthusiast Timothy Leary, consciousness and dolphin communication researcher John Lilly, and Taoist philosopher Alan Watts—all these fascinating voices swirled around the UC campus like a clarion call to spiritual expansiveness. Snyder, Lilly, and Watts were also deeply involved in the environmental movement that was just finding its voice. After exploring Transcendental Meditation with the Maharishi Mahesh Yogi, the Beatles were breaking up, and John Lennon had just released his first single, "Instant Karma," followed by the Mother Mary blessing "Let It Be."

Most of my friends easily believed in reincarnation and sometimes played a game at parties with strangers called "Who Were We in Other Lives?" Since I came from generations of teetotalers, religious poets, and schoolteachers on my Irish mother's side and Native blood on my father's side, I had no genetic aptitude for alcohol. One glass of wine was enough to make me pass out. And when I unknowingly sipped some party punch that had been spiked with LSD and felt my spirit ascending, abandoning my body, my boyfriend Galen knew what to do: he clasped my arms around an ancient eucalyptus tree and then wrapped himself around me. Half the night, until the hallucinogen wore off, I was rooted in the earth. No rapture and no wonder that I stayed sober and avoided psychedelics when everyone around me was in a purple haze. I could, however, enjoy the contact high of spiritual pursuits. It was all fascinating. But my evangelical childhood had left me with wariness toward any guru or group of true believers. On the grassy university quad, it was just as common to see someone meditating as studying.

So without any formal spiritual instruction, I simply sat cross-legged in silence and watched my thoughts, as my Buddhist high-school friend Kip had taught me. Decades later a Buddhist friend would explain it more succinctly: if my thoughts wandered, I should simply, without judgment, come back to my breathing. "It's like this," she said. "If you hear a train going by when meditating, just note it. But don't get on the train!"

In creative writing classes I was still working away on the novel about a fundamentalist snake-handling sect. I had unexpectedly fallen in love with my fervent backwoods characters, seeing them as a species that, like Neanderthals and some of the other animals I was reading about, was facing extinction. Now that I had escaped conservative evangelicals, I truly believed the whole world would too. That was evolution.

During one anthropology class Professor Raeburn showed us slides of Lascaux cave paintings. In the Great Hall of the Bulls, scientists gazed up with miners' flashlights strapped to their foreheads like bright cyclops-eyes. On a majestic panel of Paleolithic animal life were massive bulls, charcoal-edged stags, and a unicorn chasing other horses across the cave walls.

"Notice anything strange about the perspective of these prehistoric paintings?" Professor Raeburn asked.

Very strange, and for me exciting: while the animal portraits were richly drawn and realistic, the people were still stick figures.

"You see," said Professor Raeburn, letting out a good-humored guffaw, "back then we got it right. Humans realized that we didn't matter so much in nature. We were new on the scene and didn't know if we would last that long."

In the cave drawings our early ancestor hunters, with their stick spears, did seem puny and overwhelmed by the tidal wave of animal images. There was a murmur in the classroom; not a single student twittered.

Professor Raeburn paused and then said very seriously, "Homo sapiens may be a blip on the evolutionary scale, but we have dangerously reversed the natural order of things. Cave paintings now would show so many species smudged out." Professor Raeburn snapped off the projector's light, and the brilliant cave paintings disappeared into darkness. He whispered in a voice that for a scientist was surprisingly husky with emotion, "Humans have now drawn themselves so huge, there is hardly any room for other animals."

He finished the lecture by telling us a statistic that he insisted we write down because it would be on the final exam: in children, 80 percent of their dreams are devoted to animals. "We are still born with the wisdom of early humans," Professor Raeburn said. "But by the time you are all full adults, only 6 percent of your dreams will be filled with the beauty and vitality of these animals."

He flicked back on the projector, and in the wavering light the Great Hall of the Bulls stampeded out over us. We sat in hushed stillness. Our awe was as ancient as the animals. We were little stick figures, remembering.

"Our ancestors understood that our survival directly depends upon the animals and the earth," Professor Raeburn told us. "They literally kept us alive. Body and soul. We worshiped the animals—and why not." He waved his arms to take in the full panel of galloping animals. "Wouldn't you?"

"What is that creature with those big, curved horns?" a student asked, pointing to a beast drawn bold in the ocher colors of iron oxide pigment.

"That's an auroch, a wild ox," Professor Raeburn explained. "Extinct."

I was struck at how similar the auroch was to the great ungulates my father hunted. Though I protested, he had packed me off to university with fifty pounds of moose meat from his recent hunting trip to Montana. When I later found housing with some older students who also ran a health-food store, I dared not brave what I feared was their food fundamentalism and reveal the wild game hidden away in their huge freezer. Instead, I divvied up the frozen moose meat between Galen's hunter buddies and homeless people—of which there were very few in that bucolic university town.

Galen was a passionate, but earth-loving forestry major and poet, a senior who would soon ask me to drop out of school, marry him, and escape to Canada to avoid the Vietnam draft. I had no intention of marrying him and uprooting myself. I was no more a nomad, I told Galen. As much as I protested Nixon's war and right-wing politics, I was not going to leave my whole country behind. The day Galen publicly burned his draft card during a campuswide protest, I had to make myself scarce from the FBI, who searched for me as a witness for a week. When I was not enjoying high-spirited communal vegan suppers with my health-food housemates, I was out in the country with Galen on his ramshackle farm. One of Galen's attractions was his pet goat, Katie, who slept with us in Galen's hand-carved loft. The genial goat would snuggle at our feet, her large, dark eyes steadily upon us. Katie snored softly, more a guttural purr, and in our little wooden ark of a bed we sailed happily together. Sometimes Galen and I joked that Katie was in school to study us humans, just as we were in university to study other animals.

I was double-majoring in comparative literature and creative writing, with an eye to a possible minor in biology. After all, this was a school known for its science, and especially its veterinary school. Biology classes kept a firm grip on my imagination, though I was often dismayed at how so much of spirit was stricken from science, and any metaphysics stripped from physics. When I asked my father about this, he said something that we actually agreed upon.

"Science without soul is not true science," my father told me. "In my work, if a forester doesn't also believe that these trees are God's creation, then how can he manage as a good steward should?"

My father actually approved of Galen because of his forestry major and battered pickup truck. Also, Galen was a hunter, mostly of pheasant, but that was better than being some literary snob, or worse, a hippie. My mother kept nudging me to find a "good Christian congregation." I responded by describing to her the sunlit fields of corn and bright orange California poppies. Cycling by farms inlaid with wild flowers, swimming in freshwater irrigation ditches, and hiking the nearby flaxen foothills, I felt completely at home. I would put down roots here, no matter what. It wasn't my primal first High Sierra forest, but I believed that I belonged in this western landscape.

"This is my church," I informed my mother.

"But it . . . ," Mother protested, "it's . . . well, outside!"

"Yes," I told her with a fervor of my own. "Where God is."

One balmy night I was cycling across campus to a friend's party at which we were going to indulge our favorite pastime—singing. I was making extra money for tuition by singing in a folk trio, much like the one I'd seen at Glorietta, except we were all girls. I considered this my street ministry, except there was no religion, only music. We had formed an "All-Hours Lullaby Service" and were on call to come sing down other students from terrifying acid trips. Our singing was much more calming than a trip to the university health center and the dreaded shot of Thorazine. Also, we three sirens were much cheaper and didn't ding on their university record like illegal drugs.

So I was singing at the top of my voice as I cycled across gravel roads near the remote science labs and the agricultural buildings. At first when I saw the wire pen of small dogs racing toward the fence, their snouts thrown back, their voices raised to join mine, I didn't notice anything odd because my voice filled the rural evening air. Crickets and katydids chattered, and I sang all the louder, expecting by the time I reached the beagles that we'd all make a mighty animal chorus.

I cycled faster so as to reach the pups before their howls died down, and I howled out, hopefully, inviting them to harmonize. At last I was within hearing range. The beagles excitedly pressed their black noses against their high fence, heads upraised.

And then I realized something horrible, something that made me stop midsong. Silence. The beagles did not sing with me. Though their bodies trembled, their snouts were lifted, and veins and tendons were straining inside their throats, there was not a single sound coming from them except the shuffle of their small paws. Mute. Every single beagle was mute.

I was no stranger to the sight of a gutted deer carcass hanging in the family shed—I grew up believing myself more tough-skinned than most of my animal-loving college school chums. But witnessing these dumb dogs, I realized I was not. Maybe it summoned up shades of my grandpa's hound pups I had accidentally killed, or maybe the sight of dogs raising their heads to sing without any sound—whatever the reason, I was so shocked I skidded on the gravel.

In an instant the bicycle and I turned top-over-end several times before I shuddered to the ground. How long I lost consciousness I'll never know, but when I awoke, I lay gashed and bleeding from my forehead and my hands, arms, legs, and thighs where gravel and broken spokes had slashed the skin. Moving gingerly, I made certain there were no broken bones, but I was dazed and nauseated, signs of a slight concussion. I lay still, hoping someone else might bicycle by on this remote path.

It was dark now, and the only light was from the few spotlights guarding the dog pen. Hearing the silent shuffling and leaping of the dogs, I dazedly realized these must be laboratory animals. I'd heard rumors about experiments on campus with laboratory mice or beagles made to inhale huge doses of smoke in experiments to test the effect of tobacco on lungs. Other experiments were whispered to be even more grisly—genetic tests, organ transplants.

Next to the fence, several dozen beagles stood sentry, studying me closely in the most terrible silence I have ever heard. As I lay eye-level with the quiet beagles, the thought occurred to me that after some healing I would be fine, but not so these laboratory dogs. Perhaps it was the lapse of consciousness or a new consciousness, but dictionary words began echoing in my shaken brain, words that at first seemed like nonsense. "Mutt—slang for dog or mongrel, simpleton, stupid person. Mutt—mutilated or mutual. Mutant—to be changed or altered." And then the word I'd learned in biology class: *mutatis*, or necessary changes.

In my daze I couldn't quite put it all together, except to understand that because these dogs were considered stupid or less than human, all ethical considerations were cast aside to make some changes considered necessary. Scientists were making changes through animal mutilations. Were we also somehow changing ourselves, and not necessarily for the best?

While my own skin had been wounded, I had not lost my voice as these beagles had when their vocal cords were slashed. Why silence these friendly little dogs—to keep them from alerting anyone to other experiments performed upon them? In this remote area of the campus, who was there really to disturb?

The dogs couldn't even whimper without their vocal cords. But through their eyes and expressions, the beagles could still communicate, still commiserate with my wounds. I crawled over to them. It was a serene night, with only crickets singing. The beagles quietly lay down on their haunches to gaze at me. This close, I could see the neat rows of stitches running like zippers along the dogs' bellies. With some pain I lifted my arm and stretched my fingers through the chain-link fencing. Tenderly, a dozen tongues lapped at my bleeding fingers and arm, soothing me. It was their only way left of speaking—with their tongues.

For a long time the beagles comforted me—even though I was one of a species that had been returning pain for their affection. I will never forget their creature comfort. There was something exchanged between my body and those dogs that night—a simple kindness that is a wider territory than just human love. Dragging my broken bicycle and myself to a main street, I caught a ride to the health center for emergency care. Aside from the gravel imbedded in my knee and a few scars, my body healed quickly, but I was haunted then as I still am today by the wounds of those dogs.

During the following years, I would often cycle past those beagles and bring them dog treats. There was nothing else I could do but abide with them and hope that I returned to them some part of the comfort they had offered me that quiet night.

I didn't recognize it standing there with the silenced dogs, but I had turned completely away from any career in science that night. Where was the spirit in the beast expressed in even my father's ancestral hunting rituals of reverently placing a sliced apple in the mouth of a dead deer or tanning and preserving their animal skins for making our family's Christmas moccasins? Biology was "the study of life," not, as E. O. Wilson would later redefine it through the term "biophilia," the love of life. Without devotion or sacredness, science was bereft of all I believed.

I never signed up for another college biology course. And when I changed my major to focus only on literature, my father was disappointed. I feared he might force me to return to the South with him when and if he got his hoped-for promotion.

After witnessing the mute beagles, I swore I would never again stop speaking up, stop questioning my family's religion or my government's wars. I would also find a way to stay rooted in my native state, even if it meant I had to drop out of college and work in California full-time.

I was already working two jobs to help support myself—as a short-order cook and a Russian Department secretary. My Russian literature professor, Rod Patterson, was a dashing, fair-haired young man with a rakish handlebar mustache and a ravishingly beautiful blond wife. In their rural cottage, they raised white ducks whose offspring imprinted on Rod, just as did his students. Despite Professor Patterson's wife, we were all in love with him and basked in his philosophical flights. Galen and I were also devoted students of the novelist Diane Johnson, who chose both of us for her first fiction workshop there at UC Davis. Looking like a literary cross between Charlotte Brontë and a French gamin, Professor Johnson lectured us on the moody British heaths and how what haunts us also can inspire great literature. Galen was working on a cycle of nature poems, and I on my fledgling southern novel. With her genius for comedies of manners, Professor Johnson was always reminding me that irony was an option when portraying subcultures, such as my evangelicals.

"Pain . . . plus time . . . equals comedy," Professor Johnson would tell us.

I suspect she was privately as appalled as she was intrigued by my overwrought descriptions of revivals and characters riveted on salvation. She once commented rather dryly that too much intensity or belief can blind a writer to the more nuanced truths about characters—or oneself.

"For example," she explained, "our protagonists rarely see how much they resemble their antagonists. When you are portraying a villain, always look at how the villain mirrors the shadow-side of your hero."

I believed I was nothing like the holy-roller Deep South characters in my fledgling novel. It would take years for me to even consider this insight.

"People don't really argue about the state of their souls," Professor Johnson told me one class. "They argue about who lost the car keys—and *that* tells you about their souls."

I didn't quite register this then, just as I had never really understood that at other family dinner tables people did not talk about the never-ending moral Battle Between Good and Evil, the daily passion play of evangelical life. My mother had just sent me a copy of *The Late Great Planet Earth* by Hal Lindsey. This 1970 crossover best-seller inspired a new American wave of apocalypse worship. The author was an uneducated campus preacher in southern California who linked Cold War fears, assassinations, an unpopular war in Vietnam, race riots, and political turmoil. He would go on to conduct crowded seminars at the Pentagon and the National War College. The book cover promised "Incredible ancient prophecies involving this generation."

My copy was inscribed: "Read this—before it's too late! Love, Mom."

The Late Great Planet Earth seemed so sure in its predictions of Rapture. Lindsey claimed that one generation is forty years and that Jesus would return one generation after the 1948 rebirth of Israel as a state. Many believers calculated that the Rapture would occur no later than 1988.

"Listen, honey, this book gives you only eighteen more years to figure out your whole life," she told me on my visit home for Easter.

I was obliging my family by attending church service with them. I liked to sit next to my mother on the piano bench and turn the pages for her. Before the service, she reached out to clasp my hand. "I'd like to see you safely back within the fellowship of the believers," she whispered.

My mother had three teenagers at home in Berkeley in 1970, and she was working part-time as a high school study-hall monitor. Her friend Evelyn St. John had moved away to pursue other home missions work, and Berkeley was running amok with "antiwar weirdos." No wonder my mother wanted it all to end.

"Mother, none of my friends believes I'll last until I'm thirty," I teased her *sotto voce*. I was taking so many courses for my double major and staying up all night once a week, now with the help of Dexedrine, just to read.

One of the noncurricular texts I'd plowed through in the middle of the night was Alan Watts's *The Book on the Taboo of Knowing Who You Are*. In it he had written: "No considerate God would destroy the human mind by making it so rigid and unadaptable as to depend upon one book, the Bible, for all the answers. . . . To idolize scriptures is like eating paper currency."

"I might just get to heaven before you,." I teased Mother, but I was thinking about the bumper sticker I'd just seen: Speed Kills.

"Don't even joke about that!" Mother snapped and squeezed my hand rather painfully. "You're not going to die before us."

"But would you really leave . . . ," I asked, "without me?" I felt an unexpected surge of vulnerability.

Clasping her arm around my shoulder, my mother declared, "We won't have to—I hope!"

"We'll all go together when we go?" I asked, trying to make light of it.

My mother swung into a boogie-woogie version of "This World Is Not My Home" with the verse: *If heaven's not my home, then Lord, what will I do?*

Everyone in the pews sang this anthem to abandoning the sinful earth with such gusto. Looking out over the congregation, including my family sitting in the front row, I now felt completely alien, lost among true believers. But wasn't I also becoming quite a true believer myself? I just believed all that was antimatter to my family. And didn't I understand the longing to leave a family, if not a world, that seemed so wrong for me? Was that why I was speeding up my life—to make a faster getaway? They could never catch me again.

It was Professor Diane Johnson—not fears of Judgment Day—who questioned me about taking Dexedrine and cramming every other book in my head except the Bible. After staying up three nights running to prepare for Johnson's "Victorian Literature" final exam, I broke one of my own rules and took speed right before the test. Two hours and twenty-six pages later, I looked up and noticed I was the only student left in the lecture room. Professor Johnson sat on her desk, legs swinging casually. She took my scribbled blue-book pages without a word.

Later that week, she called me into her office and said, "This is publishable." She then handed the blue book back to me. It was adorned with a giant "F" in red ink.

I stared at her in bewilderment. "Why?" I managed to ask, though I knew the answer.

"You are stealing from your future," she informed me firmly. "And if I ever see evidence of any more speed in your work, I will drop you from my classes." Then she gave me her characteristic, rather crooked smile and asked, "What's the rush?"

It was a mantra I would always carry with me. And if I ever admitted during those college years that I had a guru, it would have been Diane Johnson. She saved me from what might have become a life of addiction to amphetamines, of rushing to experience everything—because perhaps unconsciously I really did believe that between the Rapture of my childhood and the revolution of my generation, the world's end was imminent.

What was really upon me, unfortunately, was my family's exodus from the revolutionary fields of Berkeley to conservative Atlanta, Georgia. The summer of my sophomore year in college my father landed his prestigious promotion to the southeast region. Would they leave me behind or whisk me off to their Promised Land of the Deep South?

Perhaps my parents believed that if they could just get their wayward eldest daughter back to the South, I would repent and be redeemed. If they could just take their beloved sinner to the proverbial

Canaan with them, I could still be saved. My trips home to Berkeley on weekends or holidays were again fraught with fear and arguments. The dinner table was a treacherous place, even with all my mother's culinary delights. I didn't want to eat; I wanted to stay in California—the land of forbidden fruit.

One Sunday morning at my parents' house, I awakened early to do my homework. I studied in the sunny rec room that overlooked acres of a grassy, steep ravine and pale hills that were home to fox and raccoons, a few deer, and ravens. I still wandered here along creek beds laden with wildflowers and blackberry brambles. Far across the wide and wild ravine was another hillside silhouetted with small houses, one of which our family had watched topple downhill in a fierce mudslide.

For some reason, Mother had called a truce of her own with pets, worn down over the years by our pleas and sulking. We doted upon a long-haired silver cat named Spunky and a feisty pup we named Shadrack, after the biblical hero who survived the fiery furnace. Surely he would need the divine aid of such a namesake to outlast Mother's now halfhearted threats to "take him back to the pound." It was with Shadrack, whose short Corgi legs nevertheless kept up with my long-limbed rambling, that I roamed the ravine. One day, right outside our house, I found a set of animal tracks I didn't recognize, although they were hauntingly familiar. Was it a bobcat?

Though I was supposedly studying that early morning, I was really looking through the big picture window for a glimpse of this nocturnal, elusive cat. Though I'd seen bobcats before, I was not prepared to look up through the big picture window and meet a pair of golden eyes gazing in through the window at me with all the curiosity of an animal visiting a human zoo.

But it was not a bobcat who eyed me that morning. It was a massive, graceful mountain lion who strolled back and forth in front of the window, never taking her eyes off me. I was paralyzed with both fear and awe. Not since my early forest days or camping trips to national forests had I seen any creature so wild. And in that one look the mountain lion restored something in me I believed I had lost long ago. I was being watched with both hunger and predatory calm. No human had ever impressed me as much as the gaze of this wild animal.

"She sure is sizing you up," my father whispered as he stood quietly behind me. "Breakfast maybe?" He let out a soft laugh.

My father's face was illumined in the early morning light, and I could see that he too was awestruck. I hadn't seen this expression on him for many years. Even so, I was afraid of what he would do. Would he take out his rifle and kill her? Would he report her to animal control to be managed?

As if sensing my fear, the mountain lion leapt over the backyard jungle gym and down into the ravine, running with such powerful, feline grace that for a moment my father and I just watched without a word.

"What will you do?" I finally asked him, more afraid of my father than of the lion.

"Not many of her kind left around here," my father said thoughtfully. "Maybe she's even the last of her kind left in these hills where she can still hide out." My father gave me a look then that I can only call conspiratorial and said, "We won't say anything about her, will we? We'll just leave her here—where she belongs."

"No." I shook my head in gratitude and surprised myself by crossing the room and impulsively embracing my father.

"Good girl," he said softly and stroked my long hair—the hair he had stopped cutting long ago, having given up managing all its wild and unruly curls. "She's a good girl."

* * *

WHEN MY FAMILY MOVED the summer of my sophomore year to what I considered a "realm of woe" in Lilburn, Georgia, my father advised me, "If you want to return to the University of California this fall, please try to help everyone get happily settled here in Georgia."

Impossible. Sisyphean. My nonradical siblings were bewildered to be greeted as "hippies" in that Georgia enclave. My mother was horrified to discover that her new neighbors in Georgia had decided that she was not devout enough. I guess her original sin was guilt by association with the West Coast.

Everyone in this backwoods southern theocracy seemed to be on the lookout for lost or transplanted souls like me. After all, I was a suspicious sinner from sun-drenched Berkeley where Vietnam draft dodgers and easy love were sure signs that End Times were upon us. To my Georgia neighbors, I was a "misfit" with tiny dark blond braids and pierced ears.

We kids were once again in such cross-cultural shock, so disoriented, that I seriously began to study Buddhism. I had witnessed enough hungry ghosts in the Haight-Ashbury to believe in all those *bardos* of the *Tibetan Book of the Dead*. But on the other hand, I was particularly taken with the concept of the soul's transmigration—more a Platonic, pagan, or Hindu notion. I hid my books under my mattress for fear Mother would discover this sacrilege and I would be forever exiled from my beloved California. If I had to transfer to the University of Georgia, I knew I would spontaneously combust.

I was already halfway there in the suffocating heat. At night we had to sleep with wet sheets wrapped around our burning bodies. No wonder hellfire and brimstone is so vivid a threat in the Deep South: it might as well be the weather report. I began to consider that the Buddhists got it right in their Niraya realms—their hot and cold hells. I wondered: *How could the Buddha have believed that being incarnated as a human being was fortunate? Had he ever been to Georgia?*

My only escapes that summer were swimming in the nearby Yellow River and grocery shopping. The Winn-Dixie supermarket was an oasis of cold air and many choices. I would loiter in the aisles, scanning shelves until my gloom eased into a cool and meditative calm. It was during one of these rather dissociative reveries that I had an idea that even my Berkeley friends might have considered far-out: what if I could transmigrate my soul into some other, unsuspecting shopper?

Getting free of my own body, like so much old karma, maybe I could become a person who just skimmed by, believing what everybody else around me did. I reasoned: Why not be a happy shopper? Why not follow the Blue Light Special to a nirvana discount? Then I wouldn't worry about the suffering just outside the single point of a perfect shelf. Without a trace of the irony Professor Johnson had tried to instill in me, I convinced myself that since I had always been a transplant, I could also transplant my soul into another person's body. Chameleon-like, I could assimilate spiritually—and just not be so odd.

One afternoon in this labyrinth of groceries, I finally found my spiritual target: a young, well-dressed mother with her toddler cooing away in his cart seat as she scanned the Bird's Eye frozen vegetables. She held a tiny clicker device that counted off the prices of each icy package she tossed into her cart: creamed corn, okra, and French fries. How sensible she seemed. How normal and certain of her path. This woman had to exemplify the Buddhist belief that we are lucky to be born human. She was obviously not a rebel or wanderer like me—who even sometimes got lost in the supermarket.

With all my might I willed my soul to lift out of my renegade body and drop into what I assumed was the young mother's blissfully ordinary life. I had read about "walk-ins"—those souls who swoop into other people's bodies. So I would be a "shop-in." She would get two souls for the price of one. And I would no longer have to suffer being myself.

Maybe it was the jittering trance induced by the fluorescent lights or the frigid *whoosh* of the frozen foods glowing off glass doors, but suddenly I saw a shimmer between me and the happy woman. For just a nanosecond, my spirit seemed to hover above the aisle, gazing down on a teenage girl in a tie-dye T-shirt with a peace symbol necklace; next to her was the Georgia housewife with a tidy bouffant, wearing a pleated skirt. Floating free above my body—my destiny—I thought I might succeed in this supermarket transmigration of souls.

But then the other shopper astonished me. Violently she began shaking her head as if fending off a hive of invisible bees. Then she started stomping her feet on the linoleum. With a little scream, she tore up her grocery list and threw her handy clicker-counter on the floor. Her toddler began to sob with her. Not just the hiccup-studded cry of babies, but a ghastly, banshee yowl.

Stock boys arrived with mops and a sloshing bucket of suds. But how could they clean up tears? The young woman was weeping inconsolably. In Berkeley, as the designated driver, the only straight person at every party, I had seen bad acid trips and even peyote gone bad at a wedding, but this woman's despair was so bottomless, so real, that it shook me back to my senses. Abruptly, and with a keen sense of my own sorrow—and some chagrin—I was plopped back into my body.

Quickly, I was at the woman's side. "It's all right," I said. Then I noticed she wore no wedding ring.

"How do you know?" she demanded.

She was right. I didn't know. I didn't know anything.

Both she and her baby were howling now like some ancient tribe singing those ululating shrills, like speaking in tongues. I recognized the sounds of pure grief, pure loss. Soul loss.

I knew then the first rule of the Buddha was true: *everybody suffers.* My Buddhist friend Kip must also have been right: *there is no way out but through the suffering.* Kip had learned this with the high school pecking order. This supermarket breakdown finally revealed it to me.

Right there in the Winn-Dixie, I wondered: *Did my soul actually transmigrate into that woman to ignite her misery?* Or was it just a coincidence that we were suffering simultaneously? Perhaps Kip was right and this was some dharmic practice—to see my own and another's suffering as a call to compassionate action. But I did nothing.

At the end of the summer, I was allowed back to California. Perhaps my parents recognized my desolation. Perhaps they saw that I was clenching my fists during every church service. Or maybe as the family found their footing again there in the familiar South, they just needed a reprieve from my liberal lamentations.

After graduation in 1972, even with all my honors in literature, I was unemployable, unless I wanted to teach. Diane Johnson had told me to avoid graduate schools, advising, "Your books will be your degrees." Without saying, "I told you so," my father arranged for me to work as a waitress in a national forest in North Carolina. That job lasted all of two months before I organized a union among the other waitresses and waiters and was fired as a "rabble-rousing radical." We were escorted off that Appalachian mountain and had to spend the night with the family of one of the waiters. They lived in a ramshackle cabin, and it was only when we all sat down to a meager meal that I realized how much they depended on my friend's waiter job for food. I was shocked by their poverty, the dirt floors like those of my own father's birthplace. And I felt some shame and guilt in knowing I had a middle-class home to land in after leading my little revolution.

"Glorietta and now North Carolina. Two jobs, two times fired," my father told me upon my return to Georgia. "Not a good way to begin your career." He seemed as concerned about me as he was cross. "Do you think you have a problem with authority?"

Because I was a rapid-fire typist, I landed a secretarial job back home in Atlanta as an engineering secretary. Numbers swirled through my head so dizzyingly that on my breaks I would stand in the bathroom, each arm outstretched against the walls, and rock back and forth, trying to steady myself for a life of dismal reality. Where were the great books of Mrs. Costarella's classes now that I needed them? What good were all the novels that filled my mind after graduating with two hundred extra units from university? Now that I was living a life of "quiet desperation," now that I felt like a cockroach scuttling to and from meaningless work, the Rapture seemed more and more attractive.

In Georgia my parents had chosen a local Southern Baptist church that was, even by my family's standards, frighteningly zealous. The pastor, Lloyd Hastrow, was a young and fiery believer who made the sermons of my childhood seem mild by comparison. He had all but convinced my fifteen-year-old brother that there was no point in preparing for college because the Rapture was upon us. One day, sitting miserably in the back pew as Pastor Hastrow regaled us with Revelation, I had an idea born of desperation: why not call the medieval literature teaching assistant, the poet Dorothy Gilbert, who had worked many years at *The New Yorker*, and plead for assistance in setting up an interview? If I did not get out of the Deep South, I suspected I might end up in my own Tennessee Williams play. Dorothy generously arranged an interview in the magazine's typing pool, called "Walden's Pond," for the eccentric woman who ran it. I called in sick at the Atlanta engineering firm and caught the first bus to New York City.

In one of the hallowed, though unexpectedly shabby, cubbyholes of the magazine, Mrs. Walden greeted me with, "We aren't hiring anybody, not even you, dear." She then proceeded to oblige me with a typing test, which I nailed at a desperate 102 words per minute. Rather dazedly, she called me back into her smoky, glass-enclosed office.

"I'll bet you could even keep up with our Race Track columnist, Audax Minor," she nodded. Mrs. Walden lit a cigarette and sat back in her squeaky chair. Intently she studied me as if I were not even there, but was a statue in a Manhattan museum. "Hmmmm," she concluded. "You'll have to lose your southern accent."

"I don't have any accent," I told her in a suspiciously lilting voice.

"People will think you're stupid," she brushed by my rebuttal. "You can start in two weeks."

She did not mention a salary, she did not explain what my job would be; she did not say anything more except, "You've just died, dear, and gone to heaven."

And I believed with all my heart and soul that I had.

seven

I Love to Tell the Story
(Baptist hymn)

WHO WANTED TO MEDITATE IN MANHATTAN AND MISS OUT ON A single New York minute? Who needed speed when subways catapulted us through black tunnels like iron slingshots? *What's the rush?* The mantra lent me by Diane Johnson in college was drowned out by the hiss and throb, clatter and screech of "the City," as New Yorkers called their home. While attentive to the chance music, like a John Cage soundtrack, I often got lost.

My first day commuting to *The New Yorker* in midtown, I caught the wrong subway and ended up in Queens. When I asked directions from a passerby, he snarled, "What do I look like, a travel agent?" Then he actually thrust me aside with his briefcase as if I were a bag lady.

Perhaps I did look a little disheveled as I dove in late to Walden's Pond. Dressed in my best dress slacks and a blue silk blouse, I still looked down-and-out compared to the stylish other staffers.

My first weeks I was assigned to Edith Oliver, the fierce theater critic. Small, quick-witted, and gnarled, Miss Oliver was an aristocratic crone out of a Grimm's fairy tale. Certainly, she seemed to hold the key to every kingdom. With one review, she could shut down a Broadway show. What could she do to a lowly editorial assistant?

Miss Oliver often snapped her fingers in my face as if I were not already riveted by her every command. She doubled as book-review editor, and her office was a garret with wall-high shelves of books longing for a *New Yorker* nod. As I dutifully logged in the candidates, I barely spoke a word, except, "Yes, ma'am," as was my southern training.

"Don't 'ma'am' me, child," Miss Oliver snapped. "I'm not Methuselah."

Once a senile writer meandered down the hall and tried to enter a door in the Books Department that had not been used for a decade; it was blocked by a huge bookcase. When at first the door didn't budge, the old man used his cane like a crowbar to wedge it open. "Move aside!" he bellowed in his theatrical baritone. "I have some timely newsbreaks!" He waved old clippings.

One more urgent shove with his cane and the door creaked open at last. Miss Oliver and I watched the slow-motion tumble of hundreds of hardback books. We had to scramble to keep from being bonked or crushed by them.

Frustrated by the fact that he could not clamber over a mountain of books, the gentleman harrumphed back down the hallway, scratching the eczema on his hands and muttering. He seemed completely unaware of the catastrophe he left behind.

Among the magazine's other, more highly functioning staff, I had never encountered such unabashed intellectual panache. During every elevator ride to the twentieth-floor editorial offices, a time when I expected to eavesdrop on learned discussions of Great Books, there was instead much dueling of wits. No wonder they called it "rapier." Because I was again trying to shed the irritating slight southern accent, I relied on Zen silence. There was also a class system that rivaled any pecking order I had ever observed among animals.

One day when Miss Oliver complimented me on my blouse, I remarked proudly that I'd just found it on sale at Lord and Taylor.

Miss Oliver stepped back in dismay, one horrified hand pressed against her chest. "My deah," she intoned in what I heard as an Edith Wharton voice, "you don't mean to say that you, you actually *live* on your salary?"

It seemed that very few staffers, including the editorial slaves, depended on their *New Yorker* salary. I discovered that my weekly paycheck that year in 1972 was $88 after taxes, and that barely covered the Lower West Side hotel I'd landed in with my steamer trunk and prized manual Olympic typewriter. It took me a week to discover that I had taken up residence in a Puerto Rican whorehouse. Of the handful of young people at the magazine, most had trust funds. One young woman arrived each morning in her father's chauffeured limousine. Many staffers admitted they would have paid the magazine simply to work there. Old money explained both the elegance and eccentricity. There was an editor who never repeated an outfit for three hundred days—in Walden's Pond we kept count—and another who only wore mohair. She left little woolly puffs everywhere she wafted.

The notable exceptions to this fashion parade down the hallways at 25 West Forty-third Street were the writers and cartoonists. They showed up as if they had just stumbled from bed or a binge. One cartoonist locked his mother in his office with him for a day, and I could hear her shouting as I hurried by with the daily "setup" sheet of what was being put into print that morning. No one seemed troubled by the scene until the police showed up, probably called by the more plebeian advertising offices on the lower floors. Editorial and advertising at *The New Yorker* were separated like church and state used to be in this country, like publishing before chains and media mogul takeovers. Perhaps that was why there was more tolerance for individuality and genius.

Another writer often appeared in the twentieth-floor editorial offices drunk and dressed in her pajamas. It didn't seem to affect her incandescent prose. A once-dazzling novelist was now homeless and living in an alcove right off the women's bathroom. The delicate old lady in poignantly bright makeup perched on her daybed smoking Gauloises and chatting with the mirror. Every now and then she would address one of us tiptoeing past her lair and deliver herself of a delightfully incoherent soliloquy.

I was one of a handful of editorial staff under thirty; the rest were in their fifties through seventies. Though the mean streets of Manhattan were pure *Lord of the Flies*, inside *The New Yorker's* run-down hallways we employees were expected to abide by a Victorian etiquette not unlike that of the British period drama *Upstairs, Downstairs*. We editorial servants knew secrets. It was a futile power.

"I count on my girls for their discretion," Mrs. Walden often schooled me, blowing a swirl of Doral Ultra Lites smoke into my face. Her glass-enclosed office was like a lab for animals being tested for secondhand smoke inhalation. The fact that two of the six of us in her Pond were young men hadn't seemed to register yet with her.

In Walden's Pond, IBM typewriters rattled under intense editorial deadlines; in diligent pairs we proofread each page out loud, even though there was an army of proofreaders just down the hall. We youngsters rotated through every editorial office from Talk of the Town to Fiction—even to stints in reclusive Mr. William Shawn's office. That was a dangerous assignment because the editor-in-chief was guarded by a southern gorgon who was as devoted to Shawn's soft-spoken and benevolent tyranny as she was difficult to fathom. Her Deep South accent was easy for me to understand after my summers in Georgia. So I sometimes got the short end of the straw for that assignment. We initiates were never allowed, however, in Fact Checking—a bastion of supernatural intellects who would have won vast fortunes on *Jeopardy*. With red pencils they pounced upon what Mrs. Walden described in disgust as "Errors in Fact." Many days at the magazine were so busy that it seemed like one blink before quitting time. But the gift of our erratic workload was that when we had no manuscripts, we were encouraged to work on whatever projects we liked, including our works-in-progress. Many in Walden's Pond would go on to become well-known journalists and authors.

"Everyone here is writing the Great American Novel, my dear," Mrs. Walden said, flipping her ashes perilously close to my elbow. She waved me back to my desk. "Feel free to try it yourself."

Mrs. Walden always carried her own ashtray as she chugged down the hallways at top speed, manuscripts in hand, smoke billowing behind her. We called her "the Locomotive."

Like those first railroads that dynamited right through stone mountains, New Yorkers propelled through crowds as if other people were not really there. Here, human nature dominated nature as I knew it. Except for Central Park and a few shady streets, I was shocked at the anemic struggle of city trees. I tried to make up for this loss by getting permission from Mrs. Walden to plant a midget vegetable garden on the office windowsill. Though sooty and struggling, it managed to produce tiny corn and cherry tomatoes that I fed to the pigeons.

One of the first things I did in Walden's Pond was pin up photos of red mud, cows, cornfields, and the mysterious Yellow River to remind myself of the humid hell I'd left behind in Georgia. While my summers in the Deep South had been unbearable, misery was good material for any novelist. Even though my main characters were based on my Ozarkian grandparents, I changed the story's setting to backwoods Georgia because it was there I had witnessed the extremes of fundamentalism, especially as an adult, that livened my first novel. I was happily writing a chapter from the point of view of a cow, like the mythic Ios, and also a sermon on the fall of the Garden of Eden from the point of view of the fallen angel serpent. Not exactly *New Yorker* material. In the magazine's archives I had looked up reviews of Faulkner—called a "flash in the pan" and "Mississippi's

Frankenstein"—and Flannery O'Connor, who, though a major American stylist, was never published in the magazine.

When I gathered the courage to submit my work to a sub-sub fiction editor, he advised me, "The magazine would never publish D. H. Lawrence if he were writing today. Why don't you go to some cocktail parties and write about real life?"

Cocktails might have come in handy, but with my embarrassing habit of swooning over a sip of wine, I resigned myself to continuing my own little opus, a parallel world of people speaking like this: "Rainin' outside, rainin' like a cow pissin' on flat rock . . . rainin' like a Devil whopping his wife . . . and she's a-cryin' up a storm!"

It was how Jessie talked, and my grandfather, a kind of Olde English that swirled through my head even in Manhattan. Needless to say, rejection slips were the result of my few submissions to the Fiction Department, whose star writer, Anne Beattie, was making a minimalist molehill out of any mountain.

"Still plunking away, are we?" one of the other staffers in Walden's Pond would ask me almost daily. After becoming an editor's protégé, he had taken to wearing a paisley ascot.

It was hopeless, but I'd determined that this was my apprenticeship and I would give myself ten years to get published. So I plunked away on my office IBM Selectric in the hope that one day my strange world would find a champion. Down the hall from Walden's Pond was an editorial luminary, Miss Rachel MacKenzie, who edited Isaac Bashevis Singer, John Hersey, and Anne Tyler. Miss MacKenzie was the kindest person I met at the magazine. She had a silver coif swept back into a bun, startlingly dark eyebrows, oversize black glasses, and a refined smile that made my speaking to her impossible. I had a frequent fantasy that if I found myself fatally ill, I would ask her to read my manuscript. Otherwise, I would simply pass her in the hallway or deliver proofs to her and stand silently in her vast office. I knew she had a delicate heart and was susceptible to noise. Her *New Yorker* piece and book on open-heart surgery, *Risk*, had just been published to much acclaim. Its last line echoed through my head, like longing: *Dear God, the miracle.*

I believed it was a miracle that I was in New York and had, as one of the other Walden Pond staffers proclaimed, "arrived." I didn't feel as assured as he of my place here—more like a survivor of shifting worlds. But I luxuriated in this liberal stronghold, believing it was an antidote to my family's conservative stranglehold. And yet— was it mutinous to notice inconsistencies in my chosen people, these liberal faithful? For example, the Ivy League elites here at the magazine sometimes seemed as self-congratulatory and exclusive as my Southern Baptist childhood churches. Whereas conservative evangelicals laid claim to a heaven not on this earth, upscale New Yorkers seemed to think they were entitled to the very best this earth had to offer. At work, I couldn't help but wonder why our editorial assistant salaries were so low. I thought liberals looked out for the poor. This was not Appalachian coal-mining country, like my first real job. Those of us who actually tried to live on this Scrooge-like salary had to take on outside secretarial or editorial freelance work just to survive.

Once I was hired to address invitations to a fund-raiser for a leftist organization whose lofty goal was protecting the rights of all religions to flourish in this country. This ecumenicist embrace was something I could believe in. Yet here again, the pay was stingy, and while I worked in the well-appointed brownstone study all day, none of the organizers enjoying lunch and tea in the next room thought to offer me anything. Finally a black butler took mercy on me and brought in crumpets and tea. I thought I actually saw him winking at me as I listened to the group's leaders run through a book, calling out names for me to scribe on elegant envelopes. It was only as I was pocketing my pay that I realized the book was the *Social Register*, which I didn't know really existed.

When I mentioned this outside job to another editorial assistant in Walden's Pond, she smiled. "Where is liberal guilt when we need it?" My friend was from Kentucky, a real-life coal miner's daughter. She would go on to great success, but not at the magazine.

Rather boldly, and perhaps as my own little class rebellion, I tacked up over my desk a modest Smokey Bear poster admonishing, Only You! I could not help but view the towering forests of manuscripts in the editorial offices as felled trees. I was also keenly aware that our offices were a firetrap and took the time to memorize all the stairways and exits.

Mrs. Walden eyed the rural exhibit above my typewriter suspiciously. "Why can't you post Picassos or Dalis above your desk for inspiration, like the other girls?" Mrs. Walden chided me, smoke chugging out in small puffs like a brushfire. "Did I say anything when you came to work wearing those tree-ring earrings?"

"My father gave them to me," I began, then quickly gave up. I had never worn my vast collection of Smokey Bear and Woodsy Owl pins and tie tacks to work.

"This Smokey Bear—he's a government agent, you know." Mrs. Walden paused and shook her head. "Never trust the government."

These were, after all, the impeachment days of Richard Nixon, and the magazine was leading other media in covering the Vietnam War with Jonathan Schell; Reporter-at-Large pieces by staff writer William Wertenbaker covered ocean pollution, and Noel Mostert profiled supertankers.

Mrs. Walden waved her arms and lit another cigarette from the one burning in her hand-held ashtray. "Listen," she said, "I know this Smokey Bear stuff is part of my staff's campaign to stop me from smoking. But it's just not going to work. You should know better than to expect me to follow advice from a wild animal." She laughed and her chest rattled. "I don't even listen to my doctor—and he's human."

* * *

NEW YORK CITY LIFE seemed to take place against a brazenly artificial movie set, not on an actual island anchored between real rivers. I was mugged three times the first few weeks I was in Manhattan, until a friend kindly advised me, "Keep your eyes straight ahead and walk with purpose—as if you are late for everything." After a scary stint in the Puerto Rican whorehouse, I had called the lead singer from our college All-Hours Lullaby Service, whose father was president of a Jewish philanthropic organization. He found a dorm room for me in the Ninety-second Street Y, but I had to pass a rigorous interview.

"You can teach those Israelis a thing or two about scripture," Mrs. Simha told me after grilling me for what seemed hours on my background. "You'll be the only *shiksa* here," she said. "Watch out that the more militant Israelis don't tear the *mezuzah* off your door in protest."

Life as the only Gentile in the Ninety-second Street Jewish Y dormitory was yet another immersion in a new language and culture. When I told my mother where I was living and that on my salary even the Y was a stretch, she responded, "You're living in the Old Testament! I hope you can save a few of your friends, dear. You know, they're still waiting for the Messiah!"

"Aren't you too?" I asked.

"Well," Mother paused, and then added fiercely, "well, at least we Christians know He came down here in the first place!" She paused, then took a milder tact. "But it's good you have Jewish friends now, honey. You know what an important role they are playing in bringing about . . . ," she hesitated, as if struggling with herself, then insisted, "well, what *some* of us still believe is God's plan."

"Do we have to talk about the end of the world now, Mother?" I sighed.

I glanced down the hallway of the top-floor dormitory. No other girls were waiting yet to use the hall pay phone. We both had time on our hands, and Mother was paying for the call. So we were off again in our End Times wrangling. Mother had recently sent me an audiotape on "the Great White Throne of Judgment" and another one of her hand-me-down thrillers. She had always been downright evangelical about her spy novels—or, as I'd heard one of the magazine critics disdainfully call it, "spy-fi." Mother had not warned me about the book's gleeful violence, but she had advised, "Just skip the sex scenes."

Propped now against the dormitory wall and tethered to the pay phone, I chided myself for falling into another family philosophical slugfest—what I'd come to think of as similar to Jacob's "wrestling with angels." The story of Jacob was one of my own and my mother's Bible story favorites: Jacob, who had already tricked his brother Esau out of a patriarchal blessing, finds himself wrestling all night with an angel. Jacob will not let the muscular angel go "except thou bless me." The blessing comes with a wound to Jacob's thigh and an annunciation. Jacob's name will be changed to "Yisrael" because "as a prince hast thou power with God and with men, and hast prevailed."

In the endless weeknight Bible studies of my childhood, I had listened to many interpretations of this story. Most of the Southern Baptist truisms centered on how Christians struggle with God and survive the mortal combat of seeing Him face to face. The emphasis was on survival rather than the dark night of the soul, the inner struggle. But living in the Y as the lone *shiksa* and listening to theological debates from another perspective had given me a vivid new interpretation of this Torah story. The focus here was on God's changing Jacob's name to Yisrael, or "one who wrestles with God." Several of my Y friends believed that it was actually our spiritual responsibility to argue with God.

"For Jews, God is not some dictator who always has to win every argument and battle," my roommate Rachel explained to me as we sat in the dormitory kitchen talking late into the night—Jacob-like.

In the communal refrigerator, we kept our food in locked metal compartments, like little safe deposit boxes. Rachel, a struggling actor and an extraordinary cook on a low budget, shared her stash with me. I had been living on tuna and bagels. And on paydays I always blew half my food allowance on challah, cheese, and deli food at Zabar's, where I had once fainted from the crush of the crowd.

"God is a good rabbi who enjoys a feisty . . . do you know the word *midrash?*"

I did not. But I was picking up some handy Yiddish and had delighted in confiding to my brother that our family was *meshuga*.

"*Midrash*," Rachel continued, "means, you know, a real back-and-forth commentary on what we believe. There are no easy moral answers. That's why Jacob has to wrestle with God."

Since I had been banished from Vacation Bible School for disagreeing that God would get personally involved in finding Mrs. Eula's contact lens, I had come to believe that doubt and questioning were as important as belief. Jacob's wrestling with his angel, whether it was the Creator or his own demons, was still one of my favorite stories because of its ambiguity, its haunting equipoise between divine and human.

"You mean, God is not the heavyweight champion of the world?" I laughed.

"God is a mystery—equal to our own," Rachel said quietly and presented me with her homemade rhubarb tarts.

I was so struck by her dessert and her words that I wrote them down. Our long, late-night discussions were one of the reasons I was so content living in the Y and would have happily stayed on for years if there hadn't been a waiting list for my room.

Now standing in the hallway of the Jewish Y, I tried to wind up the conversation with my mother on the communal phone—several other girls were now impatiently waiting, rolling their eyes. They understood mothers.

"Mother, I gotta go now, but thanks so much for your scrumptious Christmas care package."

"Maybe I should visit and cook you some real food," she held on. "Are you sure you're really getting enough to eat up there?"

"Mother, I'm in Manhattan!" I said and suddenly heard in my voice a new tone. It was only the slightest shading—supercilious, annoyed, and righteous, but it so startled me that I fell silent.

Mother continued in a softer voice. "Oh, I worry about you in that godless city."

My mother's tenderness always surprised and touched me. "Don't worry, Mother." I tried to ease her concerns. "There are preachers here on every street corner. And I'm having long dialogues about Old Testament stories here in the Jewish Y."

"Well, honey," she said, "if you wanted to live with Jewish people in some sort of commune, why couldn't you go to Israel and work on a kibbutz or something?" Mother then admitted giddily, "I've always wanted to visit the Holy Land."

My mother was not alone among evangelicals in her longing to visit Israel. Ever since the 1967 Six-Day or Arab-Israeli War—when Israel gained control of much larger territories from the Sinai Peninsula to the Gaza Strip to eastern Jerusalem—many conservative evangelical Christians had flooded to the Holy Land. They were tourists with a mission—forging a surprisingly strong, if uneasy, alliance between evangelicals who believed that Jews were God's people, chosen to bring about the fulfillment of the pre-millennialist prophecies of End Times. One of Israel's most passionate supporters was the late fundamentalist icon Jerry Falwell. The Moral Majority's Reverend Tim LaHaye, author of the "Left Behind" series, was a frequent and very welcome guest in Israel, meeting with governmental officials. This new and odd alliance of evangelical Americans and Zionists was not greeted by my Jewish friends in New York as fortuitous.

After a close reading of my mother's *The Late Great Planet Earth*, Rachel had commented dryly, "Okay, so evangelicals still believe that Jews are the chosen people. But unless we convert at the end of all the holy wars to their Messiah, we're still damned—disposable. Jews are just, well, stepping-stones on the evangelicals' way up their heavenly staircase."

"That's about it," I had said. As if in apology, I offered my roommate some homemade cherry fudge and black-walnut divinity that my mother had sent with a note: "You are too thin. Eat more desserts! And let me know a good time to come visit."

By the time Mother did visit me in New York, I'd moved from the Ninety-second Street Y to Spanish Harlem to sharing a brownstone with five others on West End Avenue. At last I finally sought shelter at the far tip of Manhattan in Inwood, a lovely Jewish, Catholic, Puerto Rican neighborhood near the Cloisters, bordering a vast park. From my tiny apartment I could see the Spuyten Duyvil Bridge and the Hudson River flowing darkly between Manhattan and the Bronx. Not since third grade in Revere Beach, Massachusetts, had I lived by water, and contemplative dog walks with my Siberian husky pup, Kasaluk, along the Hudson River were a daily retreat from city life. I had given up on my valiant midget vegetable garden on the twentieth floor of *The New Yorker* and planted a real pea patch hidden deep in the five hundred acres of the Inwood Park forests. I was finally settled, and contemplating a literary lifetime in Manhattan, when my mother insisted on a trip to the "unholy land," as she once called it.

"I'll come by train, of course," she announced in her feisty voice. Arriving in Penn Station, Mother pronounced gleefully, "This *is* hell . . . a real Sodom and Gomorrah."

Like me during my first year in New York City, my mother adored subways. Such speed and dark certainty of one's rightful stop; such a bonanza for people-watching. After all, Mother had once worked as a wartime telegrapher for the *Wabash Cannonball*, and her brother had sometimes ridden the rails as a hobo. But after two years in the city, even I had grown weary of the daily two hours of underground commuting to and from midtown. Though it gave me a chance to read and to practice calming the latent claustrophobia that had plagued me ever since we first left the vast national forest of my birth, subways had lost their dingy charm. No longer listening to John Cage rhythms, I'd taken to wearing bulky headphones big as earmuffs—long before the noise-canceling or iPod craze—and listening to audiocassettes of classical music from a portable tape recorder I borrowed from work.

I dared not tell my mother my misgivings about Manhattan. How could I leave such a prestigious job at the hub of the publishing world? My apprenticeship was barely begun, and I was determined to stay the course, even if the city was taking its toll. My parents had just left Georgia, in 1974, to return to Virginia, and my father commuted by train to Washington, D.C. While I labored on *New Yorker* articles reporting on Nixon's impeachment trial, my father was often working on forest management policies. As usual, my father and I battled over the environment and politics.

When my mother visited muggy Manhattan, I was celebrating Nixon's downfall but was careful not to betray my exultation to my mother.

"Let's not talk politics," I beseeched her, "or religion. I want to enjoy your visit here."

Mother asked sensibly, "Then who will speak for the other side?"

I sighed. The other side. That's what my life among true believers had been for so long. Was it any wonder I was more at home in this city's Tower of Babel than with my family? Everyone here spoke not only a different language but a different culture, religion, and politics. While I was tiring of New York's lack of wilderness, I would always be mesmerized by its human nature.

As I strolled arm in arm with my mother through my Inwood neighborhood—past a Catholic church where Irish Republican Army sympathizers were raising funds, past my favorite Puerto Rican bakery, past the synagogue where Mrs. Eldestein in 4F walked my husky dog when I was at work—I felt such fondness for my mother. Her Amtrak trip had happily reminded her of her *Wabash* days.

"Oh, honey, our family sure has got railroading in our blood!" She gave my arm a squeeze. "Remember, your soul just came barreling through on our honeymoon train trip out west."

I always loved hearing the story of my young parents, just married, slipping into the sleeper car berth with its own wide window as the train rocked along from Missouri to the High Sierra. By the time mother set up house in the tiny Forest Service lookout cabin, she was pregnant with me and writing a novel. It was called *All Aboard*, about her life running trains.

Sometimes I imagine I can still hear the soundtrack of my mother's cabin life accompanying the *whoosh* inside her watery womb. There is afternoon music, Gershwin, Cole Porter, the Mills Brothers, "How Great Thou Art," and "Mood Indigo." There is also animal music—elk bugling and the screech of hawks. And every morning there is the rapid-fire tap-tapping of my mother's telegrapher fingers on her typewriter, as if still sending out code to save the country. To keep trains on time. To tell her life story. She would give birth to four "babies instead of books," as she told us all. When she received handwritten and encouraging rejection notes from several publishers, she did not realize that an editor's request for a revision is still an open door. She gave up her dream of becoming a writer.

As we strolled my neighborhood, Mother asked if we could take another subway ride—"just for fun!" In the wavering light of the underground, I smiled as I watched my mother, exhilarated by the speed and the sway of riders. On the subway pole we held together I realized I had my mother's hands—fast and full of stories. Would they ever be heard? During my almost five years at *The New Yorker*, I had gotten so many rejection slips—kind but firmly stating, "not right for the magazine"—and my ten-year apprenticeship was now half over without a single publication. Perhaps my mother and I would share the same unpublished fate. But at least we both had attempted to live our dreams.

Mother had recently shocked her family by realizing her lifelong career goal: a job at the Central Intelligence Agency. This trip was actually her last fling before taking up work at CIA headquarters in

Langley, Virginia, where she would spend seventeen years as a confidential secretary working in a locked vault. She would become proficient in "dead drops"—top-secret information stowed in public places for pickup by agents—and in clandestine "airborne activities" around the world. Her evangelical zeal would find fertile ground in an agency whose mission, as I saw it, was international coercion, planting seeds of democracy and violence. Overthrowing governments, I often told Mother during her CIA years, was not unlike forcing one's religion on another culture.

"But, honey," Mother had hesitated, glancing around and then confiding, "a whole lot of the people at the CIA also believe we're doing God's work."

My disagreement with her CIA politics didn't stop me from celebrating the fact that at last Mother had a rewarding career. I was bewilderingly proud of her. No longer did she have to content herself with just reading spy thrillers and biblical potboilers predicting the end of the world. She could live the story—she could help Armageddon along.

And while Mother was saving the world, she could also make a last stab at saving me.

"We're going to find you a Southern Baptist church in this city," my mother firmly assured me that Sunday morning of her visit as she searched the Manhattan yellow pages. I could have argued with her that I had again found a place of worship in the generous forests of Inwood Park or wandering along the craggy banks of the Hudson River, but it was useless. And she was my guest.

Mother at last found one Southern Baptist church listed in all of Manhattan. It was in Harlem.

"Mother, I don't think that is a Southern Baptist Convention church," I said. "I think it's just called '*the* Southern Baptist Church.'"

"I don't care what it's called," she retorted. "That's where we're worshiping!"

I tried to tell her we were taking our lives in our hands to go into the heart of Harlem to what was called in those days a "black" church, especially dressed as she was in her polyester flower print dress, her giant fuchsia handbag, her high heels, and her little hat. She might as well have worn a sandwich board proclaiming, Mug Me! I'm from Out of Town. I was dressed almost completely in dark colors—sweater, skirt, and that Lord and Taylor silk blouse Miss Oliver had so admired. I'd noticed that the default dress code for trendy New Yorkers seemed to be black. Or maybe I was just hoping for some camouflage.

As Mother waltzed me up the stone steps of the Harlem church, every red alert bell for city survival went off inside my body.

"Good morning, sisters." A flabbergasted but genteel elderly deacon met us with a church bulletin at the sanctuary doors.

The crowded sanctuary did not reflect a single white face. "Mother," I whispered, my tiny pearl earring getting caught up in the little veil of her pink Sunday hat. "We should leave *now*. This is not a good idea."

Waving me away and at the same time deftly untangling my earring from her hat, my mother turned to the deacon and announced, "We're so happy to be worshiping with y'all today. I'm up here visiting from Virginia."

"Ah, Virginia," the deacon nodded. "That's where my wife's people come from. Whereabouts?"

"Well, Fairfax. My husband works in Washington, D.C., and we've just moved back after some time in Georgia,"

"Why, my mother was raised in Georgia," the deacon nodded.

"How did you get all the way up here?" my mother politely inquired. Her curiosity has always been something I cherish in her. "Family? Job?"

"No, ma'am," the deacon smiled. "My people came here during the Civil War. You ever heard of the Underground Railroad?"

It was as if he had given her the keys to the kingdom. They launched into a lively and long dialogue about railroads—the human line that saved his great-great-grandfather from slavery, and Mother's *Wabash Cannonball* days during World War II. I realized that as long as she and the deacon were talking like old friends, we were safe. So I stood vigilant next to my mother, scanning the congregation like a Secret Service bodyguard. I barely heard what they were saying because there were some young men eyeing us. They looked angry, yet amused. Very slightly, I shrugged my shoulders and rolled my eyes, trying to telegraph to them that I was sorry to intrude upon their territory. I wanted them to know that my mother was defenseless and naive. Lost.

I only tuned back into my mother's conversation with the deacon at the door when I heard her telling him, "My daughter here lives in the city, and we're looking for a good church home for her. Do you think she would fit in here?"

It was such a hilarious question, such a willfully color-blind and wrongheaded notion. I had to keep myself from either laughing hysterically or bolting back down the stairs and running all the way to the subway. But the deacon had fixed his eyes on me, easily taking me in—a white, liberal, probably backslid girl with whom he had nothing in common except a city. For a moment he studied me, his mouth twitching in a smile that he never showed. Perhaps he enjoyed my dismay. Perhaps he had a wayward daughter of his own. Maybe my mother's charm and complete confidence in his care convinced him to take the high, moral road. Or perhaps he was a saint.

"We welcome all souls here," he finally said. He took my mother's arm and swept her down the aisle to a pew.

There were small balconies in this church and a choir loft with an organist whose music was rapture to my mother's ears. As the organist swung into "Just a Closer Walk with Thee," my mother began tapping her feet as if she too were playing the pedals of the organ in her own church.

"Oh," Mother said happily, "she's playing exactly the right tempo for this song. They sing it so darn slow in our church."

Mother had always played her church keyboards upbeat and with soul. Her vivid and *fortissimo* style at the piano or organ often triggered complaints from the more staid Southern Baptist congregations. She really rocked "Rock of Ages," and she marched with "Onward, Christian Soldiers" and she vamped with "When We All Get to Heaven." The faster the tempo, the nearer to God. At the organ, with its many settings for percussion or instruments, Mother was a one-woman band.

"Oh," Mother whispered loudly, "she's a swell pianist. I wish they'd let me swing it like that in our church."

I had a sudden memory of early mornings at home listening to Mother warm up for her piano practice with a vibrant "Rhapsody in Blue" or "Downtown Strutter's Ball." Watching her lean toward the music like an exotic plant to sunlight, I felt a fierce protectiveness and pride in her.

Others in the congregation obviously noted my mother's musical gratitude. A few of the go-to-church ladies who make up any congregation, no matter the religion, smiled and nodded. Someone passed us a fan since there was no air conditioning and it was August. The fan, like those I'd seen in so many churches down south, was an advertisement for a local funeral home.

When the choir joined the organist in a syncopated version of "In the Sweet By and By," I thought my mother would swoon with pleasure. "Now," she said out loud and with gusto, "now that's what I call a choir!"

Though I was still wary, I was beginning to enjoy the music and the church. Even though I did note quite a few pointed glances, especially from some of the younger men, I decided that maybe we might make it out of there alive after all. Still, I was obsessing about how to get a taxi after church if we couldn't dash safely to the subway station when the thought struck me: my mother, a Southern Baptist conservative had fewer racial stereotypes here in Harlem than her liberal daughter who carried mace in her purse and was hypervigilant on city streets. Mother had entered this church with a much more open heart than mine.

On the podium the preacher, a tall lithe man in his fifties, pounced into his sermon with the agility of a lion. He roared, he whispered, he fumed and stomped. He came close to weeping. The sermon was not about hell or heaven. It was about the here and now. Specifically, a reprise of a famous 1967 speech by Dr. Martin Luther King called "Beyond Vietnam: A Time to Break Silence," an eloquent appeal to speak out against an unjust war. In that summer of 1974, we were still a year away from the fall of Saigon and the end of the war. The preacher's voice rang out to the rafters with King's words: "'If America's soul becomes totally poisoned, part of the autopsy must read Vietnam.'"

Mother leaned over and said in a loud voice, "I disagree! I support this war 100 percent!"

"Shhhhh." I almost clasped my hand over her mouth for fear that we were again endangered. "Be still, Mother."

The congregation was nodding and saying "amen" to their preacher, urging him on. Dr. King's momentous speech quoted Buddhists, the Bible, and Harlem's own Langston Hughes:

America never was America to me.

My mother opened her mouth and for a split-second I thought she might actually protest and stomp out of the service. But her good manners won out. She glanced around, frowning, and it seemed like a thousand black faces glared back at us. Maybe we would be sacrificed after all on the altar of reverse racism. Perhaps we deserved it for the *chutzpah* we showed in strolling right into their church, as if we were all the same. I could feel a current of rage running right from my mother and out through the congregation—as loud as the subter-ranean thunder of subway cars running beneath the church.

"'This Hindu-Muslim-Christian-Jewish-Buddhist belief about ulti-mate reality is beautifully summed up in the First Epistle of Saint John,'" the preacher quoted.

A stirring in the congregation, fans stopped mid-arc, eyes up-lifted toward their preacher, who came down off the stage and stood as if humbled before the memory of another Baptist preacher, now gunned down. His eyes swept his church members and then, for the first time, registered two pale faces—one frightened, the other defi-ant. The preacher's gaze rested upon us like a benediction, though he was obviously surprised to see us. In tones so soft we all had to lean forward to hear, he finished with Dr. King's words: "'Let us love one another; for love is God.'"

The preacher stood at the center of his congregation holding us still with just words. Even my mother was soothed as he bowed his head and called us to prayer. The organist, *pianissimo*, played a gospel standard, "I Am a Poor, Wayfaring Stranger."

Some worshipers, including my mother, were humming under their breath. A few people wept. I cracked open an eyelid and saw that my mother was praying silently, head nodding in rhythm to the song. It occurred to me then—*we all know the same songs.*

"Now, turn in your hymnals to page 35." The choir director took the podium, the choir stood up in their creaking loft, and the preacher sat down in the front row, eyes brimming. "I Love to Tell the Story."

Neither my mother nor I had to look at the hymnal. And this was not lost on the believers around us. As we all sang together, there were some women nearby nodding, especially when I played around with high descants or low harmonies and my mother kept to her melody with a robust soprano and a huge smile.

I love to tell the story,
T'will be my theme in Glory.

After church, we were mobbed by benevolent churchwomen, who had somehow found out from the elderly deacon that Mother was from the South. They invited us to their after-church social, and Mother satisfied her sweet tooth and complimented the coffee, which was strong and creamy, spiced with chicory just the way she liked it. Mother would later say that few Southern Baptist Convention church services came close to the grace and musical heaven of that Harlem Sunday. For years they sent her church bulletins, and they also kept me on their mailing list. I never went back, though sometimes I considered it, just to sing.

When I told my friend Emily, an African American who lived in the neighborhood, about my mother taking me up to a Harlem church, she laughed and said, "And you're still here to tell the story, girl?"

I was curious about how Emily's parents, also staunch Baptists, saw the End Times fascination that then was sweeping the country in the wake of *The Late Great Planet Earth.*

"Black people have been *through* the Tribulations," Emily told me with her wry smile. "What do you think slavery was?" She was thoughtful a moment as we walked our dogs through the generous paths of Inwood Park. "We're looking for a better life here on earth before we go zipping off to any Lord's Kingdom."

"But so many of the black spirituals also sing about being heaven-bound and longing for Over Yonder."

"That's slave code for freedom, honeychile, not death." Emily laughed and then added, "Besides, heavenly mansions sound suspiciously like plantations."

It occurred to me then that the demographics of the conservative evangelicals who believed we were entering the final days of earth were mostly white, mostly southern, and middle- to lower-class. Maybe the end of the world, which so frightens and fascinates evangelicals, is simply a world that no longer looks like them. A twenty-first-century world that, as Oprah says, "looks a lot more like me." Or a world that might resemble that Harlem church in 1974 when two white faces floated in a sea of darker shades. And yet, I still wondered why those who had suffered generations of slavery, prejudice, and often poverty wouldn't want to leave the world that perpetuated such injustices.

"The Rapture isn't our idea of being upwardly mobile," Emily told me, with a grin. "We've already had ancestors who were carried off to another world—and it wasn't so blissful." Emily paused and faced me on the forest path. "Maybe it seems to black people like we're being, well, disappeared. Or maybe it's because we've already been left behind."

Years later I would remember Emily's words when a hurricane named Katrina struck New Orleans and thousands of people, mostly African American, were indeed left behind without food or water in a sports stadium and on rooftops. The president, a born-again Christian who professed to believe in the End Times, took his time getting help to the victims. And the world watched television reports of people in makeshift rescue stations and tents calling out to us, pleading, "Where are you?" One of my relatives had commented, "New Orleans—that is such a wicked city." Tribulations.

My mother visited New York City only once in my five years there. Perhaps it was enough, yet sometimes I wished she would have visited again. I could have used a mother during some of those increasingly difficult years in Manhattan. By 1976 I was truly worn out with city living. I was tired of trying to keep my Inwood Park pea patch safe from marauders who even mugged my vegetables—tearing my spindly tomato plants to shreds and stomping on the squash and fragile staked pole beans. Now, even with my headphones on, listening to the newly discovered songs of humpback whales, I gritted my teeth during the two hours of subway travel a day.

As I haplessly typed away on never-ending piles of edited manuscripts, listening to whale songs and staring at crumpled photos of green Georgia corn and red mud, I at last recognized that I had to leave. I was still unpublished after almost six years, still receiving polite rejections notes I could have written myself since I typed them up for other hopeful authors every day. Like my family awaiting Rapture, I was only waiting for a way out of this city.

That way came when my mother rang me up at work in the Books Department to announce that she had inherited a run-down farm and five acres in a rural area between Boulder and Denver, Colorado. "You remember Aunt Ruth and Uncle Geoff?"

I remembered them well from our cross-country visits. They were odd but fascinating relatives who ran a refuge for abandoned animals.

"Someone in the family has to go live on the farm or we'll lose it. The inheritance taxes are terrible. Would you go, honey? Would you take care of the animals—now that their people are gone?"

"I'm there!" I said.

When I gave notice, Mrs. Walden attempted to commiserate with me. "I know you think of yourself as a failure," she said.

But I was obviously elated as I sat inside her smoke-filled cubbyhole and tried not to breathe too deeply. "No, I really don't."

"Well, time will tell, that's what I always say to my girls with their big dreams." She waved her cigarette vaguely toward her Pond, which was now evenly divided between young men and women.

"A farm, you say?" Mrs. Walden queried as if I had told her I was going to be abducted by aliens. "Well, keep in touch," she said, "if you can." Saul Steinberg's famous *New Yorker* cover, "View of the World from Ninth Avenue," with its city writ huge and only a few notable territories outside Manhattan, came to mind.

My last memory of Mrs. Walden is from my going-away party, a rushed affair of bagels and takeout coffee, between manuscripts. We had a big deadline that day, and I would be working late. In the middle of a Walden's Pond toast to send me off to be "downwardly mobile" and "go back to nature," as my coworkers joked, the office phone rang. It was for me.

The phone was rarely for me, since Mrs. Walden discouraged personal calls.

It was the revered fiction editor, Miss MacKenzie, calling from the hospital where she was again battling congestive heart failure. When I had given two weeks' notice at the magazine, I had bravely sent the first chapter of my novel to Miss MacKenzie to read, before she'd gone to the hospital. I had never expected anything but another rejection.

Miss MacKenzie's voice was almost eclipsed by static. "I would like to read and edit your novel." Miss MacKenzie paused to take a breath that must have cost her some effort. "When you are finished."

"But I'm leaving the magazine." I almost wailed at the irony, the injustice, my bad timing.

There was quiet, during which I actually heard Miss MacKenzie smile to herself. It was an expression I had studied when I passed her unawares in the hallways. She often walked with manuscript in hand, reading as she navigated the hallways and nodding over some author's brilliance. Or sometimes she scowled, shaking her head and jotting something in red pencil. "Lovely to meet you in the margin," she would write in her precise but tiny handwriting on a *New Yorker* fiction manuscript. And how I had longed hopelessly all these years to meet Miss MacKenzie in margins of my own. "Well, dear, can you still be reached by U.S. mail wherever it is you are going?"

"Oh, of course, of course," I stammered. "I will write you."

I wanted to shout, *I will write for you!* But I had enough decorum to thank her and say a proper good-bye. Then I exploded in a little jig that made Mrs. Walden raise an eyebrow and ask, as if she didn't already know very well, who had placed that call.

I embraced Mrs. Walden so impulsively that she dropped her cigarette. I could not tell her that I was happy to be leaving her heaven—bound only for an afterlife with other animals.

"Will you do . . . well, whatever it is they do on farms?" Mrs. Walden demanded. She was so bewildered by my career choice that she didn't bother to search for her burning cigarette somewhere on the manuscript-strewn floor. One of the young men nonchalantly stamped it out.

"Yes, it runs in the family."

"Well, E. B. White has a farm." Mrs. Walden was still the writer's personal secretary even though he was rarely in the city. "And it hasn't ruined him—yet."

eight

In the Garden
(Baptist hymn)

NOTHING HAD PREPARED ME FOR THE ECSTASY OF SNOWMELT FLOWING up to my bare knees and following my humble irrigation ditches under a full mountain moon. Here I stood on land that had been in my family for almost half a century, and it was not in the South but in my native West. These five acres in Colorado with precious water shares were still rural—dirt roads and a dilapidated farmhouse with a picket fence that had blown over in warm chinook winds. Almost all the abandoned animals—from exotic chickens like Japanese Buffs and fancy Sultans with their scarlet feathers, to stray dogs, to house cats—had vanished.

"That's what happens when old folks like your great-aunt and -uncle die so close together. Things just disappear." Mr. Vale, my neighbor, nodded as we surveyed our handiwork: little dirt dams and wooden gates diverting the clear, icy water. "Now, your kinfolk, they had more animals to lose than possessions."

The two animals who had not disappeared were an ancient hound named Dirkson, after the senator, and Bowser, a high-strung Chihuahua. Both dogs were fond of barking, which was perhaps why they were left behind. And both got along just fine as a pack with my sleek young Siberian husky, Kasaluk, who had happily traveled with me from New York City to Colorado.

My cornfield was crisscrossed with green rows. In his hip boots, Mr. Vale leaned against his shovel. His face in the moonlight was high-boned, his woven straw cowboy hat dented. He was Blackfoot and had farmed this neighboring land since the 1920s. He looked a little like my paternal grandfather, Sheriff Rory Peterson, but he was not so stern. And whereas my grandfather had once told my brother, "I'll teach you to hunt, fish, and vote the Republican ticket," Mr. Vale was a staunch Democrat who believed that tribal peoples had to learn the law and fight what he called "those damn developers" who were still grabbing their lands as relentlessly as the European settlers. Mr. Vale laid fierce claim to his native heritage in a way that my father's family did not. Though not formally educated, Mr. Vale was diligently self-taught. And he was the best farmer I had ever met. In my family, that was saying something.

Working a cornfield with Mr. Vale was not gardening as I'd known it. Cornfields were a prayer, Mr. Vale told me as I sat behind him on his tractor. Asking only that I "listen to this land," he did not charge me for plowing and helping me plant five acres of corn. I was unabashedly proud of these fields, my own little Garden of Eden. When I sent photographs back to my father, he seemed more impressed with this accomplishment than anything I had done before. He advised me about certain pests and told me how to tell if the corn was thriving. But it was Mr. Vale who taught me the mysteries of this essential native plant.

"Corn talks to you, let's you know what she needs," Mr. Vale said that night as we listened to the summer wind singing through the stalks. Tall, green music. "If the corn is dry and needs more irrigation, you'll hear the stalks talking about it. They sound parched, whispering, rattling." He lifted his boots from the mud with an audible sucking sound and strode over to fix a wooden gate, which the gush of chill irrigation water had trampled. "If the corn is too wet, she'll just flap flat in the wind, instead of flutter. When you walk in your cornfields, you should hear them growing tall. If the soil is rich and the sun is not too hot and the water is cool, not too cold, then you can hear it in every stalk and ear—happiness."

I believed everything Mr. Vale taught me because it worked. This was 1977, six years before geneticist Barbara McClintock would win a 1983 Nobel Prize for her genetics research, especially in corn. McClintock, a maverick, nomadic scholar, emphasized a "feeling for the organism" and often talked about listening to maize to discover genetic codes.

That night, running irrigation ditches with Mr. Vale, I listened to the cornstalks whisper and realized that both my crop and I were content. It made no sense. I had just left *The New Yorker* and the most prestigious job I would ever have, and now I was communing with corn in rural Colorado. When I was not irrigating my fields, I was working the night shift at a typesetting factory on newspapers like *Rodeo Sports News* and *Cattleman's Gazette*. Friends at *The New Yorker* sent condolences, no doubt seeing me as an "overnight failure."

But I saw myself differently. Upon arriving at the Colorado property, I had discovered in the tilting mailbox a letter addressed to me in the most proper, perfect handwriting. After six years of rejection, I received my first acceptance letter. George Core, renowned editor of the *Sewanee Review*, wrote: "It will be an honor to be the first to publish your work."

When I told my friends at *The New Yorker*, they wrote urgent notes: "Come back now!" they cajoled me. "There's still a job for you here. How can corn compete with the City?" one asked in utter bewilderment. I reminded him of my twentieth-floor midget vegetable garden. But how was I to explain that I had walked right into one of the photographs I'd tacked on my office wall? How to tell them that I'd found my own real Walden Pond in the spacious shadow of the Rocky Mountains? "The West is my birthright" was all I could say when I wrote my *New Yorker* friends.

For once, my family understood me more than my friends. "It's good work," my father said. "Honest. Hard. Productive."

"But there aren't many Southern Baptist churches out there," my mother fretted. "And Aunt Ruth and Uncle Geoff were not active Christians. That's probably why so many of their belongings disappeared before you could get out there. Like that credenza and lovely breakfront that has been in the family for generations. Church people would never let that happen to one of their own."

"But, Mother," I had smiled on the phone. "Ruth and Geoff don't need their things anymore. And neither do I." Or at least I thought so.

But it turned out that I did need my relatives' material blessings. Even though the farmhouse was run-down, its water pump temperamental, its sofa covered in bright feathers, and its bookshelves spackled in chicken shit, the place was nurturing. Ruth and Geoff had survived the Depression with the notion that banks were never to be trusted. So they had stashed money everywhere. Their chicken coop was a modest cash cow. In buckets of rotting feed I discovered wads of $20 bills and Indian head nickels. Every time I ran low on my meager typesetting factory salary, I would use my intuition to find another buried savings account.

My family has always been a little bit psychic—just enough to have a prescient dread of natural and human disasters that we cannot prevent. We get a "feeling," or what one of my siblings describes as "the vibe." I would call upon this sixth sense when dousing for money in the chicken coops or farmhouse. I would also double my success rate by praying to Saint Anthony, the patron saint of lost things or causes. To this day, Saint Anthony has never failed me.

That midnight, while irrigating my ancestral cornfield, Mr. Vale told me about the best farmers he'd ever met. "Ever heard of the Hopi tribe?" he asked me.

"Nope. Tell me."

The old man felt like family to me with his slight drawl and dry wit. I loved his stories and the fact that he was so proud of his native heritage. How I wished my own father would have explored and revealed to us all he knew about our mixed-blood ancestors.

My father was selective in his genealogy. He told us, "Our relatives were here to greet the *Mayflower.*"

When he followed family lines back through generations, his focus was on the Civil War soldiers who fought for both the Confederate and Union sides and on the fact that our ancestors were living in Virginia in 1720, near the humble hills of the Shenandoah Valley. He focused on gentleman farmers like the relative who served as a captain in George Washington's army, not the half-breeds deleted from American history. But still, family stories kept surfacing—the Seminole princess bride in Florida who was bought for a gold nugget the size of her skull; the "French-Canadian" great-grandmother who never spoke English. In photos she looks full-blooded, bent and collapsed into a rocking chair, all but hidden behind the younger generations. Almost out of the picture.

In my immediate family, my mother's Irish fair skin and aquamarine eyes dominate. Not so on my father's side of the family. Eloquent dark eyes and high cheekbones, tanned skin and black, wavy hair show the beauty of mixed blood. One of my father's sisters married a full-blooded Choctaw man who was always our favorite uncle. We were awestruck by his wicked sense of humor, and we craved his approval. He looked just like the Indian on a nickel and always teased my mother when she got carried away with her own moods or what he called her "missionary work."

Then there were my aunts, the very definition of high-spirited storytellers. They were a sister clan so fierce and loyal to one another that we nieces always longed for their company. My aunts on my father's side never really approved of me—except kindly Aunt Sarah. She lived in the rural South and tended her children as well as the wild animals who found their way onto her acres. Peacocks strutted around Aunt Sarah's front yard, motherless fawns took shelter under her living room couch, and often Sarah went to work in a factory with an orphaned squirrel tucked into her blouse to keep the creature warm.

I rarely talked about my own family with Mr. Vale, but I had shown him family photos and warned him that he might meet the whole gang soon enough because there were plans for another clan reunion on the Colorado property.

As we irrigated my corn, Mr. Vale used his shovel to shore up a little soil levee and let the water flow into another thirsty section of corn. "You can hear the corn just relax when she drinks her fill now, can't you?"

I closed my eyes and heard it: the green stalk filling with moisture, the leaves plumping, roots suckling, and golden tassels sighing. "Yes," I said. "I can hear it."

"The Hopi grow their corn in the middle of a high desert," Mr. Vale took up in his gravelly baritone. "In Arizona. Dry farming, they call it."

"How can corn grow in a desert?" I asked, knowing full well how much irrigating my corn needed even here, below the mountains. Almost twice a week. "Does it rain there?"

"Hardly ever," Mr. Vale told me. "That's why they have their ceremonies and dances. The Hopi believe their ceremonies, well, keep the whole world spinning." He grinned and his false teeth glimmered in the moonlight. Sometimes he didn't bother to put them in. "And you can bet their dances bring rain. Just when the corn needs it most. Like about now." He paused and gave me a rare, direct look. "You know, there's a snake dance you should see. If the tribe is letting outsiders in this year. I'll take care of your corn while you're gone."

Mr. Vale knew I was researching snake handling and southern fundamentalists for my novel. I'd always been fascinated by stories I'd heard of these backwoods bands of true believers who ritually handled snakes. The serpent was seen as the descendant of the fallen angel who first took the beguiling form of Satan and tempted Eve into original sin. In what might be called "extreme worship" today, these Christians risked painful deaths by snake venom to prove their faith and their righteousness. A kind of snake roulette. Their conquest of Satan's serpent. In my novel, I suspected that a main character, mistaking himself for a prophet, would die from snakebite—and his fanatical faith.

But according to Mr. Vale, the Hopi—revered as people of peace by many other tribes—had a different idea about snakes. Serpents were sacred messengers between this world and the underworld divinities. When the Hopi priests handled snakes in their ceremonial summer dance, it was a prayer for rain to nourish their corn and spring water for their people. The dance was a plea for divine blessing, not a battle between good and evil.

"Sure, I'll go! Why not?" I told Mr. Vale with all the spontaneity and excitement of youth. "Maybe it will help me figure out the ending of my novel."

"Let me talk to some of my friends down there in Hopi land," Mr. Vale nodded, approvingly. "I think the snake dance is on Third Mesa this year. Oraibi."

Oh-rai-bi. The sound of the Hopi village beckoned me as much as the tribal stories. En route to Arizona, I did more research on the tribe. The Hopi snake dance was a reenactment of an ancient story: A young Hopi man, White Corn, was guided by a snake into a cave where dwelled Snake People. Their land was blessed, abundant with rain and corn. Here, a beautiful girl named Bright Eyes was given to him as wife. When they returned together to his tribe, the Hopi recognized that every time there was a drought, this Snake maiden's prayers brought sweet rain. In a thunderstorm, White Corn and his wife conceived, and when her time came near they left the village for a distant mesa. After seven days, she gave birth to seven serpents.

When they returned to the village bearing their beloved snake brood, the people were so disappointed that they talked of killing these reptile offspring. But instead, an old man took the young couple into his home. Later, human children were born to the couple, and these were the ancestors of the Snake Clan, who, after many migrations, arrived at Walpi, a Hopi mesa village near the Four Corners. Here the Hopi have survived for thousands of years in the oldest continuously inhabited land in North America. Here they keep the ritual of the Snake Dance, in which the Snake Clan priests dance with the serpents in their mouths and are recognized as the most revered rainmakers in the world. As Hopi chief Don Talayesva explained, "Only the pure in mind and heart can dance successfully with the very wise and sacred snake in his mouth."

Few outsiders are allowed into the village, and then only if they are referred by friends of the tribe. Mr. Vale had contacted a Hopi family he knew through various tribal gatherings. So I had a private invitation to seek a prized spot on one of the rooftops to observe this most fascinating and earthbound of religious rites.

The Hopi cosmology locating the gods not only in the sky but also in the underworld was so welcome to me. After several decades in a family ever ready to ascend, to leave this earth behind, I felt as nourished by the Hopi cosmology as I was by my own ripening corn. Besides the native connection, I had always admired and been drawn to snakes. When I was a baby at the forest lookout station, my father often labored outside the cabin and would perch me on a sunny boulder or nestle me into some pine needles while he worked. One of my favorite photos is of my father hefting me up on his shoulder as he stands next to a tall cedar tree. Together, tree, baby, and father all rise up like a family totem pole. We are together, in full sunlight, growing like the Standing People, which was what my father first taught me to call the forest.

Once, as a toddler, while I lay napping on a warm rock ledge, a rattlesnake crawled onto my naked chest and coiled there contentedly. It is among my first memories, the delicately split tongue smelling my skin and then the reassuring weight of the snake on my small body as we both slept in the sun. That was how my astonished young father found us. He interrupted our rest with a hiss of his own to *be still!*

Suddenly the snake was lifted up by a stick my father wielded like a whip. *Crack!* He wrapped her loose length around a nearby tree, and I heard the snap of her spine. A sound so terrible I could not stop crying. I cried for days. They said it was colic. But I was inconsolable, even when my father made me a rattle plaything out of the serpent's hollow husk of a rattler.

To this day I have a little snake altar in my study, and for many years I contemplated keeping a terrarium so that I could live alongside a corn snake. But I decided that captivity would be no life for a serpent even the Bible called "more subtle." Wisdom keepers belong in the natural world. But all this was transmuted into my novel, which ends in a "snake sermon"? The serpent tells the story of the fall from the Garden of Good and Evil. It was my story too.

As a talisman for my journey, Mr. Vale had given me a little leather pouch with Hopi blue corn kernels. "The irrigation ditch is running low," he said. "Bring us back some Hopi rain for our fields."

Though the famous Hopi snake ceremony always takes place between the middle and end of August, no one knows the exact date until ten days before the actual dance. The reservation is closed to the public for nine days of this secret ceremony, which begins in the kivas, or sacred underground chambers of the Antelope and Snake Clans. Few non-Hopi have ever witnessed the kiva rituals when priests wash the snakes' heads as a kind of cleansing or baptism. It is a very dangerous ceremony, but such is the skill and traditional training of the Hopi priests that it is rare for anyone to be bitten. Nor do the Hopi have any antidote for snake venom.

One of the privileged outside observers of the Snake Dance was legendary archaeologist Jesse Walter Fewkes, who first studied the

Hopi ceremony from 1891 to 1896. Fewkes's mesmerizing eyewitness accounts swirled through my mind as I drove through what seemed like endless Arizona desert, punctuated with eerie red rock monoliths, like some lunar landscape. Though I knew from geology class that these sands and stratified limestone were an ancient sea bottom now raised high and dry, I could not shake the feeling that I was traveling through time itself. Mesa villagers believe they dwell at the Center of the Universe, having journeyed through many migrations up into this Fifth World. "World Complete," it is called, because it reveals both the beauty and sorrow that belong to any full spectrum of being.

The road to those isolated mesas was a snaking, single asphalt line stretching ahead forever. Nothing on either side but sand and every now and then a Navajo hogan. I was beginning to believe that Hopi lands didn't exist or that I had missed the turn somewhere in the vast expanse of sand. I'd been driving for many days with no real assurance that I would arrive in time for the Snake Dance. After all, the ceremonies took place over nine days, and I had only Mr. Vale's directions and the hope that I was traveling there in the correct week.

It was a blazing afternoon, not a cloud overhead, when I saw a distant slope beyond. I drove faster toward a few more rock risings, flat slabs of jutting stone awash in azure and purple colors. Suddenly a haze shimmered on the horizon. A mirage? I drove faster. There was no speed limit out here in the middle of nowhere, or the Center of the Universe. All at once the sky was split open with a zigzag of pale lightning. A long zipper of light followed by thunder seemed to buckle the road under my tires. Startled, I swerved and crunched along on the gravelly shoulder for seconds before righting the steering wheel. I stopped and jumped out of the car to stare at the horizon. Bright thunderclouds breached up over the mesas so fast it was like high-speed photography. And tucked under those dark clouds was the far-off hiss and mists of falling rain as it raced toward me.

It was over, I knew then. The Snake Dance had brought rain, wondrous rain. I had missed the dance, but the blessing now reached where I stood beside the road, raising my arms, palms upward. It rained so hard I could hardly keep my eyes open, but I held my ground. Such a downfall. Desert wildflowers seemed to surge up from beneath the sand where they had waited through a summer's drought just for this: the cool, life-giving waters described in the Psalms. I leapt back into the car and drove the last miles to Oraibi. As I got closer to the Hopi mesa, a stream of cars zoomed past in the opposite direction. All those who had been fortunate enough to witness the Snake Dance were leaving. I was the only car arriving.

As I parked and ran up the mesa trail to Oraibi's pueblos set into high cliffs, I saw pools of rainwater caught in ceremonial pottery, in empty metal barrels, in every kind of container imaginable. People from many other tribes still sat, under umbrellas and smiling, atop rooftops with sturdy ladders attached.

"Climb up here," one of the older women invited me. "You'll get a better view."

I didn't see what I'd imagined: no rainbow-cloud headdresses, no Hopi priests with snakes dangling from their teeth as other dancers close behind used feathered snake whips to distract the serpents. I saw no female members of the Snake Clan sprinkle cornmeal over the dancers to signify plant germination and assure their children protection from rattlesnake bite. I saw no gatherers after the dance respectfully carrying the coils of cleansed snakes, called Elder Brothers, to release them back into rocky hideaways. Underground again, the snakes would carry messages to their sacred kin—those prayers for rain and abundant corn.

What I did see was this: a rain-drenched desert soon to be abloom. Grateful rows of Hopi corn plants on cliffs, rooted deep in impossible crevices. Prayer feathers attached with red string to tum-bleweeds that blew across the sand like traveling caravans. I saw how the serpent and the people still dwelled divinely together in their garden.

I told Mr. Vale everything. We were picking our first sweet, white corn. Our harvest would be good.

"Well," he said softly, "the Hopi would say you saw the world truly."

"Truly?"

"Complete."

It was a concept so close to the Taoist notion that the natural world is already perfect and only a flaw in our own human vision pre-vents us from perceiving this clearly. Perhaps it is also our inability to accept or allow everything to simply be that keeps us from seeing this world truly. I would return to the Hopi reservation many times over the next years. I've never yet witnessed the Snake Dance, but I hear it always rains. Sometimes the deluge is so deep that the dry washes run with flash floods and visitors are stranded on the high mesas.

The journey to see the Hopi Snake Dance profoundly changed the way I would end my novel. After I finished my manuscript, I sent the novel off to Miss MacKenzie at *The New Yorker*. She masterfully edited it, and then she recommended it to a revered editor, Judith Jones at Knopf. After Judith read the one chapter of my manuscript that had been published in the *Sewanee Review*, she sent me an encour-aging telegram, which I thought was a hoax by one of my friends—until Miss MacKenzie called me.

"Buy some good clothes," she advised in her delicate, far-off voice. "Come back to visit New York and meet this editor. She is one of the best."

I had prepared myself for anything but this: that the first pub-lisher to read my novel would print it. I was twenty-eight years old and didn't even realize I had to pay taxes on my modest advance. I was also not prepared for what my first mentor, Diane Johnson, would tell me when she heard news of my novel's publication.

"This will not change your life," Diane said firmly. "Make sure you keep all the things that sustain you going strong."

Diane was right. I kept my typesetting night-shift job and wrote in the mornings. I planted my fields and studied the mysterious ways of corn with Mr. Vale. When my novel *River of Light* was published, nothing much changed. My family was pleased for me, but not terribly impressed. What did impress them was that I had kept a blue-collar job.

"No union organizing?" my father quizzed me good-naturedly.

"I can't get fired anymore," I confessed, realizing as I said this that the temptation to start a union among my fellow long-suffering typesetters had never occurred to me.

That next summer, Mr. Vale and I harvested a bumper crop of corn. We spent the fallow season fighting water wars to save our irrigation ditch. A neighboring town wanted our water rights, and its high-powered lawyers were buying up shares in our irrigation ditches. All around us, neighbors who had shared this ditch for fifty years were accepting cash buyouts for their shares. But Mr. Vale and I were holding out. My father held firm. For once, he and I were on the same side of this environmental battle. "That land without water is empty, useless," he said. "Keep fighting."

Mr. Vale and I showed up at endless bureaucratic meetings to protest the takeover of our ditch. I wrote letters and stood up and pleaded with other shareholders and panels of developers. At one meeting Mr. Vale shot up beside me. He said nothing, simply opened his red plaid wool jacket to reveal a holstered six-shooter. It was the only time the Water Board paid us any mind. Mr. Vale and I did manage to keep our few water shares while the city gobbled up most of our ditch.

"You've got to keep farming," my father advised as snow again changed to spring rains. "Use that water or you'll lose it to the city. Plan your next crop."

"I've already ordered seeds from the catalog," I told my father proudly. "And I'm going to try something really different for a quarter-acre—Hopi blue corn."

"What's that?" my father asked with real interest.

"You're not planting some kind of pot, are you?" My mother had joined us on the line.

Hearing my parents in stereo was the norm in our cross-continent dialogues. What was not the norm was me actually telling them much about my life outside their beliefs and limits. For example, my trip to the Hopi Snake Dance. But my enthusiasm for Hopi blue corn won out over my usual wariness. I launched into a description of the Hopi relationship to maize and to serpents and their prophecies. "The Hopi also believe in the end of this world," I finished. "But unlike your Rapture prophecy, this tribe believes they will remain here on earth. They call their mesas the Center of the Universe."

"*Our* Rapture prophecy," mother demanded. "Don't you believe in Revelation too?"

I took a deep breath. I was almost thirty years old, and it was time to tell my parents some personal truths. "Listen to me, please," I began. "I think the Bible is a great book of stories and ideas that we can interpret metaphorically."

"*What?*" they both demanded like a Greek chorus.

"The Bible may be the word of God, but I don't think it's literally written by God. Just humans who interpret and dream and disagree . . . and even edit out some of the New Testament books, especially those written by women or the most mystical believers." I was speaking so fast I could hardly breathe as I concluded, "The Bible is not the main text of my spiritual life."

I barely managed to stop myself from mentioning that I was reading William James's *The Varieties of Religious Experience* and *Gravity and Grace* by the French-Jewish mystic Simone Weil and *The Book of the Hopi* and anthropological studies of shamanism. I certainly did not tell my parents that I was fascinated by the new, groundbreaking book *The Gnostic Gospels*. I didn't discuss with them the Gnostic symbolism of the great serpent coiled benevolently around the earth or the symbolic twining of the serpent with Christ the Messiah. I did not share with them my excitement that in these two years after I had written a novel that ends with a snake's sermon I would discover that the early Gnostic texts also told the story of the Garden of Eden from the serpent's point of view. My parents' orthodoxy would never accept such heresy. They might cut me out of the family, just as those Christian patriarchs deleted Gnostic texts from their official Bible.

I did consider telling my parents that my high school Great Books teacher, Sylvia Costarella, had been right after all. I was most drawn to Taoism—a more mystical philosophy of nature and humor—than organized religion. All I said was, "There are so many other books that inspire and teach, like Lao-tzu."

"Who?" Mother demanded. "You're not turning Hindu on us, are you? And why are you running around chasing snakes? Satan took the form of a serpent, you know." She stopped, and then added in a softer voice, "Are you that lost, honey?"

I winced when I heard the pain in her voice. "I'm not lost, Mother. I'm just seeking my own spiritual traditions—and they are very different than yours."

"Didn't we give you a good enough Christian education?" she asked, perhaps as disappointed in herself as me.

A sudden memory flashed of standing with the Bible clutched in my hand, hesitating as the judge called out the next scripture in the Sword Drill. My mother sitting in the front row of the auditorium, her eager expression slowly changing to defeat.

"Yes, yes, you did. But I'm not returning to any Southern Baptist church. And I'm not pining for the Rapture. I think we're all here on earth for a divine reason." I hesitated and then said it, almost whispered it. "You know, I want to be left behind."

My father's voice was at once astonished and sad. "Why, honey, do you really want to be here for all those years of Tribulations? The Bible is very clear on this . . . ," he began and then stopped. Taking a different tack, he said, "You like stories. Let me tell you one. A woman goes to see her son march in a military parade. After he and his regiment pass by, someone asks the mother what she thought of the spectacle. 'It was fine,' she says, 'but everyone except my son was marching out of step!'"

"So you think I'm marching out of step in this family?" I asked.

"You might want to think about why you're so different from everybody else in the family." He paused and then added, as if thinking out loud, "Maybe if we hadn't let you go back out west to college. . . . " His tone was bewildered.

"Ah, the Left Coast?" I tried to make light of it, but a part of me felt forlorn.

This was the late seventies, and many of the seemingly radical causes of the sixties—women's rights, environmental concern, and distrust of government—were now more mainstream. Nixon had been replaced with a Democratic and soft-spoken Jimmy Carter. Many in my family didn't consider the more moderate President Carter a real Southern Baptist, though my father agreed with him on some conservation issues. Ronald Reagan was a far-off blip on the future political horizon, and I wouldn't have believed in 1978 that the country could ever go backward again and elect this archconservative who as a governor had run roughshod over my university days.

My mother chimed in. "Remember, honey, there are always dark forces at work in the world. I do hope you'll pray about everything you've said. Snakes and such. We still pray for you every day."

My father sighed. "Keep farming, honey," he advised. "It just might settle you down."

After that conversation, my parents didn't call me for several weeks. I missed them. Why had I insisted on bringing up what they would see as snake worship? Why not just keep rowing—not rocking—the family boat? Why not at least pretend to fit in?

My brother Dana, always the peacemaker, reported to me that Mother and Father were still recovering from my anti-Rapture heresy and that they were increasingly concerned about my straying away from their faith. Why couldn't I just let them embrace me in the family fold? My parents didn't give up hope. The next month they called about the upcoming family reunion being held on the Colorado property—my home.

"Please be on your best behavior," they pleaded with me. "This is *family*."

Thirty-odd cousins, aunts, uncles, and assorted far-flung relatives were gathering at my place at the end of the summer. "Even the Mormons are coming," my brother warned good-naturedly. He was referring to a contingent of relatives who had heartily embraced the Latter-Day Saints. They had drawn up genealogy charts and announced they were praying all of us into heaven. Mother was particularly scandalized by this since she saw Mormonism as akin to a cult.

"I promise *not* to be myself," I informed my brother, feeling a bit the martyr. Even though my family dreaded me as an inquisitor.

"You know," my brother began with his trademark humor, "the problem with this family is that every one of us wants to be right—to get in the last word." He paused. "As a writer, you understand that."

I had to smile. I'd noted this sanctimony in my friends who seemed to practice competitive meditation in the nearby Buddhist enclave of Boulder. But rarely did I catch it in myself.

"Right," I said.

"And there *is* also such a thing as the Far Left," he continued. I could tell he was feeling his way with me. When to push, when to fall back. It was a verbal parrying in our family that called upon our wit as much as our intuition. "As a conservative Christian," he added, "I don't like the extremes of either right or left. We can disagree without being disagreeable."

"You mean no more family feuds?" I asked. "No more boycotts?"

"I mean, we can listen to each other better."

"Are you asking me to be a little less evangelical as a liberal?" I asked.

"The left doesn't seem to understand the need to belong to something greater than oneself. Religion. Country." He paused. "Family. You know, humanism is just not my idea of morality."

"Nor mine," I said. "I've always believed in something more than us, our laws and ethics. You know that."

"Yes," he said softly. "But I don't think the family does. You need to sometimes reassure them of what you do believe." He stopped, then laughed. "But no more snake stories."

"Are you worried that I'll get too far-out?" I asked.

"So far, I can still track you," he reassured me with a little military pride. "But just stay in this universe, will you?"

"I promise I'll stay put."

"Good. And stay on your toes. Remember last reunion we had fistfights over who would say grace."

At the Colorado family reunion, we again had major competitions over who would bless the food before we dove into deviled eggs, heavenly hash, barbecued spare ribs, pulled pork, butter beans, and so many pies we might as well have been at a state fair. Blue ribbons to all. Aside from enjoying cool summer nights in the shadow of the Rockies, the proselytizing was as fierce as my brother predicted.

"There must be a dominant gene for religion that runs in this family," my brother whispered one night when we were all settling in for homemade strawberry-banana ice cream, my mother's favorite. We lounged around in lawn chairs every evening of our reunion, grinding rock salt and ice to churn and freeze whatever other flavors we fancied: peach-pecan, Rocky Road, chocolate–black walnut. We could agree easily on ice cream, but not on religion. Anyone who assumes that Christians are a monolith hasn't met my family or listened to all the different dialects of this one faith—Mormons, Methodists, Southern Baptists, a few Christianized Native Americans. We debated plural marriage, biblical parables, and Revelation—as if our afterlives depended on it.

One of the Mormons astonished everyone by blithely announcing, "We don't believe in all that Rapture stuff. It's just wishful thinking." In the fading sunlight, his face and his well-tended, devout family looked spit-shined.

I always enjoyed the Mormons. They had a mischievous sense of humor about everything, except their religion. I respected their collective caretaking of one another and their passion for past generations. Their religion was more inclusive, embracing Native Americans especially. And when it came to cooking, their generous and inventive potluck dishes disappeared in nanoseconds.

"So you don't believe in Revelation, but you can believe that polygamist Joseph Smith was a prophet?" The challenge rang out from one of the lawn chairs.

The argument was on. Who needed board games like Monopoly or Scrabble when we had one another to move around on some spiritual scoreboard? I supposed that many other families talked about weather, politics, and family news. But we took on the end of the world and then, of course, turned on the backsliders among us.

I spent a lot of time in the kitchen, avoiding relatives who sought me out like heat-seeking missiles for private religious monologues. For years, I had been a regular on several family prayer lists. As I served up seconds of blackberry ice cream from berries we had picked near the irrigation ditch, I was tempted simply to confess,

"The earth belongs in my religion," to all gathered here on this ancestral land.

But after a raised eyebrow from my beloved brother, who must have intuited my intent, I instead brought up our neighborhood water wars. It was a good strategy.

"Water is the most precious thing on this earth," my Aunt Arlen said. Her father would farm his southern Missouri acres until he was over one hundred years old. "You keep those water shares, you hear? They are as valuable as family."

My aunt's words would come to haunt me. But that last night of the reunion I was thinking only about how to survive my relatives. The Methodist minister married to my aunt won the right to say grace that last supper. I kept my eyes open during his long heavenly entreaty and saw something astonishing: my family, my own motley tribe, had traveled so far just to be together. Why did we do this? It wasn't just duty or expectation. It was because somehow we still just wanted to be together. Bound by blood, if not beliefs.

"All that really matters is kindness," Miss MacKenzie had once told me when I had gone to visit her in New York and realized, to my great sadness, that she was dying. From her perch on the couch in her apartment, she continued, "It doesn't really matter to me what people believe." Then she took off her huge glasses and gave me a look that I recognized as pure knowledge. "Nothing else matters so long as we find a way to be kind to one another."

I remembered Rachel's words now as I studied my relatives. Mine is not a family in which one finds rest and easy acceptance. But it aspires to be good, and every now and then we share a communal "peace that passeth understanding."

"Hey," someone called out, "we forgot something. I'm sure our hostess wouldn't mind if we were the first to pick us some corn on the cob!"

With a gleeful shout, everybody leapt up from the lawn chairs and the lean-to picnic table and ran from the backyard gathering into the gracious green stalks of the cornfield. At first I was startled by the exodus. Would they pick corn that wasn't ready? Would I have enough to feed them all?

My Choctaw uncle strode out of the field already shucking an ear of white corn whose kernels were plump. As he used his fingernail to pierce a kernel, it squirted its milky promise of ripe maize. "Just right," he said with satisfaction.

I beamed. Here was something my little tribe could heartily accept from me. Here was manna to feed my family, who would all wander away tomorrow to many different lands in their own migrations. But for now I watched heads bobbing along through tall stalks, people calling out happily to each other. All my relations.

I saw my father explaining to one of the boys that he mustn't harm a garter snake slithering down a row along the irrigation ditch. "It's good for the garden," he said.

"Look," several of the children called as they streaked toward me holding small, half-shucked ears high in their hands. "The corn is . . . it's blue!"

I knelt down next to the little girls and finished husking the corn to reveal dark indigo kernels. Then I smiled at this next generation— one with shining black eyes and straight thick bangs across her wide forehead, the other ashen-haired with blue eyes flecked with gray.

"Is it rotted or something?" one of the girls asked.

"Is it okay to eat?"

"Not rotted," I assured them. "It's perfect."

As I told the little girls about the Hopi and their blue corn, I suddenly heard singing from the cornfield, a work song that flowed into a favorite hymn. They sang out from every corner of the five acres in soaring four-part harmony:

I came to the garden alone
while the dew is still on the rose.

That sunny evening as I listened to everyone singing in the corn-field, I felt how easy it is to miss each other in the search for something beyond. Oh, the beauty and sorrow of family. World Complete.

part two

My New Testament

On the last day of the world
I would want to plant a tree.
—W. S. MERWIN, "PLACE"

nine

The Way of the Sea
(Isaiah 9:1)

AFTER ALMOST THREE DECADES OF LIVING IN SEATTLE ON THE SHORES of the windswept, often wild Salish Sea, my family voted me "Most Likely to Drown in My Own Home."

Perched here on my backyard beach that floods with amiable regularity, sending barbecue, lawn chairs, picnic table, and potted plants floating, my small waterfront studio with its wall of glass windows is more like an aquarium than an apartment. In the same way that I once wondered if ants in my miniature farm thought their curious human caretaker might be a planet, as an adult I sometimes try to fathom the point of view of river otters, seals, and dolphins. When they cruise past my window or pop their glossy heads out of the waves, just what do they see? How do they regard us terrestrials?

Often my family expresses concern about my backyard flooding, but I always reassure them. "Don't worry. I've got my wetsuit hanging in the shower, and my snorkel gear is easily accessible. I'm ready for any sea change."

"You're ready to leave us behind?" they tease.

"Does this mean you'll be making more waves in the family?" another asks.

A couple of decades after abandoning the heaven of Walden's Pond, I found work as a part-time environmental writer and editor at the Seattle headquarters of REI, the national consumers' cooperative for outdoor gear. Founded by mountain climbers, REI's multitudinous members also believe in giving back a portion of profits to environmental stewardship.

I often said to myself wearily that I was doing something I believed in—writing articles for the REI magazine *Outdoor Review* on everything in the natural world, from low-impact camping to the threats to wilderness from development.

I didn't have Mr. Vale's six-shooter, but I had my word processor. I no longer had my five acres of Colorado corn, but I had the serpentine beauty of the Salish Sea, an inland waterway that wandered almost as much as I had. Our family farm in Colorado would later be sold to a veterinarian for a proposed hospital—a fitting fate for a farm that my ancestors had once devoted to abandoned animals. I'd fled a turbulent writer-in-residence teaching position at Arizona State University, reluctantly quit a fiction editorship at *Rocky Mountain* magazine several months before it folded up its beautifully produced pages, and landed in Seattle, a city so well irrigated that it was almost underwater. Several of my friends from *The New Yorker* had also settled here, and they helped me get work—from typesetting to freelance writing.

It was in the REI editorial office that I found the way to best survive as a working writer. I passed little time at the proverbial water cooler and holed up instead in my office, often missing meetings with the valid excuse of an in-house publication deadline. Exchanging the fluorescent lights above my desk for full-spectrum bulbs, my plants and I basked in the more natural light. My day job was crammed into three days a week, and I shared a beach house with others who were rarely at home in the daytime. When my housemates were in residence, I would often hole up in my waterfront study, and if they interrupted I'd tell them I was meditating. Claiming divine communion was also how I had fended off my family as a child. But I didn't really know how to meditate. So I bought a Monet water lilies print, sat cross-legged on the floor, listened to the waves outside my window, and repeated a mantra from T. S. Eliot: "Except for the point, the still point, there would be no dance, and there is only the dance." For a long time all that happened in my meditations was that I was sharply aware of all the sports injuries to my shoulders and lower back from my childhood years as athlete and gymnast.

In my work as an environmental writer and editor, I daily had to deal with grassroots conservationists who were sometimes as hardline and self-righteous as Southern Baptists. Sometimes eyeing a stack of alerts—Save This Forest, Save That Wetlands—I felt like I was in a never-ending war: a Battle of Good and Evil between those who exploited and those who protected the earth. Was it really that simple? Or had my religious upbringing reduced me to a polarized way of engaging with the world? Forget finding common ground. And where was the humor? Was there such a thing as an environmental stand-up comedian?

One morning at work my coworker Rob ran into my office waving a newspaper clipping. "Did you see this alert that they're strip mining in a Utah wilderness area?" Rob grinned as he leaned over the light table for a photo check. "What part of the wild are we saving this issue?"

I gazed at the paste-up boards of *Outdoor Review*: an exposé of a congressional bill that would open more of the West Coast to offshore drilling; an article on dire warnings of urban sprawl; a salmon run threatened by a new dam project.

"Listen," I asked him, "do you think there might be another way to talk about the natural world besides all this fear and catastrophe?"

"Dunno," he answered. "People only seem to wake up and change when they're scared to death . . . or when they think they're going to lose something they really love: like salmon, or a favorite river. Fear of extinction is a strong motivator. And so is righteous anger—on both sides."

"Yeah, but it's too much like all the sermons of my childhood," I said and started singing a Baptist hymn. *"I was sinking deep in sin. . . . "*

Rob smiled. "Don't know that song. But we Catholics have our own version of doom and gloom. And it goes like this: we're so bad because this world is so bad, and since being here is God's punishment, why shouldn't everything else around us also suffer?"

"I don't know any Baptist song that goes quite like that," I laughed.

"That's why Catholics chant everything in Latin. Who knows what we're really saying?"

"But what if we appealed to people's better instincts . . . you know, like finding common ground in something we share—like the beauty of the world . . . the . . . well, the rapture of it all?"

I couldn't believe I'd said it, but since Rob was raised Catholic without the passion play of End Times, he didn't get my meaning.

Several days after that I sat down gratefully on my backyard beach with a notebook. The Salish Sea was at low tide that surprisingly sunny afternoon, and a Great Blue Heron stood near my driftwood perch, her bright yellow eye scanning the shallow water for fish. The magnificent bird and I shared this beach as neighbors, familiar with one another. I knew the Great Blue had a mate and a nest in the green space above our beach cottage. Frequently she and her mate would perform a wide, wing-flapping dance, stepping in and out of the water with the sinewy delicacy of ballet. It always comforted me to see her one-legged perch in the sand, that long, elegant neck so still, and then a fierce slash with her beak into the surf to emerge with a wriggling fish.

As the Great Blue fell into another watery meditation, I drew two columns in my notebook to better compare my own swirling thoughts:

Fundamentalists	Environmentalists
1. Enraptured by doom	1. Enraptured by doom
2. Apocalypse Now	2. Apocalypse Near
3. Fear of future consequences	3. Fear of future consequences
4. Righteous anger	4. Righteous anger
5. Thou shalt not	5. Thou shalt not
6. Holier than Thou	6. Holier than Thou
7. Humorless	7. Humorless
8. Blame, shame, judgment	8. Blame, shame, judgment
9. Evangelical	9. Evangelical

This list was so startling and disturbing to me that I immediately put it in the back of my notebook, feeling disloyal to all my own environmental causes. Yet I could not help but see that both sides were so busy envisioning an afterlife, or future Eden, that they took no time to appreciate the present moment. I did talk about this comparison with a few friends and began to watch myself whenever I tended to fall into the simple formulas of my heritage: black-and-white thinking, a belief that I knew all the right answers. This was a much more unsettling path; it was full of doubt, wandering a wilderness of uncomfortable gray areas. I was seeking common or even uncharted ground. Or, as Rumi says, "Out beyond ideas of wrong-doing and right-doing there is a field. I will meet you there."

About this time I met the literary ecologist Joseph Meeker. Tall and gangly, Joe looked like an old Taoist wizard. His book *The Comedy of Survival* gave me another piece of my philosophical puzzle.

"You ever see how much both the biblical and ecological heroes act out of a tragic vision of life?" Joe asked. "One's sin is evil; the other's is extinction."

Joe and I were enjoying one of our "Leo lunches." He and I were both born under the August summer sun, though he is of my father's generation.

"So what's the way out?" I asked.

"To see ourselves as a divine comedy, of course!" When Joe laughed, his craggy face was suddenly flexible with robust laughter, and the laugh lines crinkling around his eyes deepened. "You know, the tragic hero always dies at the end to fulfill some divine order that is supposedly higher than this immoral world. But the comic character just bumbles along, adapting and taking evasive action—like the animals do."

"So evolution isn't just survival of the fittest," I said. "It has a sense of humor?"

"That's one way of looking at it," Joe nodded. "To evolution and comedy, nothing is sacred—nothing but life itself."

At a time when the environmental wars were raging and it seemed that Reagan was hell-bent on cutting every stand of old growth in the Pacific Northwest, I tried looking through Joe's more bemused glasses, especially during a dinner with my neighbor, Alice, who worked for PETA (People for the Ethical Treatment of Animals). Though not a member of PETA, I admired some of the group's policies and its staunch lobbying for the rights of other animals. Together with Bill, also a neighborhood pal, we sat at a Thai restaurant on the boardwalk. We were placing our orders and happily gossiping about the politics of a new park near our backyard beach when suddenly Alice pushed back from the table, knocking her plastic chair over.

"I'm not sharing a table with anyone who eats meat!" she announced and in a huff strode over to the farthest table in the restaurant, where she placed her order as if nothing had happened.

"She's vegan," I explained lamely.

Bill, a poet whose work displays his passion for both haiku and geology, gave me a stunned look. "Does she think we meat-eaters smell bad or something?"

I was just as shocked as he and tried to keep myself from glancing over at Alice eating her pad thai with tofu across the restaurant from us. It was one of my favorite dishes, but I also ate meat about once a week because whenever I'd tried to be a vegetarian I would surrender to the family streak of anemia. Tonight I'd ordered chicken satay, and as Bill joined me with his beef curry, we found ourselves guiltily leaning together as if to hide our food from the wrath of our watchful neighbor. But when I caught myself doing this, I just burst out laughing. Why were we behaving like guilty criminals?

"Food Nazi!" Bill said out loud.

Bill stood up and strode over to our neighbor. "This is ridiculous, Alice," he said. "I happen to know that you eat ice cream—you, a card-carrying member of PETA!"

She ignored him and continued her meal as if we had both become the invisible other, the less-than-human, the sinners. We were cast out into some carnivores' circle of hell.

It was quite awkward when we all had to share the same car to drive home together. There was not much conversation. We stayed polite neighborhood friends, but no more dining with Alice. One night she did, however, make a confession.

She and I were sitting on the backyard beach and chatting about her work when she blurted out, "Bill is right, you know." She stopped, drawing an uneven breath as if it hurt her to continue. "I do sometimes just break down and hit up the Thirty-one Flavors."

"You mean you commit Baskin-Robbins?" I couldn't help but smile.

"Yes, yes." She was so penitent I thought she might weep. "I cannot help myself. It's the Rocky Road. Sometimes late at night I just jump in my car and go get a three-scooper. Chocolate-mint and strawberry. Once I even had . . . a banana split."

Alice looked so forlorn that I stifled my smile. "You'd love my mother's homemade ice cream," I said and told her about the fresh raspberries or black pecans we folded into heavy cream before sealing up the round stainless-steel cylinder, surrounding it with rock salt and ice and then grinding away.

"So you understand?" Alice asked.

"Yes. Ice cream is one of the true wonders of this world."

I didn't add that I can't abide Baskin-Robbins. All those flavors are diluted and stingy compared to Mother's homemade perfection. We agreed that the next time Alice got the urge for an ice cream run, she could call me and I would be her partner in crime. But she never did. I suppose Alice kept that her solitary sin. In fact, after our conversation Alice rather avoided me, as if I were her confessor. She did leave a PETA bumper sticker, POWERED BY TOFU, and copies of her PETA newsletter on my doorstep, as if to corral me back into the fold—what my Southern Baptist family calls "the fellowship of the believers."

But what if I don't want to be in a fold of believers who all think alike? I put Alice's bumper sticker in my collection, which includes some of my all-time favorites: TO GET TO HEAVEN: TURN RIGHT AND GO STRAIGHT and JESUS IS COMING—LOOK BUSY and GLOBAL WARMING IS JUST ANOTHER WAY OF BURNING IN HELL and COME RAPTURE, CAN WE HAVE OUR WORLD BACK?

So many environmentalists also believe that we are living in a kind of End Times for all nature and other species. The world is so polluted—what some would call "godless"—that we exist only with the haunting memory of pure nature (or Eden). Original sin among many conservative evangelicals is easily translated into pollution among environmentalists. In one story, we eat of the forbidden tree; in the other story, we cut down the sacred tree.

Both belief systems are firmly rooted in the conviction that our paradise is forever lost. God banned us from Eden; humans have destroyed the earth. What might have happened if the early Christian storytellers, who imagined this world was still a paradise, had prevailed over the state Christian empire-builders who chose crucifixion, not Eden, as their main drama? And what if environmentalists stopped portraying nature as crucified? What if both camps simply stopped all their fearmongering and found a new story? We might imagine a future in which all species flourish, along with us. A garden that is more beautiful than it is battered, more sacred than it is scarred.

I often think of Alice when I encounter fundamentalists, whether religious or environmental, who, in reaching for extremes, zoom past the rest of us who are seeking some workable middle path. In the 1990s, even though the massive Berlin Wall had fallen and the global village was rising, and even though the Internet was revolutionizing communication, there were still not many new ideas about how to find common ground or conduct a respectful dialogue between political or religious extremes. And of course, the question for me remained: how was I to deal with a family and a world that seemed bent on extremes? To my dismay, some in my family were veering even farther right.

At one family Christmas gathering around this time, I sat at the dinner table listening to their boisterous stories. They all have a dramatic flair. But this time they struck a chill in me. One sibling made a passionate pitch for a pro-life politician: "He can finally help us turn back *Roe v. Wade.*" My brother reported on a new spying device that could be implanted into a buzzing bee so as to eavesdrop on enemy conversations.

"Every day at the Pentagon," my brother said in his thoughtful, melodious voice, the voice of a true Irish tenor, "every day I have to realistically consider possible terrorist scenarios for World War III."

My father, who was now working on forest management planning, launched into a lecture on why environmentalists' lawsuits were making his U.S. Forest Service conservation job more difficult. But before he could finish one of his finer points, my mother jumped in. She announced with pride that she had just been selected that day to assist in informing a CIA operative's family that the agent had died in the line of duty.

"Oh, Mother, what a sad job," I said.

"Oh," she replied fiercely, "it was an honor. I got to present his wife with an American flag. Besides, her husband will get his own star at CIA headquarters."

She was referring to the anonymous stars at the CIA headquarters' Wall of Honor for operatives killed in the line of duty. In 1997 there were seventy. A constellation of unnamed heroes, this wall of black stars chiseled into white Vermont marble shines.

"I hardly think a flag and an unnamed star make up for a lost life," I said, walking right straight into the lions' den. "What about their poor families? Do they have to grieve in secret?"

Military honor, pride in country, the group over the individual, church and family clan—I got roaring reprimands on all sides, served up with second helpings of Mother's black-eyed peas, homemade cornbread with chili peppers, and venison stew. It was only the promise of strawberry rhubarb pie and homemade ice cream that gave me courage to stay at the dinner table and endure the majority rule of the family democracy.

"You know," I protested, "it's lonely being the only liberal in this whole family! Next life, I'm going to be born into a bookish, liberal family who adores me."

"We adore you," my youngest sibling laughed. "We just think that aliens switched you at birth."

I looked around at my family and saw echoes of the same face— intense blue-gray eyes, high cheekbones, and dark blond curls. While we mirrored each other's features, there was not a single soul in my immediate family—except perhaps my more contemplative brother—with whom I could identify. Then I gazed over at the young grandchildren around their own card table, many with more varied features from their Polish or Cuban parents. Would they grow up in the family mold and mind-set? Would I perpetually be odd person out?

Then I remembered my dear friend Susan, with whom I've swapped family stories over three decades. When I was bemoaning my family's conservatism, she asked, "So what if you'd been born into a far left family? Gentle Quakers maybe? Would you have been compelled to find your own individual beliefs?"

"You know, Behba," my other sibling now chimed in sweetly, "if we didn't love you so much, we'd just have to hate you."

"With these odds," I said, "I'm the one who should own a gun, not all of you."

At that Christmas reunion I had discovered that every single one of my immediate family owned a weapon. We had all grown up in a home with my father's hunting rifles resting across the wide-set antlers of the moose he had shot in Montana, along with some knick-knacks like a stuffed Woodsy Owl doll and Smokey Bear Christmas ornaments. But now, as grown-ups, all my siblings were armed, if not dangerous. My youngest sibling kept a pistol under the pillow at night; another packed an elegant pearl-handled gun. And my brother had his gun stored in his home safe. What so terrorized my family that they were armed even on the home front?

Years later I would read of research that correlated startle responses to one's political beliefs. Biologist Olivia Judson wrote about a study that found that "people who support warrantless searches, wiretapping, military spending and so on were also likely to startle at sudden noises and threatening images. Those who support foreign aid, immigration, gun control and the like tended to have much milder responses to the stimuli."

Was I somehow hardwired to respond more mildly to fear than my family? Because I was the only one whose first years were spent in a spacious national forest, did I have a more embracing environment during my early childhood? In a vast and diverse living forest, I instinctively knew that humans were not really in control. I couldn't believe in only one species—even if it were my own. How could I grow up to follow only One Way? And while I had the healthy fear of any prey animal for predators, I just couldn't accept that Satan was ever-lurking to torment or tempt me.

When I observe my family's religion, I see how it shapes their sense of safety and their world view. As several of my relatives are always warning me, Muslims have their own version of the End Times as they await the imminent return of the Mahdi, who will impose justice and spread peace in a corrupt world. If sin and Satan and now Islamic militants are out there waiting to destroy Christians, then we'd better circle the wagons in a tight-knit fellowship of the believers. What my liberal friends least understand about the religious right, like some people in my family, is their sense of ever-present danger and persecution—even when they are in power.

My father grinned at me from the far end of the table. "Maybe you were born into this family, honey, to learn a few things about how to protect yourself in a dangerous world."

"It's you who scare me most," I blurted out.

But then, in either a meditative or dissociative moment, I imagined floating above my family and observing myself from their point of view. Maybe I also frightened them? Was my spiritual diversity like an alien species to the family's ecosystem of one faith? Was I, like the serpent in the garden, the invader?

At that Christmas supper table my mother finally brought us back to one reason we were all together. "Ice cream?" she sang out. "We have a new machine that does the hand-cranking for you."

It was a marvel of an invention. But would the ice cream taste as good as our own hand-cranked concoction? We all left the dinner table and sat mesmerized around the newfangled contraption. Nosily grinding the ice and rock salt, it rocked back and forth as if unable to contain its happiness.

The only time I truly sympathize, body and soul, with much of my family's siege mentality is when I endure severe tree pollen allergies every March. It's quite embarrassing to be a nature writer allergic to trees when they are at their most eloquent—and perhaps most stressed—as they pollinate. It is significant that when my family left the forest for our many travels, following my father's career, it was spring and millions of trees were pollinating.

"You look like you're preparing for a nuclear attack," my father, the forester, teases me when he sees me in my face mask, sniffling and staying indoors when the bright world is abloom.

"Maybe there was so much pollen when we lived on the forest station," I say, "that I just can't take in any more." I don't mention the grief of losing my first Garden of Eden when we left the forest.

"Or," my father says with a grin, "you resist being born again."

One spring when I was hiding out indoors from tree pollen so thick it floated across the freeway like cotton, my mother called to make sure I was at least venturing outdoors for Easter service.

"Yes, Mother," I said dutifully. "I'm going to hear my friend Diana play her marvelous piano at St. Pious."

"She's Russian, isn't she?" my mother asked, always on the alert. Old CIA habits die hard. "And isn't that a Catholic church?" Mother's voice betrayed some alarm. She was particularly sensitive on this is-sue since a relative researching her side of the family had discovered that Mother's ancestors had immigrated to this country from Dublin—and they were most probably Irish Catholics.

"Catholics celebrate Easter too, just like Baptists," I said.

"You don't see Baptists taking orders from the Pope or swinging that awful incense smoke around. . . . What about your allergies?"

"I'll manage, Mother," I laughed. "Sad to say, it's the living trees that get to me each spring, not the embers."

"You'd be allergy-free after a forest fire." My father wryly joined the conversation on the other phone line.

"Listen, just stay home this Easter and read this new novel I'm wild about," Mother instructed. "You'll feel better."

The novel was *Epicenter* by the author of the prescient thriller *The Last Jihad* and *The Last Days*. It was post-9/11, and our family political dialogues were intense. We were in a new century kicked off by seeming End Times events like falling skyscrapers and airplanes.

"You see," Mother explained excitedly, "Russia joins the 'axis of evil' with Iran, which goes nuclear, and together they attack Israel in the last great battle. Just like it says in the Bible."

When my mother sent me the book, I noted that the flap copy boasted "Ten New Predictions That Will Change the World" and "Headlines Before They Happen," including: "Jews Build Third Temple in Jerusalem" and "Muslims Turn to Christ in Record Numbers."

I flipped to the author's bio and read that the author was an evangelical Christian from an Orthodox Jewish heritage. I was about to dismiss the book when I discovered Appendix 2, entitled "American Attitudes Toward Biblical Prophecy." The 2006 statistics were sobering: 52 percent of all Americans believed that the return of Jews to the Holy Land with the rebirth of Israel in 1948 was "the fulfillment of biblical prophecies." And even more alarming to me was that 42 percent of Americans agreed that Middle East wars, recent earthquakes, and the Asian tsunami were evidence that "we are living in what the Bible calls the last days."

When I called my mother to thank her for the novel, she reminded me to watch that week's thrilling episode of 24, the television series featuring adrenaline-fueled end-of-the world scenarios. The show has made addicts of our entire family, including me. It always gives us something to talk about.

"Those Muslim fundamentalists are targeting the president of the United States!" Mother said happily. "Tune in."

"It's the only time I ever watch Fox," I admitted to her. I also am a fan of the BBC British intelligence series *MI-5*.

"You see," Mother exulted, "my children take after me. Spy thrillers run in your blood."

I remembered that I had once admitted to my mother, "I don't like the Old Testament as much as the New Testament."

"How can you even say that about the Old Testament?" Mother had demanded. "It's the Word of God. It's true and eternal. The Bible doesn't need your literary criticism." She hesitated, and then her trademark curiosity got the best of her. "But why do you like the New Testament better?"

"Well, it's more mystical and full of moral dilemmas. Jesus asks the really complicated questions . . . like any good rabbi."

"But you must admit the Old Testament has a much better plot," my mother had insisted. "And you know how I like a fast-paced plot." She had paused and then added brightly, "But the New Testament does have the Book of Revelation. Now, that's really action-packed!"

For the first time then, I had understood why the "Left Behind" series was so popular among evangelicals. It was essentially a thriller for the righteous. The main characters were not prophets but God's spies who stayed on earth to kill or convert. It was the twentieth-century Crusades with the biggest plot finale of all: the end of everything.

* * *

MY FAMILY DOES NOT FIT the liberal stereotype of southerners—bumbling, black-and-white Mayberry characters. None of them live in the hallowed small towns so dear to wedge politicians. Some are pro-choice; they are not racists. My family is highly educated, and several of my sophisticated friends have been struck by how appealing and charming they are. As one of my Manhattan friends said, "I tend to think of people who are physically so refined and beautiful to look at as incapable of . . . well, being so primitive in their politics and religion."

When a New York friend threw a book party for me, my mother and niece took the train up from Virginia to also attend their first Broadway show. At the pre-theater party, my mother regaled the gathering with CIA tales. She wore a white pants suit and an elegant golden cross necklace because I had warned her about not proselytizing.

"They don't make those great old dames like your mother anymore," one of the men commented. "Spies, God, and country—she's a classic."

She holds the whole wide world in her hands, I thought to myself, the words bopping through my head like a soundtrack following bouncing balls.

On the train trip from New York City back to Washington, D.C., with my mother, I told her about the gentleman's compliment.

"Everybody is intrigued by the CIA," she said with satisfaction. "We're protecting all Americans—even the ones who distrust us."

Indeed, the CIA gift shop was one of my favorite haunts when I visited home. It was hidden inside a decoy credit union. Mother had to use her official employee card to gain entrance. Inside was a cornucopia of CIA memorabilia. Once, right after the terrorist attacks of September 11, 2001, I was caught speeding on my way to teach class in Seattle. As I unthinkingly sipped my morning tea, the policeman scribbled my ticket. He glanced at me sternly, and then all of a sudden he snapped to and tore up the ticket. "You're doing a great job!" He saluted me and nodded to my stainless-steel travel mug. It was red, emblazoned with the crest of the fierce CIA eagle, its talons clutching golden arrows. "Oh, thanks, officer," I nodded, trying to look clandestine. I had to admit that the cop's respect secretly thrilled me. No one had ever saluted me before. After the officer left, I finished my tea, fondly gazing at my CIA mug. For the first time I noticed that on the bottom it said, in tiny letters, Made in China.

Mother's working life was more on display in her kitchen and basement: official CIA coffee mugs, baseball caps, notepads, and even porcelain plates with the CIA logo. Stored in the full basement, near the Ping-Pong table and freezer full of wild game, was a working train set, which we kids had given her. Mother still set up her miniature train cars and ran them through tiny tunnels, past miniature plastic trees, and into a red-tiled station house. Sometimes she crashed her little trains, just for fun.

"Mother," I had to ask, "aren't you ever afraid?" I was about to expound on my theory that religion is too often driven by fear—of judgment, of the afterlife, of being excluded from the heavenly fold.

Mother bristled at the notion. "Honey, I'm not afraid of anything! If I could stand on a flimsy little platform while the *Wabash Cannonball* roared by at eighty miles an hour and still hold up the U.S. mailbag . . . well, I'm no shrinking violet. Besides," she gave me a meaningful look, "I know that God always has a plan for me."

* * *

WAS IT FEAR OR HOPE I FELT, or perhaps both, when, in 2004, my mother announced that she and my father would join me for my annual spring research trip with Baja Expeditions to the gray whales' birthing lagoons in Baja, Mexico. Every spring for seven seasons, I have journeyed with my "pod"—a group of naturalists, writers, artists, and cetacean enthusiasts, often led by naturalist and author Doug Thompson of Summer Tree Institute. Doug has been studying what scientists call "the Friendly Whale Syndrome" in the lagoon since the 1970s. To touch such a living ancestor is like being called backward in time to a sea teeming with marine life—mammals like us who nurse their young and breathe air.

Gray whales have been seeking human interaction since the 1970s in the Baja birthing lagoons, a protected biosphere set aside by the Mexican government. Once called "devil fish," for the fierceness with which the mother whales tried to defend their calves from harpoons, gray whales now delight people by approaching small panga boats. The whales float alongside companionably, gazing eye to eye, as if to fathom us. Sometimes they lift their long, barnacled snouts up to be touched. How many wild animals choose to seek such intimate interspecies contact? Do wild wolves or bears offer their newborns into human hands? Add to this mystery the fact that twice the gray whale has been brought to near-extinction from whalers' harpoons.

These grays are among the oldest of all whales; their fossil record dates back more than 50 million years. New scientific evidence suggests that gray whales can live up to 150 years. This means that some of the gray whales I've encountered over the last ten years in Baja's San Ignacio Lagoon may have the memory and even the harpoon scars of whaling. Why do these whales approach our boats to present us with their babies? This inexplicable trust is what keeps drawing me back year after year to San Ignacio Lagoon.

Getting to this far-flung oasis is quite a feat, especially with parents who were seventy-five and seventy-seven in tow. But my parents were spry and seasoned travelers; my father consulted all over the world on issues of forestry and wildlife. We also come from a family tradition of camping in national forests. I used to joke that my childhood was "camp or die." So the prospect of sleeping on army cots in canvas tents on a thin peninsula wedged between the Pacific and the Sea of Cortez didn't faze my parents. Nor did hopping into a tiny four-seated plane in San Diego to wing down to a dirt landing strip in the Baja wilderness.

As if to make a point that he was right at home in these mosquito planes, my father wore his Alaska bush pilot baseball cap. My mother wore her trademark Smokey Bear cap, stylish sunglasses, and a small backpack instead of a purse. As our small propeller plane buzzed low over the vast desert of the Baja peninsula, my father launched into a tale of his recent hunting trip.

Every fall he and his hunting buddies are dropped by bush plane, with their gear, rifles, and GPS instruments, in the Alaska tundra. Moose, elk, and deer are their prey, and rarely do the guys come home without meat to feed their families. Several times I've met my father in the Seattle airport en route back to his home in Virginia, and he will hand me a bloody cooler full of frozen game. I used to eat it, as I did all my years growing up; now I donate it to the city's food banks.

As we jolted along in the cerulean sky, my mother clutched my father's hand. He grinned as if we were on an amusement park ride.

"You get used to bouncing around in a little tin can in the sky," my father reassured my friend Justine, who sat next to me and opposite my mother and him in our cramped cabin.

"I've been flying with my father in his Cessna since I was a child," Justine told him. "This is like heaven to me."

Ah, he had met his match in Justine. He enjoyed her bravado. Coming from a family of strong sisters, my father has always been impressed with women who don't shrink from danger. Justine was also a transplanted southerner who, with her husband, had started a series that was broadcast on public radio stations both nationally and worldwide. She was visionary and liberal—a seemingly perfect foil for my conservative father.

After a particularly acrobatic patch of turbulence, my father took up one of his favorite subjects: politics. Kerry or Bush for president? The Bush years were my personal nadir with my family. Even though they all gave lip service to separation of church and state, they were enthralled by having an evangelical president veering toward theocracy and a war that engaged their biblical imaginations. "God chose this man to lead us after 9/11," Mother often said with the fervent gaze of a true believer. We had yet to learn that in his highly classified digests of the Iraq War, Secretary of Defense Donald Rumsfeld was cynically using Bible quotations as headlines to encourage a president whose Middle East foreign policy was so ideologically driven that it seemed drawn from End Times prophecies. The only critical comment I ever heard Mother make about George W. Bush was that he had unfairly blamed the CIA for bad intelligence leading up to his holy war in Iraq.

As my father warmed to his lecture on why Kerry was the wrong man to lead our country, I surrendered to my first moment of panic in the whole trip. Nausea or fear of flying would have been better than what I felt that moment: sheer terror. Dread. What was I thinking? Why had I brought my conservative Republican parents into this band of ultra-liberal friends? It hadn't really been my idea. Ever since I'd shown my parents a video of the gray whale lagoons, my mother had insisted that she wanted to go and "touch a baby whale." Her maternal fervor had startled me, and I was so happy to have them accompany me into my world that I hadn't really considered what the trip would be like if there was disharmony in the group.

"The problem with you liberals . . . ," my father warmed to his subject, eyeing Justine.

There was nowhere to shrink or hide in that minuscule cabin, but I must have physically retreated because my seat belt suddenly snapped tighter across my chest. I felt the siege of a claustrophobia I rarely feel anymore except when I am trapped in some family situation. *Oh, no,* I thought, *we're stuck in this tiny plane for hours in an endless political argument—with no exit!*

But Justine was laughing in her robust and good-humored way. "How about this?" she suggested to my father in her lulling and mellifluous voice. "On this trip, no politics. No religion." There was just a tinge of the aristocratic South in her tone, and a playfulness that was profoundly feminine.

Her no-nonsense voice, more than her words, stopped him. For a moment.

Then he continued, as if she had not spoken at all. "Kerry achieved nothing much to speak of in the Senate. . . . "

The zip of her seat belt as Justine leaned forward, her forefinger only inches from my father's surprised face. "I said," Justine's voice was firm and louder than the roar of the propeller blades, "*no* politics. And *no* religion!"

My father stared at Justine as if she had just suggested we all jump out of the small plane without parachutes. He seemed mystified as to what to do next.

No one said a word for what felt like hours. The twin engines roared. We seemed becalmed in the sky without turbulence or conversation. I realized I was holding my breath.

And then a revelation. My father and Justine both reared back in their seats and laughed together. It broke all the tension. The rather companionable turbulence of the Mexican skies returned, and the pilot called back to ask if any of us wanted to ride copilot with him as we were nearing the lagoon.

"I will!" I fairly shouted and climbed over both my parents to slip gratefully into the narrow seat next to the pilot. He was grinning ear to ear as he handed me a set of headphones.

I could only vaguely make out the conversation in the seats behind me. But it occurred to me that for the first time in my whole life my parents and I were going to be in a group that echoed more of my political values than theirs. When I glanced back into the cabin to see if they had throttled each other, I saw that my father was helping Justine with a cramp in her foot.

"Power bar?" my mother called up to me and tossed me her favorite sweet and salty nut cashew bar. My favorite now too, since that memorable flight.

Baja was my balancing act with my parents. It was the first time just my parents and I were together in the wilderness since that first Forest Service cabin. Since the Baja trip, and for many years afterward, my parents and I rarely discussed politics or religion. What began as a prohibition in a small plane became our practice. It was such a simple idea. Why had I never in my five decades figured that out?

My parents turned out to be the hit of the camp and were fondly included in midnight kayaking trips into mangrove groves. My podmates, as I call them, vied to include my parents in their boats. But there was one night in the mess tent when I was the one who broke the new rule. Maybe it was because I was so giddy to see the tables turned on my parents. In the midst of this liberal gang, my parents were in the minority, as I had always been with my family. Someone at my table started up a comic political pantomime. Like playing dolls with all the president's men, the salt and pepper shakers were George and Laura Bush; the squat metal napkin holder was Dick Cheney. It was such wicked fun. We knew we were within hearing range of my parents, "the Republicans." But we couldn't stop ourselves. Somehow that made it even more tempting. I played along, trying not to glance over at them. What did my parents do? Hand in hand, they stood and said their good-nights. The sweet dignity of their signing off made me bow my head.

It was awkward at first as my parents and I navigated the vacuum created between us by our lack of arguments. Still, nature abhors a vacuum—and we were in the thrall of nature.

That first night camped on the desert lagoon, the wind stilled and we heard the whales breathing—the sighs of the mother whales answering the short responses of their newborn calves. It was an otherworldly but intimate lullaby of new life. Where else in the world could we listen to wild animals sleeping so close by and trusting a human camp? It was as if we all belonged together there under the stars. It was like the beginning of the world.

The nearest town was fifty miles away. The turquoise waters of San Ignacio Lagoon were set into the bright salt flats of the Baja peninsula. Constant winds blew warmly during the March days. We vented our canvas tents with clothespins for siesta, but at night we slept bundled in knit caps and gloves, with coyotes strolling nearby.

The first day had a rhythm as our little human pod moved in synch. Dawn found us in the mess tent for spicy Mexican chocolate, strong coffee. Still sleepy, we pulled on galoshes, rubber pants, and layers of long underwear over bathing suits, then waterproof parkas, funny hats, and yellow life preservers. We barely recognized each other for all our gear. My mother had forgotten to pack any waterproof gear, and she showed up the first morning for whale watching in flip-flops, a red turban that would have made Gloria Swanson proud, and a summer blouse. She looked glamorous but completely unprepared for the windswept wooden boats and chill morning lagoons.

"I told you, Mother, riding in these skiffs is like going through a car wash—without a car!"

I piled on her the extra gear I'd brought, knowing she would choose fashion over function. My father, on the other hand, was expertly decked out in hip boots, a blue waterproof slicker, and a hat that would have been perfect for duck hunting.

Like ducklings, we imprinted on the Mexican boatman, Ranulfo, whose village fisherman father, Pachico Mayoral, had been the first to recognize the friendly whale phenomenon in the early 1970s. Pachico still runs his own eco-camp every spring for those who seek to encounter curious whales. Ranulfo has been leading whale-watching tours since he was a teenager and his father first took him out to meet the "friendlies" in 1979. Pachico and Ranulfo know more about these grays and this pristine lagoon than any scientists. They have closely observed generations of gray whales. Ranulfo also leads bird and turtle eco-tours during the off-season. He has compiled an impressive bird book of the 170 species gracing this lagoon—from white ibis to peregrine falcon to the osprey that often cruise above our boats, their talons gripping fish.

We were also accompanied by Ranulfo's niece, Lupita, the lagoon's youngest naturalist and the only female. Doug completed our crew; he was doing videography for his book and DVD, *Whales: Touching the Mystery*. We plodded single file down the blunt and sandy beach cliffs to the wood-and-fiberglass pangas awaiting us. As we stumbled over beach rocks, I saw my parents reach out to hold hands.

Once six of us settled inside the boat, the outboard motor roared us awake as we skimmed across the lagoon, our eyes already scanning the horizon for signs of blows, those heart-shaped breaths of whales. I watched my parents, big sunglasses and wide grins on their faces, full of anticipation.

"Ready for first contact?" I asked them.

"You bet!" my mother sang out.

The gray whales and their calves, being acoustic animals, often curiously approach boats that are full of singers. The whales especially seem to like lively Broadway musicals, such as *Oklahoma* and *West Side Story*. My parents joined in the harmony. We made up new lyrics to favorite songs. To the tune of "Maria" we sang, *Oh, gray whale, I just touched a newborn gray whale . . . and suddenly the world will never be the same to me!* And another favorite, sung to the tune of "Oh, What a Beautiful Morning," was *All the breaths of the whales are like music. . . .*

My father's hunting eyes were the first to spot a mother-calf pair cruising across the white-capped waters. "Whales at three o'clock!" he proudly informed us.

Ranulfo lowered the outboard motor to the soft, chugging sounds that the gray whales recognize and, if they are friendlies, curiously come to greet. Sure enough, the mother-calf pair turned toward us and very slowly swam right for our boat.

It is one thing to follow a forty-five-ton whale as long as a semi-truck. But when one is floating in an eighteen-foot skiff and the whale is navigating straight toward the flimsy bow, for the uninitiated it is always a moment between delight and panic.

"Coming right toward us," my father said quietly, his expression wary.

The only shot he would be able to take of this wild animal was a photograph. For a split-second he gave me a questioning look, as if to demand, *What have you gotten us into?*

I could just see it, my entire family blaming me for whisking my elderly parents away to their deaths by drowning, or worse, being mauled by a wild animal. I wanted to assure my father that it was all right, that he was completely safe with these gentle creatures who had not harmed any human in three decades of interaction. But reassuring him would have assumed that he was afraid. I clearly saw that it was not fear on his face but a deep discomfort from not being in his element. Humans had no control here. We were not predators. We were not prey. What were we?

As the huge whale surfaced, her double blowholes exhaled a prismatic rainbow misting over us all. "Baptism!" I shouted.

"Thar she blooooows!" my mother called out in pure pleasure.

She leaned so far out of the skiff that I had to grab on to her red life preserver as the mother whale rose up near us, her huge head barnacled, baleen-stripped mouth dazzling.

In the back of the boat, many eager hands scratched and stroked the supple gray skin, which felt as smooth and cool as melon.

"Shift your weight to the opposite side of the boat for balance," my father commanded. Everyone obeyed.

It really did feel as if we might capsize, though we never had before. But with my mother halfway out of the boat, her hand reaching, reaching for that gray head and me holding on to her, the boat tilted low. We took on a little water. Thus, the galoshes.

The mother whale rose up several feet from the bow. She floated, watching us. Her eye was dark, unblinking. That eye gazed at us as if from the bottom of the ocean. My mother's hand was stretched so far, but the whale skimmed right past my mother to let herself be stroked by Ranulfo, who fondly greeted her by name.

"Welcome back!" he called out to her in his soft baritone.

The mother whale turned on her side, showing her flank spackled with white barnacles and a raised pale harpoon scar along her flank.

We all gasped.

Then the mother whale did something I'd never seen before in all the seasons I had been visiting Baja lagoons. With a deep inhalation, her blowholes closed as she turned upside down, underwater. As if on signal, her calf rolled atop her belly. Stretching a pectoral fin out like a wide wing, the mother lifted her newborn way up to us, at eye level, in the boat. We were too astonished to respond.

Time stopped. Only the cries of cormorants and pelicans, the lapping of mild waves against the boat.

"She is giving her baby to us," Ranulfo said in the softest voice.

Why? This belly-up cradle of her newborn by the mother is usually a behavior observed only when a predator, like an orca, is menacing the mother-calf pair. The mother gray whale lifts her calf on her belly and holds her offspring away from the orca's teeth with her last, withheld breath. But here the protective gesture was an offering.

"She's big," my father said, "and she's brave."

Ranulfo leaned over and rubbed her vast belly. "She is a good mother," he said, as if reciting his own family's genealogy.

Balancing on her mother's belly, the calf was practically in the boat with us, inquisitive but shy. She was brand-new—no more than a few weeks old, with short baby whiskers and no barnacles. At fifteen feet long, the calf was nursing on milk so rich she would gain one hundred pounds a day. When the calves are two to three months old, they embark on the perilous 2,500-mile round-trip journey between Baja and the Arctic, an obstacle course of orca attacks, supertanker boat propellers, Russian and subsistence hunters, and other hazards. Thirty percent of the calves do not survive.

"Reach way out, honey!" My father had lost all sense of caution as he clambered across the boat to join my mother as she again leaned, her hand stretching toward the calf. He lifted his camera to capture the image:

My mother's fast hands—hands that once typed out Morse code, that passionately play across the piano keyboard—now seem to float in slow-motion stillness, midair. It is the calf who rises up to her outstretched hands as if seeking a blessing, a laying on of hands. My mother's face is radiant with sunlight and surprise.

"Her skin is so soft," she marveled. "Like a real baby's."

"No barnacles," laughed Ranulfo. "Not yet."

Breath from the calf's double blowhole was strangely sweet, and her pectoral fins were still a little awkward. Inside each pectoral were the skeletal remains of a hand, a reminder that these grays once walked on land.

Slowly the mother sank beneath the boat and emerged on the other side. She lolled nearby, her calf now playing and pirouetting beneath our hands. I sat on the other side of the boat, balancing my parents and the other whale watchers, who were laughing and gently touching the calf. My mother started singing a song I had told her the whales always seem to enjoy. One of the mother whales is even named after this hymn.

Amazing grace
How sweet the sound

Now both my mother's and father's hands were resting tenderly on the bobbing whales, my mother's hand on the calf and my father's hand on the mother. My father joined in with his beautiful baritone, and everyone was singing as the mother and calf raised their heads higher, their eyes holding ours. I was so proud and happy to belong with my parents. They were now part of my pod. It reminded me of long ago before I had words, when all I had were images: I am the only child of young and strong parents. We are at the beginning of the world and live together as a trinity in a forest lookout cabin surrounded by wilderness. My parents sing to me in the fierce sunlight surrounded by tall trees. I am the firstborn and know that I am welcomed to this magical world.

Ranulfo instructed my mother to reach right into the baby's mouth and scratch her bright baleen. "They like it," Ranulfo shrugged and smiled.

Without hesitation, my mother scrubbed the baleen up and down. She grinned and said, "It's like brushing my kids' teeth."

"But this is not a toothed whale," explained Ranulfo. "Her baleen strips are keratin, just like our fingernails. Mother Nature makes all of us out of the same stuff."

"Yeah," Mother echoed. "The same stuff."

The calf then turned toward her mother, and the two of them sank gently to swim beneath the boat. Then they rose up and headed toward a nearby skiff. A happy hooray went up from the other boat as the mother-calf friendlies headed their way.

Exhilarated and spent, we all rocked in the boat. Most of us were drenched in saltwater, but under the constant sun our clothes dried quickly.

"Why do you think they want to be near us?" my father asked Ranulfo and his niece Lupita, who was our naturalist.

"It is mystery," Lupita said in her halting English. "I think maybe *las ballenas* . . . the whales . . . are like God. They forgive us." Her dark face was wide and full of wonder. "They forgive us *todo* . . . everything."

ten

Fire from Heaven

(Revelation 20:9)

Perhaps inspired by this Pacific adventure, a year later, for his seventy-ninth birthday, my father took his children, and all the grandchildren, on a Caribbean cruise.

"I could have bought a brand-new pickup truck," he told us. "But I wanted to be with you all."

Of course, I earnestly protested this family vacation. Every season in Seattle I curse the gargantuan cruise ships that use my home city as their port. Sometimes I even startle myself with fantasies of blowing them up. At times like this I realize I don't really have what it takes to be a pacifist. "You know, Dad," I lectured, "cruise ships dump tons of waste into the ocean. Besides, you should save all that money for your old age."

I could just hear my father winking over the phone. "Well, honey, I hereby appoint you our onboard environmentalist. You can attend the daily waste-management lectures the ship's engineer gives . . . while the rest of us are having fun."

As we clambered onboard the gigantic cruise ship docked in Miami—twenty-two of us schlepping way too much luggage—my father said, "All I ask of you is that we come together every night for supper."

"It's formal dining, you know," Mother said brightly. "So dress up." It took several of us to lug her oversize red suitcases up the gangplank. She cast a preemptive eye on several of the grandchildren. "No T-shirts. And we're going to take family pictures. This is the cruise of a lifetime."

Boarding the cruise ship, which seemed the size of a glacier, we were dazzled. There were nine decks, each of which was louder and more stimulating than the next one. Even the ship's library was noisy. I felt as though I were trapped in a multilayered shopping mall. Everything whizzed or whistled like a Las Vegas casino, and I noted that many of the three thousand people onboard had the hungry, dazed look of people playing slot machines. There was, in fact, all-night gambling on one of the top decks. Some of the more psychic elements of my family would make a lot of money.

Our daily itinerary was daunting, including more destinations than some of us had traveled in our lifetimes: Haiti, Jamaica, the Bahamas, and Cozumel. Each day we were not at sea there were onshore adventures—from swimming with stingrays off Grand Cayman island to climbing a waterfall in Ocho Rios. We could choose to gang up with one another, gossiping about those of us left onboard, or we could avoid family altogether if things got too hot.

The weather was hot enough. Our Caribbean cruise was in August, off-season. As one who dwells in a temperate rain forest, I was stunned every day at the weight of the humidity, but few of my southern relatives seemed to mind. True to my father's request, we all gathered each evening to dine together. The way they fed us, you'd think everyone onboard had just been rescued from a tropical island and deprived of food for months. I'd read that most vacationers gain 5.4 pounds each on cruise ships, so I was determined to lose weight on this cruise by climbing all seven decks and forswearing elevators.

One night at the bacchanalian banquet, when I heard a neighboring diner order two meals and three desserts for himself, I practically levitated with indignation. But then I remembered that rather recently one of my friends had opened my own refrigerator and decried, "There's more food in your fridge for one person than for my family of four—and most of it is rotting. Are you stocking up for doomsday? Or a Southern Baptist social?"

I rather liked the ocean-view cabin on the seventh deck that I shared with my niece Elizabeth. We both despised air conditioning, so our room was sultry and somewhat salt-encrusted from the sea mists. Other family members complained about it. But I could sit for hours and gaze at the rippling turquoise waves—nothing on the horizon but clouds.

Midway through the cruise, and perhaps because of the unrelenting heat, at the dinner table talk turned to global warming. Unfortunately, not everyone in the family had taken the "no politics, no religion" tack that my parents and I had so enjoyed ever since those Baja lagoons. So the debate, as usual, was heated.

"Global warming is just a liberal plot," someone suggested, and all heads swerved toward me.

I considered my position. That day I'd enjoyed kayaking with my nieces and nephews to a Haitian village, and I was not really in the mood to fight. Besides, I could plainly see that some of my family had sunburns and seemed to be in pain. Suddenly I remembered my grandmother's tactic whenever her family squabbled. She would talk about the weather. "Well, this has been a very hot year for the Northwest," I said, hoping it was mild enough to turn away wrath.

"Environmentalists act like this planet is the *Titanic* and we're all going to go down with the ship," someone added. "Blub, blub, blub. . . ."

I couldn't help but warm to the subject. "Funny you'd think of the *Titanic* at a time like this." I really shouldn't have joined the fray. It wasn't as if I could hop a helicopter back to Seattle. This was seven straight days of family. It was not *The Love Boat*.

"Well, the science is not yet all in on global warming," one of my siblings picked up the cause. "Didn't you get the e-mail I sent, Behba, by the University of Virginia professor who believes it's all a hoax?"

Everyone eagerly waited for my retort. In my family we tease that in any argument someone must always be sitting in the "hot seat." Sometimes it is my designated chair. I considered saying that even *Scientific American* had declared that the climate debate was over: greenhouse gases had reached record, unsustainable levels that were destroying the planet's delicate climate. But I hesitated. Forget global warming—what were my own chances of surviving this hot seat? I stared at the tower of sliced pineapple and the three-layer ice cream cake someone had set before me.

"Yes," I began with a sigh. "I got those e-mails. You know, global warming skeptics are not really scientists; they're from think tanks funded by the world's biggest polluters. It's like the way the tobacco companies tried to cast doubt on cigarettes and lung cancer research."

"What about that e-mail I sent everybody that proved Al Gore's movie is full of factual errors?"

I found myself thinking that whoever had invented the "Reply to All" in e-mail should be shot. Being on the family distribution list is like having a virus of Fox News invade my in-box. I had received the endless loops of e-mails from family members citing the very few scientists who still questioned whether global warming was real or human-caused.

"Yeah, I saw that one," I grinned. "That's why they invented the 'Delete' button."

"Hey," one of the nieces delicately tapped her fork against the crystal water glass. "Simmer down. Do we really have to figure out global warming on our Caribbean cruise? Can't we just . . . well, enjoy the scenery? Or each other?"

She was right, of course. But she was immediately drowned out by the debate. I addressed the table with what I believed was a call to common ground: "On climate change, we're all in the same boat."

But my remark was received as criticism. This struck me as odd, until I glanced at a sibling's sunburned face and recognized a put-upon expression. As the eldest child, I tend to believe it's my responsibility to enlighten my younger siblings. They often tell the childhood story of me flouncing in as they labored over Dick and Jane reading assignments. "That's nothing," I informed my siblings with a flourish of my heavy book bag. "Just wait until you get to *third grade!*"

"I suppose you think you're the captain of this boat?" my youngest sibling quipped.

"Sinking, we're sinking!" one of the nephews shouted playfully.

Another family member took up the banner. "It's the sun that's really responsible for global warming, not us."

"Besides," Mother agreed, "maybe it's God's will."

Code word for End Times, I thought glumly and tackled a piece of glazed pineapple. If I tried to take on global warming and the Rapture at the same time I was sure I would capsize.

"You know," someone began, "Revelation says the world will end in fire. I always thought that was nuclear war, but maybe it will be global warming . . . one of the Tribulations. I mean, if the science is really true."

I surprised myself by reflexively quoting Revelation: "Fire came down from God out of heaven. So you mean we're right on schedule?" I asked. "No worries. It's God's plan?"

"Maybe so."

Even with the blast of air conditioning in the ship's dining room, I was burning up. I turned to the table. "How come you can doubt evidence of global warming, but you don't ever doubt all these End Times interpretations of Revelation?"

"Well, honey, the Bible says we will be swept up to meet Christ midair," my mother jumped in. She is always exhilarated by the good fight. "We truly hope you'll be lifted up to heaven with us."

I was about to protest, but suddenly I was distracted by the thought: What if I was wrong and my family was right all along about the Rapture? What if while floating on this little cruise ship of a world, the tropical heavens suddenly parted wide and I saw my whole family ascending on chariots of fire? Wouldn't I want to be with them? I pictured myself on an upside-down, tilting *Titanic*, like in the movie with all the passengers clawing their way to higher decks. Wouldn't I take a lifeboat or a chariot of fire if it were offered, especially if my whole family was onboard, reaching their loving arms out to me?

Then the sad but somehow bracing thought struck me: no, I would want to stay onboard and go down with the ship. Perhaps this was where the rather blissful memory of having drowned as a child came in handy. I realized that I would want to sing along with those *Titanic* musicians who serenaded everyone as they sank.

With this realization I at last understood: my family was my first love. Without them, I would be inconsolable. Perhaps if there ever were a Rapture I'd face my first Tribulation—living on this beautiful, battered earth without my family.

"Do you want seconds, honey?" my mother asked. "The dessert table is divine."

Was she trying to rescue me? Or simply end the global warming debate? Whatever, her reminder about the abundant desserts sent many of us stampeding from the table. On the buffet line, an ice sculpture of a swan was slowly melting, infinitesimally.

One of my nieces, Sasha, who has spent her summers between university studies working in African clinics, came alongside me. I had once asked Sasha what she believed were the greatest problems facing her generation. "AIDS," she had answered, without missing a beat. Then she added, "And global warming fits right in there too."

In the dessert line, Sasha now took my arm companionably. "You want to climb the waterfall with us in Jamaica?"

"It's an uphill battle," I said. We both knew I didn't mean the waterfall.

Back at the table I was strangely relieved that the talk had turned to hunting. For one of his fishing trips with my nephew to Alaska I had wanted to present my father with a baseball cap that asked FISH WORSHIP—IS IT WRONG? But instead I gave my nephew a T-shirt with a Ray Troll drawing of a salmon sporting a turban. The caption read: WANTED DEAD OR ALIVE: OL' SALMON BIN LADEN.

At the head of the table, my father sat happily surrounded by his family, his silver head haloed by the light from a porthole. He had retired from the U.S. Forest Service and had worked on international wildlife conservation issues. After his second retirement he'd accepted a temporary position as the interim director of a wildlife museum in southern Missouri. Mother sat next to him, eyeing three bowls of ice cream that were woefully substandard compared to her own glacial creations. Ice cream, melting ice caps—it all swirled in my head as Dad launched into a story of a recent hunting trip near the Arctic Circle to shoot musk ox. "The bush pilot dropped us off in the wilderness with just our guns, our tents, and our GPS navigational devices." He glanced at the table—tenderfoots all. "You know, kids, the musk ox is kind of a relic from the Ice Age."

I did not mention that these creatures from the Pleistocene have complex, matriarchal societies like elephants, or that their populations that year in the National Wildlife Refuge had crashed down to a single animal, or that in Canada 20,000 musk ox had died several winters ago from what scientists called "icing events with rain on snow." I just stared resignedly at my pineapple upside-down cake in its sugary pool of pistachio ice cream. A bad combination.

"The Arctic Circle?" one of my nephews asked. "Isn't that where all the ice is melting?"

Oh, no, we had circled back to climate change. I again felt compelled to launch into a little science lecture of my own. "Yes, arctic ice caps are melting at an alarming rate."

"Arctic ice *is* shrinking," my father acknowledged, "but in the Antarctic the ice is expanding. No one knows why."

"But we do know why!" I protested.

"You just *think* you know," someone said.

I half-expected to be called "smarty pants." I was about to say that I had just read a news story that polar bears were drowning as the arctic ice disappeared. And that in fifty years, two-thirds of the ice bears would be extinct.

Instead, I found myself obsessing about the new *National Geographic* credit card I had just gotten to afford the airfare and other expenses on this cruise. The shiny plastic square was imprinted with a vivid photo of a polar bear poised on an ice flow. On the cruise ship, we used a single credit card as collateral to underwrite all of our on-board purchases. No actual cash was accepted on the ship. We were issued a Royal Caribbean white card on a lavaliere to wear around our necks—as if we had been radio-collared by our creditor. No pretty photos of floating polar bears. The cruise ship card seemed somehow less real. It was so easy to spend mindlessly on the ship— "like Monopoly money," said my brother, who worked in finance at the Pentagon. I feared that my cruise card, minus polar bear, was already maxed out.

"There've been a lot of big climate changes and even ice ages in this planet's history," someone piped up. "It's just cyclical."

"How can you say that?" I finally snapped. "If you still doubt global warming evidence, then you're just in denial."

"Hey, Behba," my brother tried to toss me a life preserver, "did you see that greeting card, 'I'm not living in denial . . . I'm just visiting'?"

Sometimes I imagine families as a kind of Olympics in which everyone has an event. Always the subtle competition, the power struggles, the rivalries and shifting alliances. While I may think my family's event is synchronized swimming, they probably see me as a lonely, long-distance runner—probably running in the wrong direction. In the obstacle course of my own immediate family, the next generation has learned to be less strident and more nimble. Once when the family was debating something by e-mail, my niece sent a note: "I have no comment," she wrote about the raging family feud, ending her sentence with a smiley face icon.

Back at the family dining table, a usually taciturn nephew who is studying aviation ventured into the global warming debate. "You know, we're all addicted to foreign oil."

As the talk turned to automobiles and gas mileage, I breathed a little easier and kept my head down. This was the year that renowned biologist E. O. Wilson published his letter to a Southern Baptist preacher called *The Creation: An Appeal to Save Life on Earth*. Wilson wrote movingly about "the gravitational pull of the natural world on our spirit, and on our souls." He pleaded with the Baptist preacher to find common ground on which "the powerful forces of religion and science can be joined."

In the same year, the "Evangelical Climate Initiative" was launched, acknowledging human causes of global warming and asking Christians to get involved in decreasing carbon dioxide emissions. Our family Caribbean cruise was right on the cusp of the 2008 "Declaration on the Environment and Climate Change," co-authored by James Merritt, a Baptist seminary student and once a self-described "enemy of the environment." Merritt had an epiphany during a university lecture when his professor proclaimed, "When we destroy God's revelations on earth, it's like tearing a page out of the Bible."

The declaration urged Christians to engage in "creation stewardship" and to respond to the climate crisis with "moral passion and concrete action." It caused a rift with more conservative evangelicals; they countered with a resolution that fiercely denied any human responsibility in causing climate change. In his own conservative hometown of Nashville, Al Gore's Nobel Prize for his work on global warming went unacknowledged and his laureate speech was not covered. Yet in Atlanta he was hailed as a "Baptist prophet" by the New Baptist Covenant Celebration and given a Bible with a green cover. And now many so-called "Inconvenient Christians" are working together to face climate change in such groups as Creation Care and Earth Ministry.

How this religious rift plays out in my family is generational. In 2006 my parents and most of my siblings were still debating global warming while the next generation was going green.

At the ship's dining table our ice cream was melted. Feeling somewhat cooler and calmer, I decided I could turn back to the subject of climate change without going down with the ship. So I asked my forester father for some help. "Dad, you're always talking about being wise stewards of the natural world. You were the one who told me the aspen tree colonies are dying out from drought. Do *you* still doubt all the evidence of global warming?"

He eyed me a moment and then answered, "Honey, I won't be around to see if it's as bad as some predict. For now, I'm more concerned with conservation, what we can all do on a practical, everyday level. Like conserving gas, electricity, heat—things that can make a difference every day." My father glanced around the table and seemed gratified to note that all eyes were on him. "One possible solution to lowering greenhouse gases is using more nuclear energy."

"But what about toxic waste?" I asked. Someone had to say it.

My father grinned. "Have you been attending your onboard waste management seminars?"

He had me there. I'd been too busy kayaking in Labadee, hiking in Ocho Rios, and singing at "Family Karaoke" on the ship. I shrugged and said lamely, "Even environmentalists take vacations."

With a nod my father switched the subject back to his hunting trip. "It's weirdly beautiful way up there in the Arctic," he told us. His dark blue eyes seemed more mysterious than usual. "So few people, so much land and water. I flew up there with the guy who owns a huge hunting and fishing store. He flies all over the world on his own jet to go hunting. He's also a major funder for the wildlife museum."

As he talked, I remembered my recent trip to the Ozarks to visit my folks and tour the wildlife museum he had come out of retirement to direct. It was impressive—so many live species of exotic fish and forest animals. My father had proudly showed me around—"We've got a bald eagle, beavers, river otters, bobcats, tropical fish . . . say, honey, we even have a shark"—from the educational woodlands exhibits to the huge aquarium. I was particularly fond of the hammerhead eyeing us.

It was good work he was doing, rescuing both the animals and the people in a museum that was facing bankruptcy. "So many people don't have the money or the equipment to go camping," my father said. "So they come here and get up close and see the animals. Learn about wildlife firsthand."

I've always loved my family's fascination with animals. My parents' house is so full of animal sculptures, paintings, antlers, and bird and chipmunk feeders that it too looks like a wildlife museum. As I'd stood with them in front of the aquarium tank watching a moray eel gnash his fanged teeth, I'd felt the contentment of the wild forest we had first shared together half a century ago—our little family triangle of three living on a million acres of wilderness. As he named each flickering fish, I realized that my father had expanded his conservation from land to sea. I was also proud of his recent work to set aside ocean areas for future generations. He had once invited me to attend a conservation conference on protecting marine ecosystems at Monterey Bay Aquarium. My father took some obvious pride in me, as I observed a fisheries-management roundtable.

For years, my parents have lamented that I could have "used my God-given talents to become a missionary." I always respond that I am a missionary—but from the animals to the humans. Over time my folks have come to embrace my work for wildlife.

I was quite touched to find that at the entrance to his museum, my parents had set up a card table with a stack of copies of my *National Geographic* book on gray whales and my love letter to my Northwest home, *Living by Water*. As visitors entered the museum, my father was like a congenial carnival barker holding up my books and saying, "My daughter here wrote this." I hid rather shyly behind a barricade of books as my father commiserated, "This is kind of like having a lemonade stand . . . except you're a grown-up."

After some long hours of book signing, my father announced heartily, "Let's vamoose. I'll take you for supper at my favorite restaurant. It's right inside the hunting and fishing shop."

As we walked in the door of the gigantic store, a cheerfully rotund woman greeted us like a game show host.

"Fudge?" she asked, pointing to a fortress of chocolate bricks studded with pecans. Then she held out a casual hand. "Check your gun?"

My father grinned and wrapped his arms around my shoulder. "My daughter left *her* gun at home," he told the official welcomer.

Remembering this museum visit with my parents, I listened to Dad finish his musk ox hunting tale to an enthralled family table. He marveled, "Seeing that shaggy musk ox is like going back in time." Then he added fondly, "It's like shooting a wooly mammoth."

"Are you going to make us eat musk ox, Grandpa?" one of the nieces teased. She and several of her sisters are vegetarians.

"Nope," my father laughed. "I didn't get to keep that musk ox. It's hanging on someone's trophy wall. Besides, musk ox doesn't taste so good."

Then someone asked my brother to tell a story that is a family favorite, one that reveals the evolution of hunting in our family. "You all remember when Dad and I went hunting up in Alaska a couple of years ago?" my brother began. We all knew the story. Still, we hung on every word, especially my brother's four daughters, who, like all children, enjoy hearing stories with themselves as main characters.

On that Alaska hunting trip my father had bagged an elk, and my brother shot a small buck. Someone snapped a photo of the father and son standing proudly with their trophies. But when my brother's four-year-old daughter Miranda saw the photo with the small buck strung up right next to the much bigger elk, she mistook the pair for a mother and fawn.

"Why did you kill the baby deer, Daddy?" she had wailed inconsolably.

Patiently my brother tried to explain to his girls that this was not a fawn but a fully grown male deer who could be legally taken. He reasoned with them that deer were overrunning many areas and that hunting was like pruning or culling. Besides, it was a tradition in our family. Fathers putting food on the table for their children. His daughter only wept louder. Miranda wanted to have a funeral for Bambi. She could not believe her father capable of such cruelty.

In the midst of her tears, Miranda came up with a sudden rationalization. "Daddy," she asked, "was that deer trying to hurt you with his horns? Is that why you had to kill the baby deer?"

My brother saw a way out and came up with an idea that seemed right, at the time. "Yes, honey," he said. "I had to protect myself. It was an *attack deer*."

Miranda had instantly accepted this explanation and stopped crying. But several months later, when one of her relatives took her to a wild safari theme park in Florida, the jig was up. With perfect poise, Miranda—who has always been addicted to Animal Planet—gazed happily at black bears, pythons, and tigers. She was not at all afraid of the fearsome predators. But when she got to the exhibit of white-tailed deer, she began screaming in terror, "Attack deer! Attack deer!"

It was then that my brother had to confess that there was no such thing as an attack deer. He had pulled Miranda into his lap and admitted, "Deer are very gentle. They will not harm you."

At the cruise ship's family table, my brother now raised a toast to our mostly teetotaling family. "No more attack deer," he said.

Then someone remarked, "You know, being afraid of a deer attacking is like the environmentalists always warning us the sky is falling."

"Or the seas are rising."

"Well," one of the nieces piped up, "they are . . . the seas are rising."

"Then we'll just float," somebody said. "We'll live on a cruise ship like those elderly people do instead of going into nursing homes. They just book a cabin and sail the world. A good end."

"But what about us?" a nephew asked.

Like many in their generation, my nephews and nieces are very sensitive to environmental issues. They send me green petitions and health alerts: pollution-related asthma is up 400 percent; grassroots organizations are cleaning up salmon streams; activists are protesting Japanese whaling. Once, at a niece's wedding reception, my three nephews raced out of the bar to witness green sea turtles coming ashore to lay their eggs. They sat on the sand half the night in their best dress suits, mesmerized by the mother sea turtle digging a safe deposit for her next generation.

"Hey, speaking of underwater, who wants to sign up for swimming with stingrays tomorrow off the Bahamas?" my nephew now asked everyone.

I was not surprised that all ten of my nieces and nephews raised their hands. Over more dessert, we were eagerly planning our Grand Cayman adventure when I glanced over at Catherine, who was happily eating a lobster tail drenched in butter.

"It's my second helping of lobster," she announced with gusto.

Several minutes later Catherine stood bolt upright from the table, her face drained of all color. She is always the tannest of us all, favoring her mother's darkly elegant Eastern European features. So it was shocking to see my niece go pale as paper. Catherine clutched at her throat.

"Daddy," she said in a strangled voice, "it's happening."

She meant anaphylactic shock. For all of her eighteen years Catherine has suffered from asthma and food allergies. A half-dozen times she has ended up in the ER, and the last time before our cruise she almost died. While it sometimes seemed that she was allergic to almost everything, Catherine had never had any reaction to lobster.

"Where's your epinephrine kit?" My brother was at his daughter's side in a nanosecond, propping her up and dragging her from the table.

Catherine shook her head, tears streaming down her face. She began to tremble uncontrollably. "Cabin," she managed to say. "Left it . . . "

My brother signaled to me, and I immediately took Catherine's other arm, my own heart pounding. The three of us moved together like a centipede with one body and many legs as my brother and I maneuvered Catherine through the dining room and toward the elevators.

"I think the ER is all the way down on the first deck," my brother said, his voice very calm so as not to further alarm his daughter. But his blue eyes were blazing, pupils dilated with fear.

"Faint . . . ," Catherine said and her knees buckled between us.

We knew we had only minutes to get her down the six decks to the ship's emergency room. Where was the elevator?

"We're going to have to walk her down the ship's stairs," my brother said grimly as Catherine began to slump and stumble.

How we dragged Catherine down six grand stairways I'll never know, but we did. All the while I was talking to her as my brother did most of the heavy lifting. Catherine's half-closed eyes fluttered, and she nodded. But her lips were tinged blue, and my brother was now completely carrying her weight. Any moment she would slip into unconsciousness. We might lose her this time.

By the time we staggered into the ER, Catherine was shivering, her skin cool and her pulse erratic. The ER doctor, a South African woman, immediately recognized the extreme danger. "Lay her down on the table right now. We've got to find a vein for an IV push of epinephrine."

The doctor strapped an oxygen mask over Catherine's face and told me, "Keep talking to her and keep her with us."

Slowly Catherine began to find her breathing rhythm again, but her blood oxygen and pulse were still quite low and her vital signs sluggish. My brother began singing to his daughter as he stroked her arm—little ditties and then our grandfather's lullaby.

Lu, La Lu. . . . My brother's beautiful tenor floated above the chitter and blink of the emergency room equipment.

Under her oxygen mask, Catherine's eyes streamed tears. "Behba," she called my family nickname. Her breath was ragged.

"Remember when we went whale watching off Monterey and you had an asthma attack?" I asked, holding her hand. It was cold. "You breathed your way out of it."

She nodded, tears streaming down her cheeks under the oxygen mask. I had an idea. I ran up the seven decks of stairs to my cabin and grabbed my laptop. Back in the ER, I perched on Catherine's hospital bed and set the laptop on the stainless-steel bed table. Then I played her a video of a recent whale-watching cruise I'd taken with my Summer Tree Institute "pod" off the coast of southern California. I'd been promising to play this video for my nieces and nephews for the whole cruise; I never expected that I would be showing this footage in the emergency room.

Catherine's eyes, still full of tears, fixed on the small screen as she watched the video:

On the open ocean, a colorful crowd of us lean way over the bow rails, laughing and joyfully calling to a sudden super-pod of dolphins surrounding our whole boat. "Everywhere you look!" I am shouting as I lean way out of the boat. "Dolphins everywhere you look!"

Wave after wave, a tsunami of dolphins rises up on every side of us. Our boat is just a miniature metal cork bobbing in a sea that is primal, blessed with abundance—like at the beginning of the world. Three thousand dolphins, both above and below water, surf and leap over the white caps, following a school of fish. There are newborn calves sailing in their mother's slipstreams and an ultrasonic thunder we can only barely hear as the dolphins talk right over us. In synch they soar and pirouette and splash down so that the spray of all those sleek, silver bodies rises up and drenches us. Sunlight and saltwater shine in rainbow prisms, and we are bedazzled, hanging over the rails with unabashed happiness.

"Oh." Catherine now breathed and breathed and breached up from her body's collapse. "I want to see that . . . thousands of dolphins . . . in my lifetime. You think dolphins will be here?"

"They will," I said firmly and held her hand. "And you will."

She was warmer now, and rosiness was returning to her cheeks. Gone was the shallow breathing of shock.

The ER doctor, who had joined us to watch the video, nodded to the nearby machines. "Vital signs stabilizing," she said, and there was a touch of awe in her voice. "Beautiful."

My brother was grinning with relief. "Can we get a copy of that video for medicine?"

Catherine gestured for me to lean nearer. She whispered, "Remember what I used to want to be when I grew up?"

"Yes," I smiled and kissed her forehead. "I remember."

Ever since she was a child, Catherine had wanted to be a dolphin trainer. Now she was a college freshman majoring in sociology. But after this last near-death experience on our cruise, Catherine recognized that she was at a turning point in her life. She decided to take a temporary break from college. Instead, she volunteered as an intern at the Dolphin Research Center in the Florida Keys. Every day she studied and worked with bottlenose dolphins and helped educate the public about the plight of cetaceans in polluted seas. She sent us all e-mail albums of the dolphins and a huge green sea turtle she helped rescue from fishing nets. My favorite photo is of Catherine with a dolphin tattoo.

Catherine and her big sister Elizabeth are now both considering careers involving wildlife, following in a family tradition. Catherine wants to continue her work with dolphins; Elizabeth is majoring in psychology and hopes that she and her sister will use their education to combine psychology and animal welfare. They dream of perhaps even opening up a business together to help animals. Elizabeth is particularly interested in the new trans-species psychology, like the post-traumatic stress studies now being done with elephants by ecologist-psychologist Dr. Gay Bradshaw of the Kerulos Center.

The next day, as we peacefully swam alongside dozens of mysterious stingrays off Grand Cayman Island, Elizabeth confided, "I always pray for the animals as well as us humans."

* * *

ON THE FINAL DAY of the family cruise, my brother and I toured the Mayan ruins of Tulum. "You know, sis," he told me, "the Pentagon is taking global warming very seriously. When we get back to the ship, you should Google 'General Zinni.' He's working with retired generals and admirals to study the military threats from global warming."

"Why should I Google the general when I've got you?" In the heat we were both drenched in sweat. I leaned against my brother as if for some slim shade.

Seven years younger than me, my brother Dana is tall, good-looking, and thoughtful. Though he was my live doll when we were children—one of my hips is permanently tilted from carrying him as a baby—he has grown to become a mature voice in our family. He is often the family mediator. Not what one usually thinks of in a military man. Soft-spoken, he nevertheless is firm in his beliefs as a conservative Christian and moderate Republican. By his own admission, his social politics are sometimes less moderate than my parents. He is the only one of my siblings with whom I can actually talk about my own more mystical inclinations. He also has inherited my mother's far-ranging curiosity about the world; in his military job he has traveled abroad much more than any of us. It did not surprise me that Dana and I were the only ones in the family who opted for this Mayan temple tour.

It was a voraciously hot day, cloudless, with the sun blaring down on us as we stood before the ancient stone steps of El Castillo, the rock tower dominating the cliff above the Caribbean. El Castillo didn't deter the Spaniards who arrived here on the Yucatan coast in 1518 to convert and conquer. But the heat did almost stop us. Already we had seen several people, one a young girl, faint from the 105-degree temperature.

"Maybe climate change is the real terrorism." Dana pulled me into the slight shade of a tree. "Hurricanes, flooding, water shortages, diseases, environmental refugees—that's a recipe for military disasters around the world. A lot of guys in the military are saying that global warming can cause wars—that's why it's a real threat to our national security."

"How come you didn't bring this little detail up at the dinner table, bro?" I demanded. "I could have used some reinforcements."

"Well," Dana smiled and readjusted his sunglasses, which had slipped off his nose to reveal a wink, "I figured you were holding down the fort okay. Besides, you've got a continent between you and the family and can escape after this cruise. I'm always in the fray."

Nearby a Mayan guide was shouting to a red-faced gaggle of other tourists so we could easily eavesdrop.

"Tulum is sacred to Mayans," the guide said. "Before AD 700, it was the most important religious and commercial center on this coast, with really sophisticated cities and irrigation systems and over a million people in city-states that rivaled ancient Rome."

"But why did the Mayans die out?" a little girl demanded.

"We didn't." The guide grinned and squatted on his knees to speak to her at eye level. "Some of us descendants are still right here, *muchacha!*"

The guide then went on to explain that there were several reasons for the decline and fall of this once-mighty civilization, including a drought that lasted over 150 years and royal infighting between superpowers who were also family. "With such terrible droughts, there was a lot of petty warfare," the guide explained. "We've learned from Mayan hieroglyphics that one royal brother actually ritually sacrificed another."

My own brother nudged me and playfully pulled my straw hat down over my eyes. "Better watch out, sis," he said.

As we listened to the guide go on with the grisly details of the dynastic spat, I couldn't help but think back to the family dinner table. While we all hotly argued global warming and the gospel according to the Book of Revelation, were we just a ship of fools sailing toward environmental apocalypse?

In the shadow of these Mayan ruins, I wondered: do people have to get so close to extinction to change? The meaning of the word *apocalypse* is "revelation." Is it possible to have revelation without apocalypse? Can we really learn from the environmental collapses of past civilizations? If so, perhaps we can imagine more than the destruction of the world. Perhaps we can envision our way into a future in which the earth survives *with* us—a natural world in which extinction (the wrong kind of rapture) is not the only option. When the Bible promises, "We shall all be changed," why not consider this a form of skillful and soulful adapting rather than simply dying out?

Once when I was teaching creative writing in the bright deserts of Arizona, I was troubled by the fact that my university fiction students simply killed off so many of their characters instead of trying to imagine alternative lives for them. It was as if they were practicing Pac-Man instead of storytelling. So for an entire semester I forbade anyone to kill off a character—*no matter what.*

My writing students had complained mightily. But soon they began to attach to their characters more empathetically and to expand their characters' possibilities. Plots changed, relationships between characters opened up, there was a commitment to continuing lives. A love scene was much harder to write than a death scene, they discovered, and a life was much more complicated to complete than one cut short by lack of imagination.

"You know," the Mayan guide concluded his talk, "some scientists are saying that Mayan civilization was destroyed by a big swing cycle when the sun got way too bright and changed the climate."

"So let's get out of this sun." My brother grabbed my arm again, and we fled along the stone path toward the nearby *cenote*, or underground springs.

In the cool *cenote*, my brother and I floated on our backs, buoyed by saltwater. We floated, sun-blessed, beneath a still-benevolent sky.

"Admit it, sis," my brother splashed me. "You're actually having fun on this family cruise."

"Yeah," I said slowly, just realizing it myself. "I am. I didn't expect it."

"You didn't expect the Spanish Inquisition?" Dana said, quoting Monty Python. "Think of it! We didn't sink the ship."

As my brother and I drifted, I reached out a hand to take his as we used our yellow plastic flippers to propel ourselves through a rock tunnel.

"Remember when we climbed Dunn's River Falls in Jamaica?" I asked him dreamily.

Was it only a few days ago that we had stood warily at the foot of the two-story-high waterfall, encouraging each other as we climbed? Slipping on the moss, falling on the narrow ledges, completely soaked by the cascade of chill water, some of us doubted we could finish the climb.

"Hold hands," a niece called out.

"No . . . if one of us slips, all of us fall down."

"Let's do it," a nephew ordered. "We can make it if we create a human chain."

Hand to hand, my nieces and nephews and my siblings all held each other steady. Again and again when we stumbled on the slick stone we found our footing, even as the waterfall crashed over us. We ascended, laughing. And no one was left behind.

eleven

When We All Get to Heaven
(Baptist hymn)

"DO YOU REALLY WANT TO DROWN . . . AGAIN?" A RELATIVE ASKED ME
when I announced that I was off to the Grand Canyon for a rafting
trip down the mighty Colorado River. "What is it anyway about you
and water?"

As always when talking with my family, I carefully considered my
answers. Sometimes I imagine a multiple-choice quiz to calibrate
which response will be the most "family correct."

My options were: (a) Taoists naturally follow the "Water Way";
(b) as an amateur Jungian astrologer I'd discovered that my birth
chart has a Grand Trine in Water, so this element is my greatest gift
and teacher; or (c) it was a free, once-in-a-lifetime trip with other nature writers. In return we would each contribute an essay to an anthology entitled *Writing Down the River*.

For once, I didn't engage in an endless loop of spiritual debate.
Besides, I knew this relative disapproved of astrology as "of the
devil." Perhaps I've learned a little over the years. So I considered my
answers and chose the one that seemed the least charged.

"Well," my relative laughed. In our family radar I could hear perhaps some relief on her part. "Who can turn down a free trip?"

Our rafting guides on the Colorado River spoke of "the River" as
one might the Almighty—with a respectful sense of its sacred power.

Some of them had lost friends on the river or they themselves had capsized and been at the mercy of another kind of liquid gravity. Over the two weeks of camping and river rafting, we had all fallen into a kind of trance akin to worship. I was reading my waterlogged copy of Lao-tzu's *Tao Te Ching* in a new translation by Ursula LeGuin.

Water and Stone

What's softest in the world
rushes and runs
Over what's hardest in the world.

These pastel limestone canyons were so ancient that there was no carbon-dating them. Striated in lavender, rose, and green, the steep walls revealed the slow sculpting of glacial force, from Mesozoic layers down to the bottom of Paleozoic time. Edging the river was black, volcanic schist like the scrawling of a giant. "No one knows how old this stone is," our guide said. "Older than anything human, that's for sure." Her eyes were hooded with reverence.

That first week on the river we spent our days looking upward at the slim chasm of blue sky, like the suggestion of another world far above. But that gazing upward soon gave way to keeping our eyes steadily on the ever-changing river—the Almighty. One moment it was mesmerizingly flat, like a lagoon reflecting the pastel purples and dark rose colors of the embracing canyon walls. The next minute we descended into the frightening glory and roaring blur of whitewater as we hung in the air, almost upside down.

One day, midrapids and midair, our river raft shot up at a perilous right angle to the roiling Colorado River. Stomachs lurching, we then dropped the height of three stories, splashing into the watery zigzag and turbulence of Tiger Wash Rapid.

"Do we need to do a woman overboard drill?" our river guide shouted, leaning hard against her oars to keep the raft pointed straight through the churning, blood-red waters. I glanced around at everyone in my boat to do a quick head count. All eighteen of us were still attached to each other in toboggan-like postures—a little human train of bodies wedged within each other's legs. Our orange life preservers were soaked, and our faces were dazed and grinning, much the way chimpanzees grin when terrified.

Eighteen of us adventurers—mostly strangers to each other—were rafting down the Colorado for two weeks, along with several elders, a young and adventurous family—"river rats," as the repeat runners called themselves—and our stalwart crew. Lava Falls Rapid, the mightiest and most dangerous of all the rapids would be our last near the end of the river. Even our guides were uncharacteristically serious as they prepared us for this rapid rated five for difficulty.

"Sometimes we capsize at Lava Falls," they had told us. "It happens to the best of us. If it happens to our boat, stay calm and swim toward the light. Sometimes if you're sunk in a keeper, you can't tell which way is up."

A "keeper" was their word for the sometimes fatal whirlpools that pull people and boats into them like a black hole. "A place of no return," our guide said gravely.

"That's what they always tell you when you die," someone tried to make a joke of the warnings. "Go toward the light."

"Good advice," our guide said in a voice like a snapping turtle. Then she added more amiably, "All I'm saying is, this is not Disneyland."

Whether we were drifting lazily, bodies stretched out on pontoons to sunbathe or shivering in our bobsled positions as a chilly wave pummeled us, I kept my eyes on the woman who always perched in the front of the boat. She was our matriarch, Maude, and we had quit volunteering to sit in the bow and take the brunt of the river because Maude had so fully claimed this perilous place. At seventy, she was the oldest and seemed too frail to take up this post—half lookout scout, half sacrifice. Maude was the first to get dunked. She was also the first to see around the next bend to what awaited us all.

"I'm the elder," she had explained simply. "I go before you."

What she told only a few of us and did not share with everyone was that she was dying of kidney cancer. This was to be her last trip. She told us she came to her beloved Colorado to "memorize the river so I can learn how to move between the worlds when my time comes."

Time did not seem to exist here. Just the river. I could understand how Maude, as her own time grew near, wanted to be in a place that felt eternal. Sometimes the river was calm and sunlit; other times it was hard going, relentless. We just hoped to keep afloat, keep our heads up. Go toward the light.

"What I like about the river is that everything makes sense," Maude had said the night before we dared Lava Falls Rapid. "Perspective, you know."

"Don't sweat the small stuff?" someone ventured.

"Yeah, and you realize that you are in the presence of something much greater than yourself . . . call it God or nature."

"Or the river . . . ," someone finished in a soft, dreamy voice.

That last night, as on all the nights before, we had made camp in the shelter of red rocks on the shore of the Colorado. We had all grown accustomed to the river's voice. Unlike the rhythmic rise and fall of ocean surf, it was a constant baritone, like the seesaw of huge, watery cellos. Fluid, but forceful. We bathed in the river daily, and our bodies were caked in the dry red of river mud. If some of us had started out this trip with tidy khaki or primary-colored shorts and tank tops, we all now appeared downright aboriginal in the monochrome of our rusty skin and clothes. Like creatures whose colors change to fit their habitat, we all now resembled the river.

It was even hard to tell who was old and who was young because our skin was sun-baked and layered with fine sand. Ageless, timeless, with no distractions from the world above. We had no cell phones, only one satellite phone for emergencies. No radios that worked this deep inside the canyon, and no computers or any other way to keep track of the doings of other humans. It wasn't just "no politics, no religion," it was close to "no people." Except us. And we weren't exactly people anymore. We belonged to the river. We were creatures who needed the shelter of stone, the comfort of an evening fire, the sustenance of the food we carried with us. We were more animals or early humans who depended on water for thirst, for travel, and sometimes for burial.

In a way, Maude told us that last night that she was experiencing her own last rites, while she was still alive. Her husband and several of her family members were on this river trip alongside her. "Who says you can't take them with you?" Maude had teased.

She was comfortable talking about her imminent death. It was a done deal—the next rapids—and she was matter-of-fact.

We whittled sticks for toasting tiny marshmallows over the fire. "This is my idea of heaven," Maude said.

"S'mores?" someone asked with a laugh. "That's heaven for a sweet tooth."

"No." Maude was serious. "Here, this river, this camp, this canyon. It's the closest place to heaven that I know."

Maybe it was the sugar, maybe it was the dread of Lava Falls Rapid the next day, maybe it was Maude as our guide to the beyond. Somehow we all got on the subject of the next world.

"What do you think heaven looks like?" a young man asked Maude. "I mean the heaven that's after this earth?"

"Ah," she smiled. In the firelight, her smooth face was ageless. "You're assuming there *is* another heaven besides here."

"Well, yeah, that's what most people think, isn't it?"

"And what do you think?" Maude asked the man. He was German, and we teased him that he was "travel-mad" because he had been almost everywhere we could name. He already had his next trip planned—to Ethiopia.

"I don't know," he answered. "But I like to plan and prepare for my trips." His face lit up and he grinned. "Even my afterlife. I would like to know where I'm going. And what it looks like."

"So you can pack?" our guide suggested.

"So I can know how to live," he answered.

"Good idea." Maude burst out laughing and took a few minutes to make an utterly perfect s'more. We all clapped at the luminous ooze of marshmallow between chocolate and graham crackers. "But really," she continued more thoughtfully, "how do you all imagine heaven?"

"I think maybe it's like a huge intergalactic train station," the German traveler suggested. "You can decide which train to take and where. But perhaps someone puts you on the train you deserve to take."

"Heaven is a giant, glittering city with no slums or poor people," someone else said. "You can build your own house, work if you want to, and there is so much love no one ever feels lost."

As the campfire itself glittered, we all leaned closer for warmth and to listen to one another. Most of us sat cross-legged now, sleeping bags wrapped around our shoulders. Beside us the river rushed by on its own way to eternity.

"What if there's nothing?" an older man asked, his face a play of light and shadows from the fire. "I mean, if you just go back to being part of the cosmos. Not some individual soul, but some kind of consciousness that is absorbed into the whole?"

"Could be," Maude nodded, rocking back and forth on her knees. She reached in and adjusted the wood, its white ashes disintegrating at her touch.

"I think heaven is a kind of school," I offered, joining in the dialogue. "You review your life with guardians or guides and then wisely decide what lessons in your next life you'd like to understand."

"Yeah, but what if you flunk out of heaven?" someone chimed in. "Do you believe in hell . . . like the worst detention hall ever?"

"I think heaven and hell are here," another fire-tender answered. "And there are all sorts of prisons . . . or detention halls. Sometimes they are called religion."

We fell quiet, letting the river talk. It occurred to me that we were in a kind of geological underworld and the Colorado was the River Styx ferrying us to our destinies. But this underworld, unlike Hades, was lush with life and beauty. Being here on the river was a vigorous meditation. Far above us was the world we had left behind, the "rim life," as our guides called it, almost as an afterthought. Its busy distractions and demands seemed irrelevant here, even silly. No news. No possessions. If a nuclear bomb went off, we might not even know about it. We rarely even saw a plane zip by. We were a small tribe of travelers who belonged more to the river than ourselves, like the original dwellers, the *Anasazi*, whose rough-hewn doorways stood sentry in the pink granite cliffs.

The novelist and poet Linda Hogan, who was also on this trip, seemed to have this in mind when she reminded us, "Native people believe that spirits can come back to watch over us and the earth."

In Seattle my desk looks out on the Salish Sea at the island birthplace of Chief Seattle, a nature preserve of ancient cedar. I remembered his words:

> Our dead never forget the beautiful world
> that gave them being.
> They still love its winding rivers,
> its great mountains, and its sequestered vales,
> and they ever yearn in tenderest affection
> over the lonely-hearted living
> and often return to visit and comfort them.

Chief Seattle's words echo the Buddhist concept of the *bodhisattva*, or those enlightened beings who volunteer to return to this world to help others achieve wisdom and liberation. As we continued our late-night dialogue imagining heaven, I was struck at how few people brought up any sense of judgment day, or punishment for earthly deeds. There were no circles of hell or limbo. Someone did mention the *bardos* of the *Tibetan Book of the Dead*—not as chastisement, however, but as a kind of spiritual maze in which the soul struggles to find peace and clarity.

No one asked Maude how she imagined the afterlife, since she seemed closer to that mystery than we were. "Well," she finally took her turn, "I may be in heaven before you . . . unless Lava Falls takes us all together. So I'll go first and say this: I think the afterlife is a bright and powerful river that carries you anywhere in the universe you want to visit."

"Like the Milky Way?" someone asked.

We all smiled and lay back on our sleeping bags and stared up at the narrow slit of night sky far above. Most of us slept under the stars with no tents, luxuriating in the cool desert air. For a long time I gazed up, trying to figure out half a constellation visible between canyon cliffs. Was it the Pleiades?

*   *   *

IT OCCURRED TO ME that night deep in the canyon that in all the decades I'd discussed religion with my family we had never had a dialogue imagining the afterlife. I mean, what did it really look like after we all got Raptured? Or as the Baptist hymn proclaims:

> *When we all get to heaven*
> *What a day of rejoicing that will be.*

Besides rejoicing, what was going on up there? My memory scanned every sermon I'd ever heard as I tried to recall any story describing heaven itself. All I could remember were Christ's words that "in my father's house are many mansions." There was also some mention of streets of gold and semi-precious stones. Would everyone have a mansion, no matter their class on earth? Would the meek also inherit heaven? Would there even be the concepts of more or less in such a paradise? I remembered reading the Greek tragedy *Antigone*, in which Sophocles, through his anguished heroine, asks if after death we are all equal. I also recalled a Russian friend of mine telling me a Ukrainian joke: In heaven everyone is having fun flying around and enjoying their afterlife, but a boy asks his father why there is a big wall on one side of heaven. "Christians built it," the father replies. And when the boy asks why, the father adds, "Because the Christians believe they are the only ones here."

In college I'd studied Dante's *Inferno*, with its well-organized circles of hell, I'd dutifully plowed through Milton's *Paradise Lost* and *Regained*, and I'd wandered amid William Blake's mystical visions. But in these books there was more symbolism than actual details of daily (or eternal) life. I was also familiar with gospel spirituals expressing the hope of immigrants or slaves, who had lost so much in this world, through visions of sunset mountains, exotic gardens, and rivers over yonder. The river imagery was particularly poignant since so many slaves in the South were forbidden to learn to swim for fear they might just float "down river." That is where the saying "sold up the river" comes from.

I'd noticed that even in the best-selling "Left Behind" series, the drama still takes place here on earth. Why, if it is their fervent destination, do the Rapture folk never focus on heaven itself? One would think that in trying to sell salvation and a better world than this, there would be more enticement than "it's better over yonder." Do we sign up to be guardian angels for those we love and have left below? Or do we just rejoice in our own luxurious mansions while leaving sinners to suffer? Where is the compassion of the New Testament Christ, or the mercy?

And where is the commitment? Is the best that an End Times believer can offer another person the conditional promise: "I'll stay with you until something better comes along. I'm just passing through, you know." Isn't it possible to have a relationship with others and with the earth that is loyal, generous, and long-lasting?

I often wonder if the magnificent seer of the Book of Revelation, John of Patmos, might be branded a false prophet today. He was writing at a turning point in history when Rome was killing early Christians and the battle was over allegiance to Caesar or Christ. Adopting the popular apocalyptic style, John the prophet offered Revelation as a vision of victory for the oppressed faithful few. The poet's visions are a pageant of deliverance and a dramatic prediction of the downfall of Rome. My favorite definition of the word "prophet" is this: someone who simply tells us the way things are.

When Revelation was written, Christians were a persecuted minority, so the book offered hope of freedom from any worldly governments that would destroy them. But too often for the 47 percent of Americans who are said to believe in the Rapture, Revelation is no longer a poem of suffering and stamina for a small group of early Christians but instead the party line. For Rapture believers, heaven is a gated community.

Once I heard a theologian ask, "What if the Bible was written symbolically and we are taking it literally?" Literal-minded interpretations of John's magnificent poem of Revelation have reduced it to "the Good, the Bad, and the Ugly." In the same way that we need not just technicians but poets, musicians, and painters to be the first into space to look back and describe our watery planet to us, we also need interpreters to study Revelation as the timeless poetry it is. We need prophets who tell us the way things are so that we can prepare for the future. Too often Revelation is interpreted in a narrow way that is like holding up a tiny magnifying glass to one iota of geologic time written in Grand Canyon stone and proclaiming a prophecy for how our one tiny trip down the river would turn out.

*   *   *

THAT LAST NIGHT OF our Colorado River trip, I was delighted to listen to people's visions of the afterlife. Having this discussion with Maude, our matriarch, who would bravely go before us, was an honor. Her attitude was both practical and playful.

"I'm just so *curious* about what comes next," Maude said as we all watched her face in the firelight. She smiled. "Sometimes I can almost glimpse it, just out of the corner of my eyes. But then, like a dream, it's gone."

"But what do you see in just that glimpse?" the young German man asked. Possibly he was booking his travel there.

Maude paused, cocking her head as if listening more than seeing. We listened with her: the cascading roar of the river, the wispy breeze through tamarisk trees, and the delicate trill of a canyon wren. "Light," she finally said very softly. "A different light."

We did not press her for more details. It was late and Lava Falls Rapid awaited us next morning.

"Time to turn in," our river guide told us with the authority of a mother putting her wound-up children to bed. "No more talk of heaven now. We need to give our complete attention to the river."

"Give it to the river"—we all echoed the motto that was our answer to almost everything here in the grandest of all canyons.

Dutifully, I lay in my sleeping bag, my eyes wide open to memorize the slip of sky: there was the top of Cassiopeia and Orion's Belt. I couldn't sleep. Instead, I remembered the closest description of the afterlife that I had ever heard. It was from Rachel MacKenzie, my beloved first editor.

The last time I had said good-bye to Rachel in her New York apartment, I felt her spine shift as if she were already untethered from her body. Startled at her frailty, tears blurred my eyes. But Rachel shook her head, and from her couch sickbed she had motioned to me that it was all right to leave her. "But keep the door open when you go," Rachel whispered in her delicate voice. "So I can listen to your footsteps on the way out."

The night before she died, I had a dream that Rachel came to perch rather professionally at the end of my bed. She looked exactly as she had the last time I saw her: luminous hair swept up in a bun, black glasses perched low on her nose, that familiar, faint smile as if she was pondering some kindly private observation.

"You?" I was so happy to see Rachel. In my dream, I sat up in bed. "Are you really here?"

"No," Rachel answered softly. "I'm not. I'm in a different place."

"Where? What's it like? Are you all right?"

"Yes," Rachel nodded thoughtfully. "And I want to tell you something important."

"Tell me!"

"Where I am, there is still suffering." Her expression was fiercely tender. "But . . . but you understand everything."

And then she was gone. The next morning I got a call that Rachel had died from the congestive heart failure that haunted her final years. To this day I keep her last handwritten note to me framed on my desk. And sometimes Rachel still visits my dreams, as if to edit my life.

That last night in the Grand Canyon, when I could not sleep, I found myself asking Rachel if she might consider being a guardian angel for our descent into Lava Falls Rapid. And we also had Maude with us.

*   *   *

As usual, Maude took her position in the bow of the boat. She was dressed for the dangerous occasion in her brilliant red slicker with a yellow rain hat tied under her chin. Along with the water sandals we all wore, she had added long waterproof nylon pants, and she had clipped her fanny pack to her life preserver for easy access. Despite all the sensible gear, Maude had added Hopi silver earrings that dangled spiderweb turquoise stones. As our raft rose and fell in the increasing turbulence, Maude's earrings made a little silver melody.

Sitting strapped to the boat behind Maude, I held on to the ropes on either side of me as if the river were a rodeo ride.

"Wahoooo!" we all hollered out loud as our raft hit the first rapids of Lava Falls Rapid's 900-foot run. Short, but brutal.

These falls are legendary for their sideways gravitational pull. That is why our river guides had warned us that to avoid capsizing we had to veer to the right shore and sluice down along the bank.

Swept into this watery tornado, our raft first sank in a dizzying descent and then stood upright on its stern. We all shouted out in alarm as the boat spun around like a rubber top, then sashayed vertically down the roiling red waves. The water might as well have been a trampoline as we bounced into midair and then free-fell the precipitous thirty-seven feet back into the rapids with a body-jolting splash.

Gripping the ropes for dear life, I looked for Maude and saw that she had hooked her feet rodeo-style under the boat straps and was hollering. She threw out her arms to the cold, muddy water swamping us. "Hallelujah!" Maude sang out as a wave whomped her.

We all disappeared into a whirlpool that sucked us downward. We swirled underwater for what seemed hours, but was really only seconds, before the river spat us back up into the air. As we ascended up into this world, Maude was still there riding point on our raft. We had not capsized. We rode the rapids.

Maude's face was radiant as she cried out, "Isn't this everything you always wanted?"

twelve

Song in a Strange Land

(Psalm 137:4)

YEARS LATER I WOULD THINK OF MAUDE AND THE CONVERSATION ON that Colorado River rafting trip when we tried to imagine heaven. My family had gathered together in a Forest Service cabin on a lake near Ocala, Florida, for a Christmas reunion. No familiar rapids of family debating faith, just the still waters of a natural lake.

The nieces and nephews whom I'd taken swimming with dolphins as children were now in their twenties. While they were almost all evangelical Christians, they had as keen and concerned an eye on this world as on the next. To my great relief, not one of this next generation had yet tried to save me.

Still, I had my doubts about spending the holidays in one cabin with the whole family gang. But my anxiety eased when I noted that the cabin, with its large room of bunk beds, generous kitchen, and stone fireplace, was embraced by acres of tall trees. I could always escape into the forest's hot springs and swamps, these lush "wet prairies" where *The Yearling* was filmed. And after enduring Seattle's winter-long rain shadow, it was exhilarating to gaze out from the sunlit pine cabin. Its tin roof was bright as a mirror, and its sensible brown wooden siding reminded me of the cabin I first lived in as a child. Its wide windows overlooked a lake surrounded by national forest. Adorned with the ancient lace of Spanish moss, stately euca-lyptus trees seemed to breathe for us.

We spent most of our time on the sturdy dock or in rowboats that could seat four of us at a time. One morning, as I rowed lazily across the lake with several of my nieces, I listened to them tell stories of their summer mission work in Africa. All three had spent their sum-mers volunteering in AIDS clinics in Africa or in Mexican or Cuban missions. All three were fluent in Spanish and their university studies were devoted to public health, English literature, and education. The youngest, Sissy, was taking a course in Islam to better understand that faith.

As we slowly circled the lake, morning mists were drifting up from the warm water like spirits. I teased my three nieces, "Our fam-ily is living proof that there must be some kind of God gene."

"Actually, there is a God gene," Sasha, the young scientist, com-mented. "Our brains are hardwired to believe."

She went on to explain that some neurologists believe there are genes that influence the brain chemicals associated with an emo-tional sensitivity to what they call "self-transcendence."

"You know," Sissy interpreted, "a sense of oneness . . . a connec-tion to something bigger than us."

"I know, honey," I smiled. "And I think it must be hereditary."

"It is," Sasha concluded. "But it's also built right into our brains. Prefrontal and temporal lobe stuff. You know, we can feel God's pres-ence when some brain circuits—like those tuned to fight or flight—are quiet, like when you're praying."

"Or rowing along on a lake," I smiled, as our boat glided in the water with hardly a sound. Only the creak of the oars, the trill and chirp of a white ibis, wings rippling the warm air.

It occurred to me that the spiritual solace that I sought in nature and my family found in religion might be much the same. If my brain was wired to circuits most mystical, wasn't it also always tuned to the earth? Did my beliefs and my physical sense of belonging to this world run along the same neuropathways? "Hey, couldn't just one of you devout Christians have turned out to be a wild pagan or a Buddhist or something?" I asked. "Just to keep me company?"

"I like the Dalai Lama," Sissy answered with a grin. "He's doing a lot of good in the world. I just don't believe he's any kind of god."

"Neither does he." I turned to Sasha the scientist. "Have you read about the Tibetan Buddhist monks meditating in labs while they run imaging tests of their brain waves? Super attention and concentration. Very high states."

"Are you . . . are you Buddhist now?" the eldest, Adrienne, asked with a kind of polite scrutiny.

"Nope, still too much of a male hierarchy for my taste," I answered. "And I just can't wrap my mind around the idea that all of this is an illusion"—I opened my arms to include the clear slope of sky, encircling cypress trees, and some of the last stands of Longleaf pine—"or *maya*. But I do like meditating."

"What are you then?"

"Well . . . ," I began slowly, searching for my response. Though I'd started the discussion, I somewhat resisted the spiritual drilling and thought longingly of the Dalai Lama's response to a reporter when asked to describe his faith. "It's private," he'd said and then laughed.

I rowed a few minutes in silence and then at last answered my niece. "Well, I do believe in a divine presence in this and all worlds. And I believe that every faith is sacred."

I hesitated when I saw that Adrienne expected something more—an alliance with a specific tradition. I did not mention that my hometown of Seattle was the most unchurched city in the country or that many people all over the whole country, especially in New England, were following the Pacific Northwest template of considering themselves spiritual rather than religious. Soon *Newsweek* would run a cover story on the diversity of religion, calling this trend a "post-Christian" America.

When Seattleites are asked on surveys to check the little square box beside a specific religion, 90 percent check "none such." Yet spirituality, if not religion, thrives there. I've never met so many meditators or conflict mediators as in my rainy, pensive city. Sometimes, gazing out through the violet-gray mists as a luminous Mount Rainier floats above us, it seems like the whole city is levitating. And they say that Seattle is the best place to have a heart attack because more people have trained in CPR than in any other city. Fewer churchgoers, more compassion.

I didn't tell all this to my nieces. I just said, "Well, for my part, I prefer private contemplation to organized religion."

"So you're more a mystic than a true believer," Sasha announced simply.

It seemed an astute and sympathetic assessment, and her perception took me back a little.

My nieces all rested on their oars and laughed as a pelican swooped down, his comical bill clenched around a tiny, wriggling fish. Suddenly there was a swarm of pelicans that arranged themselves into a "V" formation to cruise the circumference of the lake. With their oddly outsized beaks, the pelicans seemed somehow comic—a feathered patrol.

Then Adrienne asked me, "Remember when we were little we used to call you Aunt Wu Wu because of your strange ideas?" My niece fondly splashed me.

I suddenly remembered Adrienne as a three-year-old on one of our family train trips. Adrienne had fixed me with her azure eyes and demanded, "*Behba*, is God everywhere?"

"Yes, Adrienne," I had explained. "I believe that the divine dwells in every tree and stone, in animals and rivers . . . and in all of us."

"Well, then," she had asked me fiercely, "if God is everywhere, am I in His way?"

I was stunned by her intuitive leap. "Honey," I answered, "you *are* the way."

My words had elicited only a deep frown from my niece. I could hardly explain the idea of the Tao to myself, much less to a three-year-old. So I tousled her hair and said, "Listen, God is big enough for all our ideas."

This had seemed to satisfy my thoughtful niece. Unlike her sister Sasha, the budding scientist who, as a child, often lay in bed at night calculating complex math problems in her head, Adrienne would always be a philosopher and reader. When Adrienne was in elementary school, she organized a recycling club in a wealthy city that did not recycle. In high school she lugged around a trademark backpack that bulged with books, including a gargantuan Bible. In college she majored in English literature and braved her fear of flying by traveling to Egypt to teach English as a second language.

Though she is half-Hispanic, Adrienne has her mother's long Palomino mane and fair skin. Her sisters are dark-haired, but have blue and green eyes. All three are bright, lithe, and elegant. They could easily be models, but each sister has devoted her life to non-profit public health or mission work.

Boating together at Christmas on that tropical lake, my nieces and I rowed far from shore and relaxed. We drifted like the translucent swirls of water lilies adorning our oars. The winter sun was just burning through the morning mists rising off the water. A Great Blue Heron sailed by, sitting like a feathered skipper on a floating tree branch.

"*Tranquillo.*" The youngest sister, Sissy, breathed deeply and lay back against her oars, letting her life preserver cushion her. "*Paradisio.*"

I dared not break the companionable silence by asking my nieces how they felt about any other paradise, like that promised biblical heaven, or whether they believed the End Times were due in their lifetime, or whether they looked forward to it as others in the family did. It was enough that we were here together, afloat in our own little ark. I wanted only to abide with this next generation who so loved the world that they were giving their lives to nourish it.

Several years later a younger relative would send me a *Time* magazine article that seemed to say it all for her and perhaps for this next generation of new evangelicals. Called "Christians Wrong About Heaven, Says Bishop," the article included an interview with N. T. "Tom" Wright, the Anglican bishop of Durham in the United Kingdom. A Cambridge theologian and world-renowned conservative Christian, Wright does not believe in heaven or the Rapture portrayed in the "Left Behind" series that so enthralls many American evangelicals. Wright finds a very different biblical truth in the New Testament, which describes a "life after life-after-death" or "ultimate resurrection into the new heavens and the new Earth." Paradise is not a final resurrection or rapture away from this world. It is an intermediate stage before Christ's return to join the "new heavens and the new Earth together."

In Wright's interpretation of Revelation, "God wants you to be a renewed human being helping him to renew his creation . . . you won't be going up there to him, he'll be coming down here." That is why it is so important to care for this earth, God's creation. This world, not a "disembodied heaven," is the one to which Christ has already returned in the resurrection.

So why not help out in creating the new heaven and earth? That's what Bishop Wright asks in his lecture "Farewell to the Rapture": "Is not the 'Left Behind' mentality in thrall to a dualistic view of reality that allows people to pollute God's world on the grounds that it's all going to be destroyed soon?" If the earth is joined with heaven, if eternity with the divine is already here in this world, then we cannot leave the earth behind—ever.

The fact that the next generation of my family is not so enraptured by End Times theology gives me much hope for the future. Perhaps in my parents' generation, which survived two world wars, and in my generation raised under the shadow of nuclear Armageddon, apocalyptic worldviews helped us contain our terror. Even though our next generation witnessed the horror of 9/11, that did not turn them away from their devotion to this world. They are not plotting their escape. They are even more determined to do their spiritual work here, not for some future reward, but because they can actually help. They are still young enough to know they can change everything.

*   *   *

THAT WINTER NIGHT, as we all converged in the Florida cabin's huge kitchen to rustle up Mother's favorite beef chili, her guacamole "with a real zip," and enough tossed salad for a small battalion, the whole family started singing. To the sizzle of the skillet, the drumsticks of the wooden salad spoons, and the snap of the stone fireplace, we fell into a familiar repertoire—a song list that included such family favorites as "Over the Sunset Mountains," "Precious Lord, Take My Hand," "Do Lord," and the rather mystical "I'll Fly Away."

As my niece and I cut a miniature mountain of vegetables for the ranch dip, Sasha told me about her recent trip to Africa to work in an AIDS clinic. She had befriended a young woman known as Queenie, whose wayward husband had left her with the terrible disease. Queenie turned her illness into a teaching tool.

"Queenie would hitchhike and get picked up by truck drivers who thought she was a prostitute," Sasha said. "Boy, did they get a surprise! Instead of sex, Queenie gave the guys some AIDS brochures and a big lecture about the risks of unprotected sex for anyone they loved." Sasha grinned. "Queenie is well known in Africa for her work. I wish there was some way we could get her on *Oprah*."

"More salad!" one of my siblings shouted and tossed another head of lettuce toward us for chopping. "I'm making Mother's blue cheese dressing. Killer cholesterol!"

We fell into singing more hymns, and then we easily segued into a songfest of Broadway show tunes. Mother has long been an ardent fan of musicals, and we all joke that we could have made fortunes on

Name That Tune because we grew up memorizing the stereo sound-tracks to *South Pacific*, *Oklahoma*, and *The King and I*. We can chant and sing every word in four-part harmony. Singing in my family is the an-tidote to the dissonance of all our religious or political feuds. We cannot argue when we are listening so intently to try to find the per-fect blend of our harmonizing parts.

As we swung into a syncopated version of "Swing Low, Sweet Chariot," someone shouted out, "Where's the tenor?" I glanced ex-pectantly at my tall nephews. They grinned and shrugged, adding their baritones. My brother usually sings a sweet tenor, but he and his family had stayed in Virginia this holiday.

"If Grandpa were here," someone said wistfully, "he'd sing tenor."

We all stopped singing for a moment, remembering Grandfather Horace, my mother's father. He was a tender man, devoted to Baptist church and family. During the Great Depression he managed to sur-vive by selling life insurance—a sign that he, unlike the banks, was to be trusted. Grandfather Horace was not a rousing storyteller like so many in my family, but he more than compensated with his Irish tenor and the caramels he always carried in his pocket for us. What Grandfather Horace lacked in imagination he made up for in kind-ness. Originally from Tennessee, he often sang us to sleep at night with his mammy's lullaby, "Go to Sleep, My Little Pickaninny." He swore this lullaby was his best legacy to us—the song like a potion with the power to cure fevers and calm any fear. We still sing his mammy's lullaby to our children.

When Grandfather Horace was on his deathbed, I spent many hours with him reading his World War I diary. As he lay in his oxy-gen tent, struggling to breathe, he asked me to read each entry out loud, especially the stories of the young German soldiers he had bat-tled to stay alive.

"They're all here in this room," he murmured to me as I sat by his bedside. "All those German soldiers. They were just boys, like me.

When I bayoneted them . . . their eyes went still and so soft. I was the last face they would see in this life." Grandfather's eyes streamed as they often did. During the war he had lost a tear duct from a puncture wound to his face by a rampaging dog. "You hear me, girlie girl?"

"I hear you, Grandpa," I answered and slipped my hand under the plastic oxygen tent to hold his arm. It was studded with bruises from the IVs.

"I was an angel of death for these German boys," he coughed, and there was a rattling sound that was scary. "And now . . . well, now they're my angels. They will carry me over to heaven . . . these boys who were my enemies so long ago . . . these boys who I sent to heaven." My grandfather gasped for air, and his pale blue eyes fixed on what he only could see in the air around him. "But first, they have to forgive me. That's why you've got to read my diary to them, girlie. To let them know that someone still remembers them."

So I read aloud to him each and every page of that diary, each and every description of a soldier's wounds. Had I any illusions about the glory of war, that diary dispelled them. Mundane descriptions of horses and caissons, of eating cabbages in fields when rations ran out, were interspersed with harrowing details of soldiers' deaths. I read the entire diary to Grandfather Horace until at last he seemed to feel some peace. The last afternoon I saw him, he reached out his skeletal hand to seek mine.

"Sing me," he whispered. "Sing me my mammy's lullaby."

And I did, just the way he taught me when I was a child. In that Florida cabin, at the mention of my grandfather, we all instinctively shifted into a more meditative mood. In one voice, without missing a beat, my family switched songs to sing Grandpa's lullaby:

> *Lu, La Lu, La Lu La Lu La Lu Lu*
> *Underneath the silver, southern moon*
> *Rockabye, hushabye*
> *Mammy's little baby*

The lullaby was so soothing that soon we found ourselves sitting closer together before the fireplace with huge bowls of chili, home-made cornbread, Caesar salad, and brownies for dessert. We fell into a nourishing silence. Then Dad told stories about our ancestors from his genealogy studies.

My niece Sissy cuddled next to me on the sofa, her head on my shoulder. We were bundled up in a plush Smokey Bear throw that Mother had brought. On my other side Sasha and her new husband relaxed in obvious contentment. They had found each other and their life's work in Africa together.

Later there was more singing from the open kitchen as my siblings did the dishes. "I'm Gonna Wash That Man Right Outta My Hair," they belted out in Broadway style.

"Behba, will you teach me to sing harmony?" Sissy asked in a soft voice. "Everyone else in the family can hear it, but I just can't."

"What do you hear now?" I asked as we listened to the singing in the kitchen. "Do you hear how their parts fit together perfectly? That the sound is richer with harmony? Think of harmony as another dimension of melody."

Sissy cocked her head like an alert animal, her silver earrings dangling. She listened as my siblings danced around the counters sashaying and strutting in show-tune style, acting out the lyrics. *Cancel him,* they sang, *and let him go . . . yeah, sister!*

In frustration, Sissy shook her head. "I can only hear the melody."

I decided to teach Sissy using the song "Do, Re, Me" from *The Sound of Music.* Over and over, we sang it together to the protests of the others. After about an hour of practice, we made some progress, but still Sissy found it hard to hear her alto harmony. At one point, I noticed that every time we fell silent in between drills and gazed at the fire, outside there was an accompaniment of crickets and a slight wind. I suddenly remembered my father telling me once that the wind blows a different song through each tree. The breeze's harmony depends on the leaves through which it plays. The wind is accompanied by each tree's melody. How to translate this into human singing?

"Listen, Sissy," I began, "when you work with children in your mission AIDS clinics, don't you have to listen very deeply to what they might *not* be saying? Aren't you also paying attention to their body language, their faces, and the stories they are too afraid to tell?"

"Yes," Sissy nodded thoughtfully. "I have to listen to what they say but also try to hear what is really inside them. Child psychologists call it *attunement*."

"Well, that's the way you find your harmony," I told her. "You listen with all of your attention to the part that is *not* being sung, that's hidden just inside the melody, that's waiting and wants to be heard. Then it is revealed."

We again took up our singing drill, and Sissy listened to my melody so intently that it was almost comical—the only wrinkle in her young face creased across her forehead in profound concentration. Her eyes were still points, hardly blinking, reflecting the firelight.

In the middle of the umpteenth drill on *Fa, a long, long way to go . . .* , Sissy jumped up from the couch, almost upending the rest of us and shouted out: "I've got it!"

By George, she's got it, someone sang out and segued into *My Fair Lady*, singing, *You said that she would do it . . . and, indeed, she did!*

"Stop it, you're distracting me!" Sissy held up her hand. "One more time, from the beginning."

She did have it. Sissy was tentative, but she was singing her fifths or thirds to blend with my melody. Her voice was clear and robust, as if she had found not only harmony but also a missing part of herself.

"Let's do another song," Sissy insisted to a general groan. During the next few songs, my niece was ebullient at her success and kept repeating her alto part with such pleasure that we finally had to stop singing, exhausted.

About midnight, when various nephews and nieces were shuffling off to tents pitched outside or the bunk beds inside, Sissy finally called it a night. She embraced me warmly and whispered so as not to wake up our already slumbering family.

"I understand it now," Sissy said. "Finding another part to sing is like that Bible verse, 'the evidence of things not seen.'" She smiled. "Well, harmony is the evidence of things not heard."

I stayed up late that night in paradise with my family. With a little shock I realized that as much as I'd struggled against my parents' beliefs, I was grateful to them. Inheriting my mother's moral universe and my father's love of the land and all animals, I hadn't wandered far from Eden.

Sitting before the stone fireplace and listening to the music of soft snores syncopating the night sounds of crickets, I saw that in our way my family was enraptured—without leaving each other or this earth behind.

Epilogue

We Shall All Be Changed

(1 Corinthians 15:51)

HERE ON OUR ALKI BEACH, THE SMALL NEIGHBORHOOD VIGILS THAT began years ago with just a few of us sitting with seals have grown into a devoted force of citizen naturalists. The seal-sitters have become a real community, some of them kids. We call the teenage volunteers "the Boys Brigade," because they skateboard the boardwalk while keeping an eye out for the pups. Over 100 neighborhood volunteers have taken the seal pup conservation training from NOAA.

And in the spring of 2009, the National Wildlife Federation recognized our neighborhood's diverse community conservation work, including many other grassroots organizations of birders, salmon-friendly gardeners, and Seattle Parks and Recreation workers, by certifying Alki Beach Park as an official wildlife habitat. It was the first community in Seattle, and the thirty-first in the nation, to receive this certification. Of course, we had a beach party—and seal-sitters joined the Audubon Club, Whale Trail organizers, and other citizen naturalists in celebrating.

Recently, my niece Elizabeth and her new husband, Alec, joined me in seal sitting, on their honeymoon. When I picked them up at the airport, one of Elizabeth's first questions was: "Hey, any seal pups on your beach?"

"As a matter of fact, there is one hauled out at the point," I replied, smiling at her in the rearview mirror.

As we drove from the airport to my Seattle neighborhood, I noticed a bumper sticker, with the Christian fish design, that read: Extinction Isn't Stewardship.

Elizabeth was still as radiant as she had looked on her wedding day, with her curly hair and rock band T-shirt. Her husband, Alec, matched her with his mop of Beatle-cut hair and slim, muscular body.

We didn't go straight to their honeymoon suite from the airport. First, we swung by the wharf near my home where a late-season pup was resting on the sand behind some driftwood.

"Oh, he's so little," Elizabeth laughed.

At that moment the pup stretched and gave a great yawn, revealing a full set of tiny, sharp teeth. We would have clapped with pleasure, but instead we stayed very still.

Against the cityscape backdrop of Seattle, the pup looked even smaller. The uninitiated might have missed him completely because the pup was so well camouflaged against the gray gravel and black beach rocks.

"Have you named him yet?" Elizabeth asked, and when I said no, she made a suggestion.

"Yes, we will call him George." I smiled fondly, thinking of my neighbor whom Elizabeth had not met.

"Yeah," my niece nodded. "Someone named George just seems like he'd stick around, you know?"

"I know," I sighed. Rumor had it that George might be transferred to the East Coast.

We were joined by a few other seal-sitters—Ned, a fireman, and Aimee, his nine-year-old daughter. Aimee was here every day looking for her pup, Ned told us. "It's what she cares about most." Softly he added, "It's kind of saving her life right now."

I did not ask why. Even though we seal-sitters spend hours on the beach together, we are careful not to pry into each other's lives. Sooner or later the hours on the beach and the intimacy with these wild animals make friends of us all. I trusted that as the season progressed I would know why Aimee needed saving.

"You know, we think we're saving the seals," Robin, our tireless and talented photographer, told me one day. Robin's photos help identify and document illness, bullet wounds, and other human-caused injuries. "But really, the seals are also saving us."

She was right. As neighbors have bonded together to watch over and share the beach with seal pups, we've come closer together. During the off-season we still seek one another out. We have helped one another through divorces, job loss, retirement, broken bones, and illness. When I had a bad cold, seal-sitters dropped off chicken soup along with daily seal pup photos. Janette, one of the most diligent seal-sitters, organized a *Sex and the City*–style outing with a sleek black stretch limo to fit all of us in as we sipped champagne and rested up from a particularly stressful week on the beach.

Sometimes seal sitting strikes me as a bit like the church socials of my childhood. Though not bonded by religion or politics, we are still a little "fellowship of the believers," as my mother calls her Women's Missionary Union. As in the original meaning of the word religion, "to bind together," the neighborhood naturalists are close-knit, though we all have such different takes on faith, politics, and even culture. We joke that if it weren't for the seals we would never have found each other.

My niece and her husband studied the pup as he flopped a little closer to the surf and scanned the waves. "It's like a secret," Elizabeth said softly so as not to disturb George. "Knowing how to look, I mean, really knowing how to see the world with others . . . besides just us . . . here."

As we watched the golden pup stretch and preen and yawn, I remembered my brother, Elizabeth's father, telling me, "You know, all those hours that you wait on the beach for the mother seal to return to her pup . . . well, isn't that kind of like the way we Christians wait for Christ to return for us and restore heaven here on earth?"

I had never thought of it that way—and with my upbringing I should have. But now, watching this pup, I thought it made perfect sense.

"Hey, little buddy," Alec breathed. "Hope you make it."

"We'll also pray for this pup," Elizabeth whispered.

And then the newlyweds held the newly weaned pup in their true and tender gaze.

*   *   *

ONE THANKSGIVING WEEK we were concerned to see another late-season pup haul out on the beach. It was a startlingly sunny Sunday, and hundreds of beachcombers were rather desperately seeking the strong autumn light of Alki Beach. The seal-sitters were swamped with questions and concern.

"Is the pup okay?" people asked.

I watched our well-trained seal-sitters calmly reassure the crowds. "We hope so," Nancy, a retired high school teacher, explained.

"Will he live?"

Nancy responded, "You know, harbor seals can live up to twenty-five years. This little pup here seems perfectly healthy . . . just napping. Please try to keep your voices down and let him rest."

With this Thanksgiving seal pup, Robin used her telephoto lens to discern that most of the pup's teeth were sprouted—a sign that he was almost weaned. We worried that he was too late in the season and might have trouble learning to fish for himself in the winter storms.

That holiday weekend we also gave thanks for the pup's health. We marveled at his plump belly, his trusting snooze as throngs of people gathered around him, generally keeping a respectful distance behind the yellow tape. As I settled in my lawn chair on the beach, binoculars trained on the napping pup, I thought of those hound pups long ago who lost their lives under my watch. Maybe I had made up for that carelessness, for forgetting the effect of heat on all living things.

I also reflected on how much had changed—not only on this neighborhood beach but also in the world. A new American president promised a sea change in green energy and climate change. Interfaith groups around the world had signed a "Climate Change Manifesto of Hope." The declaration asked: "Can the Planet Earth be healed? Our answer is yes." In my family, my father now talks about global warming and its devastating effects on fisheries and the world's oceans; my brother's church welcomed a scientist to talk about climate change.

Of course, many in this country have not changed. They still think global warming is God's code to the faithful that the End Times are here and that Barack Obama is the suave, sinister Anti-Christ. America's premier evangelist, ninety-year-old Billy Graham, announced that his ministry would focus on End Times in 2009. His website posted a Q&A with Graham that considered whether the world would end in 2009 and offered to prepare believers for life in the Last Days.

Then there are the green doomsayers who still use fear to compel us into conservation. On many television stations there are popular apocalyptic shows, such as *Future Earth: Journey to the End of the World* and the eerily fascinating *Life After People*. One of the myriad environmental e-mail alerts I've received warned that it was already too late to stop global warming. These prophecies sometimes make me wonder, why try? Then I remember that this environmental gloom can be a mirror version of the religious fundamentalists' abandonment of earth.

On the beach now, as I watched the pup's steady breathing, the rise and fall of contented sleep, I reminded myself: even if these might be those last days, what alternative do we have in this world but to hope, to imagine—keeping our watchful eyes on what is most beloved and beautiful? To be grateful for an earth we share with what is still wild, still trusting.

The pup showed an almost feline contentment as he stretched into the banana position, scratched his whiskers with his little wing of a fore flipper, and then gave a great yawn. The pup seemed to believe the beach was his refuge, as it had been for thousands of years.

"These are urban seals now," Brent Norberg of NOAA Fisheries told us at a meeting between the seal-sitters and this government agency charged with federal protection of marine mammals. "NOAA counts on grassroots organizations to help protect seals."

One of the seal-sitter kids, ten-year-old Anasophia, was so inspired by the pups that she made a wildlife calendar featuring our favorite pups of the season—Neptune, Spud (named after Spud's Fish and Chips), and Liberty (named after the smaller-scale Statue of Liberty replica that graces our busy boardwalk). From the sale of her calendar, Anasophia raised $2,000, which she donated to the PAWS Wildlife Center. The tireless rehab workers at PAWS take care of the injured or ill pups in the hope of rehabilitating them back into the wild. Of the pups that we seal-sitters were granted permission by NOAA to rescue, few survived. Taking a pup off the beach is traumatic, so it is only done in extreme cases of human-caused injury or if there seems a good chance of recovery.

But one lucky pup was successfully rescued by Kristin, our Northwest stranding expert, and flourished under PAWS rehab. Officially the pup was number 07-2094, but unofficially we used the name Edmond, after the seal's harbor city habitat. When we found out that Edmond was in fact a female, the name still stuck. Edmond had been hanging around a fishermen's wharf in Edmonds, Washington, near Seattle. At NOAA's marine mammal hotline, Kristin had been called numerous times to retrieve this pup after she had swallowed barbed fishing bait. The fishermen had grown rather fond of the wily pup and didn't mean to snag her with their lines, but Edmond was now attracted to their wharf. So she had to be moved for her own safety. We hoped that in a less urban habitat, Edmond wouldn't get into so much trouble.

When Edmond arrived at the PAWS wildlife rehab sanctuary, she was emaciated and lethargic. Her jaw and mouth were pocked with puncture wounds that were badly infected because of the polluted inshore waters. For a time, Dr. John Huckabee, the PAWS wildlife vet, didn't think Edmond would thrive. Every morning the staff opened her kennel, afraid the pup would not have survived the night.

Edmond not only thrived in rehab but grew into a butterball on the 350 pounds of large herring fed her at PAWS. After fifty-three weeks of countless blood tests, X-rays, and constant care in rehab, Edmond was at last ready to be released back into the wild.

Every seal-sitter's dearest wish is to join the PAWS wildlife rehab team in a seal pup release. I had the great fortune of joining PAWS for Edmond's return to the sea. As I greeted Dr. John again at the PAWS Wildlife Center, we exchanged a look that I imagine is common to anyone who works with wildlife—sorrow and hope. "Well, at least this little one made it," Dr. John said kindly. "This seal we can bring back to where she belongs."

"Yeah, let's get this show on the road," Kevin, the wildlife rehab leader, said with pure happiness. He and his partner, Julie, one of my ex-students, were directing the release.

Kevin was a tall, muscular man who was used to lifting the seals and bear cubs and bald eagles who found their wounded way to PAWS. He and Julie chatted with Edmond, who was swimming in the PAWS rehab swimming pool. Deftly, Kevin slipped a huge net into the pool, then lifted up the startled—and very fat—pup. In seconds, the fifty-pound pup was transferred to a wildlife kennel, covered with a white cloth, and carried to Kevin's van.

As we drove the half-hour or so to a nearby island, I talked with Julie, who has worked in wildlife rehab along with Kevin for many years.

"Even when Kevin and I eloped," she said, "we printed out the directions to all animal rehabs in Las Vegas, because everywhere we go we always seem to find animals in trouble. This is our life."

Of the fifteen harbor seal pups taken in for rehab by PAWS that season, four were released and two were transferred to another wildlife center. The others were either dead on arrival or in such poor condition they had to be euthanized. At the Everett harbor, we were greeted by a good-hearted park ranger whose boat was revved up and ready to go. Kevin and the ranger carried the kennel, still covered, onto the boat. Inside, the pup made little barks and snuffles.

"Edmond knows she's home!" Julie said with a grin. "She can smell the sea."

Even we could smell the fragrance of saltwater, kelp, and briny depths. It was clear and crisp this Halloween Day, the time when mystics say the veils between the worlds are thin and spirits can pass between realms. How I wished some of the seals we had buried that season on our beach were also onboard today with us. But after all, this was the Day of the Dead, so maybe their spirits were still swimming nearby.

As the boat rocked on gentle waves, Edmond's kennel rocked back and forth with the pup's excitement, like a child barely able to conceal her pleasure. Edmond knew what was awaiting her: the emerald waters, chill and familiar. Fishing again for herself, diving fathoms deep—not in a swimming pool—and dreaming as she slept, drifting in kelp forests with the one pulse of the sea like a watery heartbeat.

At this moment the world seemed perfect. Was it always so, if we could but perceive it?

I remembered the running philosophical dialogue that I enjoy with my friend Sarah Jane, who is Jewish and also well versed in Buddhism. "Do you know the term *tikkun olam?*" she asked.

She explained that this was the Jewish concept of repairing or transforming the world. "If you believe that we are here to repair this world, then we cannot long to leave, can we? The world cannot be repaired without us."

She paused and smiled. "Then there's the whole notion of *bodhisattva,* or those beings who, out of compassion, make a conscious choice to return to earth. Buddhism says it is only in the human form that there is any possibility of enlightenment. It's the most beautiful concept, because it means that we are an extension of the divine."

"Do you believe that animals can be enlightened?" I asked her.

"If enlightenment means knowing and generosity, maybe animals are more capable of it than we are."

"Sometimes I think my cats are ascended masters."

"Here's my favorite quote," Sarah Jane continued, "and I think I made it up: 'All things observed closely enough turn to good.' If you observe anything long enough, you become intimate with it. Isn't perfection really just the ultimate intimacy and understanding—so much that you simply become a part of everything?"

On the boat for the release of Edmond, we were all part of everything—the haunting caw of the blue heron, the slap of the waves against the bow, the happy snuffles of the seal pup. Even though the wind was cold, each of us was smiling ear to ear as the boat with our precious cargo motored slowly through the freezing Northwest waters. And then we were there—on an isolated island with no fishermen's wharves, only an expanse of rocky beach, chatty crows, and bald eagles. Just as we landed on the island so that some of the PAWS volunteers could take pictures of the release from shore, a seagull with a broken wing practically walked right into Julie's arms—as if recognizing that help had arrived.

Julie shrugged and expertly lifted the seabird, careful of his wing that hung at a crazy angle to his feathered body. "This gull must have dialed 911 for animal rescue. Happens all the time. We come to release one animal and another needs help."

Repair, transform.

The boat motored out again into the cold waters as Kevin eased the kennel to a lower step at the stern. Then, with a move like a magician's, Kevin prepared to lift the blanket from Edmond's carrier.

"Ready!"

In one graceful motion the veil was lifted, the kennel door was unlocked, and the pup sniffed once more—poised between two worlds. And then she slipped out of her container as if it were no more than a second skin. Edmond glided off the end of the boat without even a splash. She was that smooth, that fast, that knowing. The pup surfaced and then very slowly circled the boat. For one long moment, she swam near us. Great, fathomless dark eyes held ours, and then, in the twinkling of an eye, the pup was gone. She dove deep. Far off, a glossy head surfaced, pirouetted, and disappeared.

* * *

IT'S BEEN A QUIETER seal pup season this year. We haven't seen as many pups this summer and are troubled by reports along the West Coast of record numbers of stranding seals. No one knows the cause of these deaths—another El Niño cycle or climate change? Triple-digit temperatures have shattered all Seattle weather records. Seal-sitters are on alert, especially watching out for injured or underweight pups.

My good neighbor George and his family did move away. We still keep in touch by e-mail, and I send him photos of this season's pups. I teased him that his new job assignment in Florida was not as close to the Rapture as he was here on our beach.

"Yeah, but in Florida there are more true believers like me," he promptly wrote back.

As much as I resisted George's hope of taking me with him come Rapture time, I often find myself remembering my neighbor's beach beatitudes. As we both watched over the seal pups we also witnessed one another's daily lives.

Sometimes, sitting over a pup without George, I can almost hear his End Times soliloquy. Of course, he would call it his "still, small voice," telling him the world is so full of tribulations and terrors that we are truly due some rapture. But I also still hear his wonder when he tells me about seeing the Everglades in his new home state or being startled when a manatee raises her bewhiskered snout in the backyard canal.

"How could any sailor have ever confused these creatures with mermaids?" George wrote me in a recent e-mail. "Too long at sea, I suppose." Then he added, "You know, sometimes harbor seals wander this far down the Atlantic. Hey, can John and Bill send me the revised design dimensions of the life rafts they built for the pups? My daughter and I want to make one for her high school science project."

"Build it and they will come," I wrote back.

Suddenly it struck me that I should ask George a question that I never had while we sat together all those hours on our backyard beach. So I again took up our spiritual dialogue as if we were still perched together on driftwood keeping vigil:

> Dear George,
> Pup on the beach.
> Wish you were here.
> By the way, I never asked, but
> now that we are sailing waves of cyberspace
> instead of the Salish Sea, do you believe that
> the animals will be Raptured with you?

And within a twinkling of an eye, in the time it takes for a text or instant message to zing back and forth, George zapped me his note.

In George's answer to my question I heard the echo of my mother's fervor, a flashback to Sword Drills, and the music of his ministry to me, which I surprisingly missed, in the way that one longs for family and then wishes to escape them:

> Dear Seal-Sitting pal,
> Balmy here and 73 degrees.
> Sun—but alas, no seals.
> Just joined SaveOurManatees.org
> You still read your Bible?
> See 1 Timothy 4:4—"Every creature of God is good."
> Your neighbor for eternity,
> George

Acknowledgments

All the names in this memoir are actual, with the exception of some changed for privacy. A very few details have been changed for the same reason. Otherwise, I've depended on diaries and family stories and the ever so selective offerings of memory.

My elegant and abiding editor, Merloyd Lawrence, called this book forth from me and was a guiding spirit in its creation—we shall gather at the river. My literary agent and dear friend, Sarah Jane Freymann, read the first chapter of this memoir at her family Seder and inspired every other chapter. Daniel bravely read along, listened with all his heart, and offered his own spiritual insights to help balance this book.

I was also blessed to have a community of keen-eyed and valiant readers accompanying me on this book's journey, and all my gratitude goes out to them: Rebecca Romanelli, for her metaphysical sophistication, which was its own nourishing manna in this memoir's wilderness; Vanessa Adams, for her straightforward compassion and for not letting me take myself too seriously; and Sy Montgomery, for the strength and steadfast inspiration of her own memoir and for lending me her good, good eye. Maureen Michelson of NewSage Press generously gave this book her bracing editorial red pen and asked "the hard questions." Jessica Sinsheimer's reading of the manuscript was crucial at several turning points. My *Animal Heart* editor, Linda Gunnarson, advised and encouraged all along the way. Anne DeVore's erudition and psychological gnosis strengthened my spirit. And as always, Susan Biskeborn gave this book its wise, finishing touches.

I am grateful to my supportive *Seattle Post-Intelligencer* editor, Kimberly Mills, who first published a sketch from this book. *Orion* magazine editors Aina Barton and Emerson Blake and my old Graywolf Press editor Scott Walker were the "editorial brothers and sisters" who advised me through several drafts of "Saving Seals" (the prologue). Sister author Mary Swander of the University of Iowa's "Earth-Animal-Oracle: Symposium on Wildness, Wilderness, and the Creative Imagination" gave me courage and funding to finish this book.

Several communities nurtured me through the long "lost in the funhouse" adventure of memoir: my students with our creative and far-ranging dialogue; fellow writers and scholars at the Black Earth Institute, especially Professor Patricia Monaghan and my inspiring co-author Linda Hogan; my "pod" of naturalists and writers devoted to the natural world, especially Summer Tree Institute's Doug Thompson and Robin Kobaly, Justine Toms of New Dimensions radio, biologist Stacy Studebaker, and earth advocate Zappo DeMoll of Ocean Haven; my conservation circle of seal-sitters, especially Kristin Wilkinson of NOAA, wildlife photographer Robin Lindsay, and marine mammal biologist Dr. Toni Frohoff of the Trans Species Institute and Terra Mar Research; our Twelfth House Club of poets and seekers, Taoist healer Jim Dowling, Sufi poet Hafiz Lu Leland, and opera singer-teacher Gerald Halsey; my Seattle Metropolitan chorale, especially Seattle Glee Clubs founder Bert Gulhaugen and Metropolitan director John Gulhaugen; also accompanist Diana Shvets, whose Russian food and artistic friendship fed my soul. Thanks to Diana for the reminder that the Tibetan monks teach, as part of their spiritual practice, to laugh every day.

For finding neighborhood and divine comedy in daily walks and companionship, I am grateful to Tracey Conway, canine saint LuLu,

Bill McHallffey, and the feline ascended masters Loki and Tao. As always, I am grateful to the Salish Sea, my muse and mentor. This memoir is written in loving memory of my very first editor, Rachel McKenzie, whose rigorous but kind eye is always within me.

And I am grateful to my family, even though they might not agree with some things in this book. Finally, I owe much to my friend Joseph Meeker, whose *Comedy of Survival* is so often a subtext of my life.

About the Author

BRENDA PETERSON is a novelist and nature writer and the author of fifteen books, including a *New York Times* "Notable Book of the Year," *Duck and Cover*. Her memoir *Build Me an Ark: A Life with Animals* was chosen as a "Best Spiritual Book of 2001" and translated into Chinese. Her nonfiction books include *Living by Water* and the National Geographic book *Sightings: The Gray Whale's Mysterious Journey*. Peterson's most recent novel is *Animal Heart*.

Peterson's work has appeared in many national publications, including the *New York Times*, the *Chicago Tribune*, the *Utne Reader*, *Sierra*, *Orion*, and *Oprah* magazine. Since 1993, she has contributed environmental commentary for Seattle's NPR stations. For the past three decades, Peterson has studied and written about interspecies relationships. She is the founder of the grassroots conservation group Seal Sitters (online at: www.sealsitters.org). Her new children's book *Pups on the Beach* (Henry Holt) is due out in 2011. Peterson lives by the Salish Sea in Seattle, Washington, and her website is www.literati.net/Peterson.